DIVORCE LAWYERS AT WORK

DIVORCE LAWYERS AT WORK

Varieties of Professionalism in Practice

LYNN MATHER
CRAIG A. McEWEN
&
RICHARD J. MAIMAN

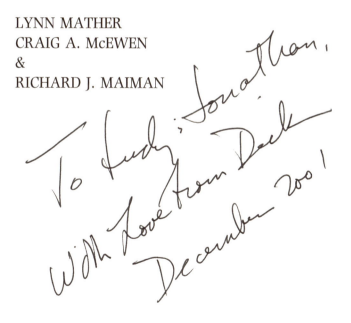

To Judy, Jonathan,
With Love from Dick
December 2001

OXFORD
UNIVERSITY PRESS

2001

OXFORD

UNIVERSITY PRESS

Oxford   New York
Athens   Auckland   Bangkok   Bogotá   Buenos Aires   Cape Town
Chennai   Dar es Salaam   Delhi   Florence   Hong Kong   Istanbul   Karachi
Kolkata   Kuala Lumpur   Madrid   Melbourne   Mexico City   Mumbai   Nairobi
Paris   São Paulo   Shanghai   Singapore   Taipei   Tokyo
Toronto   Warsaw

and associated companies in
Berlin   Ibadan

Copyright © 2001 by Oxford University Press

Published by Oxford University Press, Inc.
198 Madison Avenue, New York, New York 10016

Oxford is a registered trademark of Oxford University Press, Inc.

Library of Congress Cataloging-in-Publication Data
Mather, Lynn M.
Divorce lawyers at work : varieties of professionalism in practice / by Lynn Mather,
Craig A. McEwen, and Richard J. Maiman.
p.   cm.
Includes bibliographical references and index.
ISBN 0-19-514515-1; ISBN 0-19-514516-X (pbk)
1. Divorce suits—United States.   2. Lawyers—United States.   3. Practice of law—United
States.   4. Professions—Sociological aspects.   I. McEwen, Craig A.   II. Maiman, Richard
J.   III. Title.
KF535.M38   2001
346.7301'66—dc21   00-052448

9 8 7 6 5 4 3 2 1

Printed in the United States of America
on acid-free paper

PREFACE

This book explores how lawyers understand and arrive at many of the decisions that they make in their daily work lives. For lawyers, these decisions ultimately constitute the heart of professionalism in practice, and they vary significantly among attorneys. The importance and the variability of these practice decisions raise important questions about what "professionalism" means and about how professional work is guided or controlled to ensure quality and accountability. Our account, drawn from a detailed study of divorce attorneys in two states, pursues these crucial questions for both theory and practice.

Our book was written with two primary audiences in mind. First, we wish to contribute to the efforts of social scientists who study work and the professions in general, and the legal profession in particular, to better understand the complex forces that shape discretionary choices in work. Second, we hope that leaders and members of the bar who are concerned about issues of professionalism will find in this book a fresh way of thinking about how to strengthen the norms that guide lawyers' behavior and the challenges in doing so. We also believe our book will prove useful to law students who are studying professional responsibility, legal ethics, and family law and trying to prepare for the challenges of everyday practice, as well as to lawyers already grappling with the difficult decisions that we discuss here.

Our book would not have been completed without the patient support and encouragement of our spouses—Mike, Maggie, and Susan—who made space in their lives for a project that exceeded its original life expectancy. Despite our intense concentration on the task at hand, it has not escaped our notice that our children turned into adults as we wrote this book. We express our deep appreciation and thanks to Katie and Eileen, Ian and Kirk, and Elizabeth, Catherine, and the two Justins, for enriching our lives in countless ways.

We wish to thank Ken Kressel and Heather Wishik for contributing to our early thinking about the nature of this project, a fact that they have probably long forgotten. Many of our colleagues have provided encouragement and support along the way by commenting on papers, responding to presentations, or reading articles emerging from our research. Particular thanks go to Susan Apel, Richard Brooks, John Conley, Clark Cunningham, Robert Dingwall, John Eekelaar, Cynthia Epstein, Lee Epstein, Michael Freeman, Hazel Genn, Herbert Jacob, Robert Lee, Carrie Menkel-Meadow, Charles Miller, Frank Munger, Mack O'Barr, Gerald Phillips, Joe Sanders, Ulrike Schultz, Peter Teachout, and Celia Wells.

We appreciate the opportunities we have had to present earlier versions of chapters from this book at American Political Science Association and Law and Society Association panels, and at faculty colloquia at Bowdoin College, Cardiff University, Dartmouth College, Lake Forest College, University College, London, the University of Maine Law School, the University of Nottingham, The Ohio State University College of Law, Vermont Law School, and Washington University. The feedback we received from colleagues at each of these venues helped us enormously in suggesting new interpretations of our data and clarifying our analysis.

Several scholars gave our manuscript a careful reading and made invaluable suggestions for revision. We are grateful to Richard Abel, David Chambers, Christine Harrington, Sandy Levinson, Mavis Maclean, and several anonymous Oxford University Press reviewers for their detailed and constructive criticism. Our book is better because of their thoughtful comments.

Many other people have contributed to this project along the way. Students at Bowdoin, Dartmouth, and the University of Southern Maine helped in collecting and coding data from courthouses, in doing library research, and in assisting with the preparation of the manuscript. They include Julie Amstein, Robert Bordone, Elizabeth Day, Steven Franklin, Chad Fischer, Carolyn Gardner, Jennifer Hickey, Jesper Johansen, Melania Kasfir, Michelle Lundeen, Amanda McGovern, Karen Nevers, Zoe Oxley, Todd Sisitsky, Anne Sosin, Jason Spitalnick, Alison Thoreson, and Barbara Ucasz Fiacco. We thank them for their care in completing what was often tedious but nonetheless essential work. Thanks, too, to Kathleen Donald and Barbara Mellert for administrative and computer support.

The National Science Foundation (Law and Social Sciences) made our work possible by awarding us research grants that supported the collection of our data. Generous support was provided by the Rockefeller Center at Dartmouth College and by Dartmouth's Presidential Scholars program. We also thank our universities for granting us sabbatical leaves that provided precious time for research and writing.

Earlier versions of some of the articles we have expanded into the chapters of this book were published by the following journals, to which we express our appreciation: *Droit et Societe, International Journal of Law and the Family, Law & Society Review, Legal Ethics,* and *Maine Law Review.* The articles have all been substantially revised for this book.

We could not have done this research without the cooperation and support of the court clerks, marital masters, and judges in Maine and New Hampshire who provided us with access to their workplaces and assisted us in understanding what we found there. Finally, we most gratefully acknowledge the indispensable assistance of the 163 lawyers in Maine and New Hampshire who were willing to share their time and insights with us. These "reflective practitioners" helped us to find our way to identifying and answering many crucial questions that we perceived much less clearly at the start of this project.

CONTENTS

1. Debating Professionalism and Control over Lawyers' Work   3

2. The Many Faces of Professionalism in Divorce Practice   16

3. Communities of Practice   41

4. The Boundaries of Expertise   64

5. Maintaining Control over Clients   87

6. The Meaning of Advocacy   110

7. Serving Clients while Protecting the Bottom Line   133

8. Constructing Professional Meaning and Identity in the Practice of Divorce Law   157

9. From Professionalism to Collegial Control   175

   Appendix: Studying Divorce Lawyers at Work   195

   Notes   203

   References   227

   Index   239

DIVORCE LAWYERS AT WORK

1

DEBATING PROFESSIONALISM AND CONTROL OVER LAWYERS' WORK

A prospective divorce client appears in a lawyer's office for an initial consultation. She has a sad story of domestic violence and a clear need for legal assistance, but only a limited capacity to pay for that service. *Does the lawyer agree to represent this client, knowing that she may have to reduce or even waive her usual fees?*

A divorce client frequently tries to use his meetings with his lawyer to unburden himself about his unhappiness over his divorce and the direction his life is taking. *Does the lawyer listen to the client and offer him emotional support, or does he insist that the consultations focus on the client's legal case?*

A divorce client refuses to consider a negotiated agreement and demands that her lawyer fight her case in court as a way of punishing her husband. *Does the lawyer pursue the client's demands in court, or does she try to persuade the client to rethink her goals and expectations for the divorce in order to reach a settlement?*

A divorce lawyer is preparing for settlement talks with an opposing attorney with whom he has never negotiated before. *Does the lawyer significantly inflate his opening demands, or does he make a more modest proposal that he considers fair and reasonable?*

A divorce lawyer has a client who wishes to talk directly with her spouse about the terms of their settlement. *Does the lawyer permit her client to take part in fashioning an agreement, or does she insist that all negotiations be strictly between herself and the opposing counsel?*

Decisions such as these lie at the heart of lawyers' day-to-day work. Whether they are made reflectively or reflexively, such choices underline the substantial discretion that results from the indeterminacy of attorneys' professional roles. Ultimately, legal practice is constituted out of these many small judgments. How do lawyers think about and actually make these decisions? What guidelines and standards do lawyers use in deciding how to relate to clients and to opposing attorneys; about when, how, and with whom to negotiate; and about how at the end of the day to evaluate their own work? Do the answers to these questions flow more or less automatically from the lawyer's formal training and expertise? To what degree do they reflect the lawyer's own self-interest, the particular interests of the client, or the broader public interest? Such questions lie at the heart of discussions among scholars and bar leaders about the meaning of professionalism. They are the central issues of this book.

Simply put, the debate over legal professionalism revolves around the degree to which general professional identities, formal training, and rules of conduct guide the choices of individual lawyers in practice. Professional bar rhetoric suggests that the most powerful influences on lawyers' decisions come from law school socialization and formal codes of professional responsibility, which promote and enforce shared expertise, norms, and obligations. An alternative perspective points to economic incentives as the crucial determinants of lawyers' conduct. That is, through their conditions of work, lawyers' choices, like those of many professionals, are shaped by their own material interests or those of their employers or clients, even though they may be rationalized by reference to professional norms. Yet a third perspective emphasizes the role of personal identities and values in lawyers' decision making. In this view, lawyers' individual values or personal characteristics such as gender, race, religion, or class influence their professional conduct.

Each of these viewpoints yields a different explanation for the choices lawyers make in their daily work lives. Consider, for example, the attorney who is trying to decide whether or not to represent a poor client. If the lawyer agrees to accept the case, the professionalism account might suggest that she has internalized the legal profession's norm of public service and feels obliged to help those who cannot afford a lawyer. However, the workplace version might see a struggling sole practitioner who cannot afford to pass up even the possibility of a modest fee. Alternatively, the personal identity perspective might attribute the lawyer's decision to take the case to the fact that as a woman, the lawyer empathizes with the abused wife and seeks to use her legal skills to help women in difficult situations.

Similarly, if the lawyer decides against representing the client, it might be because, having already achieved the American Bar Association's aspiration of 50 hours of pro bono work for the year, she feels that she has done her professional duty. Or perhaps the attorney rejects the case because as a junior law firm associate she is under considerable workplace pressure from firm partners to meet her annual quota of billable hours. Or it may be that she is tired of doing divorce work and does not want to be stereotyped as the advocate for all women.

What about the situation in which a divorce client badly wants and needs help in sorting out his personal life? How should the lawyer respond? Perhaps he declines to provide such assistance because he believes his legal training did not prepare him to be a therapist, and that it would be unethical for him to pretend to do so. Or maybe it is because in his low-cost, high-volume practice, the lawyer simply cannot spare the time to talk to clients about their personal problems. Possibly, the lawyer discourages his client from venting his feelings because he finds such issues painful and difficult to talk about. If, however, the lawyer decides to engage in counseling the client, is it the result of a family law course in law school that opened his eyes to the psychological effects of divorce? Is it because his experience as a divorce specialist has taught him that affluent clients expect to be provided with emotional as well as legal counseling—and are able and willing to pay for it? Or is it perhaps because this lawyer is naturally sensitive and empathetic and would not dream of silencing a person in distress?

Questions about the basis for these independent decisions are in essence ones about the nature of control over work and are central to an understanding of the professions and how they relate to other kinds of occupations. These questions are also important to the legal profession in its attempt to assure the public that it serves and protects their collective interests. Clearly, each of the three perspectives on lawyers' decision making—the "professional," the "workplace," and the "personal"— could make sense in the individual circumstances that we describe. But each perspective alone is inadequate for generalizing more broadly about how lawyers define and conduct their work. In our research we sought to discover the forces shaping attorneys' choices through a detailed study of the work of divorce lawyers. Based on this empirical research and building on other sociolegal scholarship, we advance a fourth alternative, a general explanation that draws something from each of these three perspectives.

In this book we argue that divorce lawyers understand and make choices at work through *communities of practice*—groups of lawyers with whom practitioners interact and to whom they compare themselves and look for common expectations and standards. These groups or aggregations of lawyers are numerous and their norms quite variable, even inconsistent. They range from the bar as a whole, to lawyers who practice in a particular locality, to groups of specialists (or nonspecialists) in family law, to law firm colleagues.[1] It is largely through these communities of practice that divorce lawyers exert limited collegial control over one another and thus help to shape the day-to-day choices that constitute legal practice.

Unlike the universalistic version of professionalism that legal scholars and bar leaders advocate, worry about, and struggle to define, we examine more particularistic forms of professionalism, what we call *professionalism in practice*. That means to us the making of discretionary judgments in reference to some standards or norms that are thought to be shared among other practitioners. Most research on legal professionalism has addressed the organization and ideology of the American legal profession as a whole and has paid far less attention to the everyday practice of law. By contrast, this book examines professionalism through the routine decisions of individual divorce lawyers. By studying lawyers at work, exploring their own descriptions of how they understand and make discretionary choices, we show how professionalism in practice is both constructed and enacted in the day-to-day work of divorce attorneys.

Traditional Professionalism and Lawyers' Decisions

"Professionalism" has provided one answer to the question of what influences lawyers' choices in their work. From this viewpoint, law schools teach the norms and values as well as the expertise that guide and constrain attorneys' decisions in their practices, while the formal rules of professional responsibility and organizations of the bar reinforce this socialization. Bar leaders and scholars frequently invoke this ideology of professionalism, even though they seldom agree about its precise meaning.[2] For many, the central questions about professionalism have been normative in character, as they have struggled to capture its essential qualities. This search for the normative core of the concept of legal professionalism identifies it with a varied set of values and aspirations including public service (American Bar Association 1986), independence (Gordon 1988; Linowitz 1994), objectivity (Zacharias 1995), and statesmanship (Kronman 1993). To those who espouse this normative approach, such ideals may be associated with bygone days when the practice of law was perceived to be a calling rather than a mere occupation.

Even the firmest advocates of this professional account have doubts, however, about the viability of such norms in the face of competing pressures from the workplace: economic self-interest, the demands of consumers of legal services, and the expectations of organizations that employ attorneys. Indeed, the fragility of such control based in the formal organizations and institutions of the legal profession may help to explain why the "crisis in professionalism" has been a recurrent theme in the organized bar in the United States throughout much of the twentieth century (Solomon 1992). Commenting on that crisis in recent years, the American Bar Association has asked rhetorically: "Has our profession abandoned principle for profit, professionalism for commercialism?" (American Bar Association 1986: 1).[3]

The ABA's worries about the self-interested conduct of individuals and law firms have been mirrored in the concerns raised by state bar associations and legal scholars who bemoan not only the disappearance of the ideal of public-spirited service but also the replacement of collegiality and independent judgment among lawyers by self-interested competition and subservience to client demands.[4] The widespread agonizing about the decline of professionalism reflects "a sense that the organized profession has lost control over key aspects of professional behavior" (Nelson and Trubek 1992a: 178). Time and again, however, the organized bar has demonstrated its reluctance to surrender its belief in the efficacy of formal norms and rules. Even when confronted with evidence of the weakness of existing codes in controlling lawyer conduct, the predominant response within the legal profession has been to propose more thoughtfully drafted rules or more rigorous enforcement of existing standards.[5]

The Workplace and Lawyers' Decisions

Many critics challenge the bar's heavy reliance on formal rules of professional responsibility, noting the indeterminacy of many of these norms and the inherent difficulties of collegial enforcement of rules.[6] Even when the norms are straightforward and consistent, the facts and issues in cases frequently are not.[7] Also in doubt is the existence of a unified professional community that can shape the identities and claim the loyalties of individual attorneys. Research has shown that the work lives, practices, ethical commitments, and reward systems of American lawyers vary significantly, depending on who their clients are. Sociologists have identified a sharp cleavage between attorneys with corporate or business clients and those with individual clients (Carlin 1966; Heinz and Laumann 1982; Heinz et al. 1998). To a degree, this separation overlaps the one between lawyers in large law firms and those in small firms or sole practice (Seron 1996). The work lives of lawyers from these two divisions differ so dramatically that it is difficult to conceive of any overarching professional identities or ideals that would have practical significance in guiding the choices of all attorneys.

Indeed, the large firms as well as the government agencies and corporations that employ increasing numbers of lawyers not only help to divide the profession but also compete with one another to establish standards for conduct. Kelly argues that the law firm has become the mediating force between lawyer, clients, and the community at large (1994: 21). Such practice settings challenge the individual independence of lawyers that is central to the ideology of professionalism and increase the possibility of bureaucratic or organizational control over work decisions (Nelson 1985; Galanter and Palay 1991; Kronman 1993; Trotter 1997). Spangler pointedly asks how salaried lawyers can reconcile accountability to their employers with their own professional judgment (1986: ix). In the years since her work was published, this question has also become applicable to law firm partners whose autonomy may be constrained by their responsibility for the firm's profit margin.[8]

This workplace and organizational perspective has been encouraged by a tradition of research about the legal profession that gained momentum in the 1970s. A rich array of empirical studies provides glimpses of lawyers at work in different settings. While little of this research has examined the forces shaping lawyers' discretionary practice decisions, the findings have clear relevance to that question. Some of this research underlines the importance of lawyers' economic self-interest in decisions about how to negotiate and when to settle civil cases (Rosenthal 1974; Kritzer 1991). O'Gorman's (1963) pioneering study of matrimonial lawyers shows that their varying role conceptions are molded in part by the structures of their practices.[9]

The picture of lawyers that emerges from this research and commentary differs sharply from an idealized vision of a unified professional community that shapes lawyers' conduct and with which all lawyers identify. What is portrayed instead is a highly differentiated world of legal practice in which lawyers' day-to-day decisions about their work appear to be rooted in the various work settings themselves. Thus, we have a second account of lawyer choices, one in which the workplace is "the crucial determinant of lawyer behavior" (Nelson and Trubek 1992a: 184). In this account, there are multiple conceptions of professional roles that reflect the incentive structures and organizational settings of varying work contexts.

Personal Identities and Lawyers' Decisions

To the extent that different kinds of people are attracted to practice in different areas of law or in varying legal work settings, expectations about professional roles may be shaped in part by the personal qualities of practitioners. Thus, a third account of lawyer choice incorporates personal identity into our thinking about professionalism in practice. In the traditional view—what Levinson (1993: 1578) calls "bleached out" professionalism—lawyers' personal characteristics such as gender, race, class, or religion have no bearing on their professional identities and practices. Indeed, the basic "notion of professional ethics" is that they, "by definition, supersede personal ethics" (Freedman 1966: 1482). But how tenable is such a view? Although held up as an ideal by much of the bar, it has been challenged on a number of grounds. As Postema (1980: 63–64) argues, it simply may not be possible to separate one's personal and professional personalities and still engage responsibly in professional work, since sound judgment requires not only professional training but also personal reflection and experiences. Luban (1988) also contends that professionalism must incorporate lawyers' individual consciences and views because lawyers cannot avoid sharing responsibility with clients for actions taken in law.

Beyond the familiar conflict between personal and professional morality, however, is the particular tension that women and minorities may experience in conforming to professional standards that were constructed largely by white men of a particular class (Auerbach 1976; Harrington 1993; Sommerlad and Sanderson 1998). Indeed, the social fragmentation of the legal profession has serious implications for ideas about legal professionalism (Pue 1998; Alfieri 1999). According to Wilkins (1998), for example, racial identity inevitably shapes lawyers' conduct. Not only is it difficult for people to ignore their own personal identities when they become lawyers, he argues, but other lawyers, clients, judges, and juries tend to perceive lawyers in terms of their racial and gender identities.[10] Religious identity could also affect lawyers' decisions, just as it did for the Catholic lawyers that Carlin (1962) studied during the 1950s who would not handle the divorces of Catholic clients without "clearing" them through the Church.[11] Moreover, both the ambiguity of professional rules of conduct and the wide range of workplace rules for lawyers permit them to emphasize different aspects of professional identity according to their own personal qualities and self-images. Thus, we should not be surprised to observe variation in lawyering according to who occupies the role.

Debate about women in the legal profession has similarly reflected competing views about the emergence of a particular woman's legal sensibility versus the strength of legal professionalism as a gender-neutral socializing force. While considerable research on women lawyers has documented their difficulties in advancing in the profession as a result of sex discrimination and/or family situations (Taber et al. 1988; Hagan and Kay 1995), fewer empirical studies have examined the relationship between gender and attorney decision making.[12] Menkel-Meadow (1985; 1989; 1995) has suggested that women's entry into the legal profession might redefine professional ideals and roles. Drawing on Gilligan's (1982) distinction between an ethic of care and an ethic of rights, Menkel-Meadow speculates that women lawyers would be more likely than men to bring an ethic of care to their legal work and thus would tend to make different kinds of decisions.[13] Research on a distinctive woman's voice in the legal profession has been inconclusive, however, and it is essential to examine the situational and contextual forces that intersect with gender to influence lawyers in their daily practice (Cahn 1992; Rhode 1994; Sommerlad and Sanderson 1998).

When we view lawyers not as a single monolithic professional group but as divided into many smaller groups differentiated by conditions of practice, we can see more clearly the expression of personal identities, values, goals, and preferences in legal work. Professional decision making permits sufficient discretion, for example, in choosing and relating to clients, that individual practitioners may be able to act out their roles quite differently. Moreover, like-minded individuals may reinforce one another through communities of practice.

Communities of Practice and Collegial Control of Lawyers' Decisions

A major challenge in studying lawyers' decisions is to understand the ways in which varying conceptions of professional roles and obligations both develop in response to and shape specific work contexts and work decisions.[14] We use the concept of communities of practice to suggest that while the formal norms of the legal profession as a whole affect the behavior of its members only selectively, other layers of collegial control operate in work settings and interact with personal identities to help lawyers resolve uncertainties about appropriate conduct. Collegial standards and norms provide grounding for independent decisions and legitimate them so that they are neither entirely self-interested nor idiosyncratic.

The importance of these collegial reference points for decisions is highlighted when one recognizes that many law jobs require substantial discretion. As Schon (1983) has pointed out, images of professionals-as-technicians fail to take proper account of the intractability of many problems and of the imaginative, problem-solving work in which professionals must at times engage. This view of choice is reflected in Glendon's description of the legal realist Karl Llewellyn's approach to legal professionalism: finding an appropriate balance in the face of the many competing claims on time and loyalty (1994: 3–4). But who is to judge the "appropriate balance" or to evaluate the rightness of a particular approach to problem solving? Professional colleagues presumably do, either directly through observation and comment, or indirectly, as lawyers examine their own choices in the light of what they think other attorneys would do in similar circumstances.[15] Thus, collegial influence and control appear to be central vehicles for shaping day-to-day decisions of lawyers. Collegial control plays out in the context of communities of practice.

A modest research literature about lawyers and courts has established the importance of localized groups and of shared "local legal cultures" in shaping the conduct of lawyers. This research reveals loose networks of interdependent lawyers who establish shared expectations for conduct through repeated interaction in common activity. Studies of criminal courts, for example, identify courtroom workgroups that grow out of continuing relationships among prosecutors, defense attorneys, and judges

(Eisenstein and Jacob 1977; Heumann 1978; Mather 1979; Eisenstein, Flemming, and Nardulli 1988). In these workgroups, or communities, of judges, prosecutors, and defense lawyers, colleagues constrain and enable each other in accomplishing the work of criminal law practice. There is a normative dimension to criminal court workgroups as lawyers in them take seriously the professional ideals they create for themselves about how to "do justice" in criminal cases (Utz 1978). Efforts to explain delays in civil courts have similarly led to the concept of local legal culture to describe common understandings about the pace and character of civil litigation among lawyers, judges, and clerks in a particular jurisdiction (Church 1985; but cf. Kritzer and Zemans 1993).

Gilson and Mnookin (1994) use concepts from game theory to argue that continuing relationships among practitioners in a field such as divorce law will create groups of lawyers with mutual obligations that might constrain adversarial conduct and take precedence over some of the demands of the formally defined professional role. Carlin's (1966) pioneering study pointed to the social setting of lawyers' work to explain their understanding of professional norms. Handler (1967) also found that continuing relationships and homogeneity of the bar in a middle-sized community led to a widely shared local interpretation of professional obligations and ethical rules.[16]

Taken as a whole, then, research about legal practice emphasizes the significance of various forms of collegial influence over lawyer decision making but provides a sharp contrast to the image of a single professional community. It reveals instead a picture of many groups that are based in the organization and institutions of legal work and that help to define appropriate behavior for attorneys. Nelson and Trubek suggest that "workplace contexts develop widely varying and often mutually contradictory 'local versions' of professionalism" (1992a: 199). These groups may develop as well out of the shared personal perspectives of similarly minded practitioners. As a result, Wilkins writes, "there is a plurality of overlapping and interacting normative communities, each with a semi-autonomous approach to interpretation, conduct, and professional role" (1990: 513). This book is largely a study of such overlapping, interacting, somewhat inconsistent, and loosely defined communities of practice, and of the ways in which they assert limited collegial control over day-to-day work decisions of divorce attorneys.

Our perspective draws selectively from the professional, workplace, and personal identity accounts of how lawyers make decisions. We believe that traditional professional ideology usefully identifies a normative and collegial dimension to law practice in assuming that members of the legal profession respond to behavioral cues from and expectations of colleagues. However, the professional account overstates the power of formal rules, does not sufficiently acknowledge their indeterminacy, ignores the weakness of enforcement of rules, and fails to recognize the fragmented nature of the profession. We find the workplace account helpful in pointing to the widely varied conditions in which legal work is performed and the significant effects of those conditions on behavioral choices and norms. But to the extent that such a viewpoint dismisses formal rules as irrelevant and offers economic self-interest as an over-riding explanation for behavior, we think it goes too far. The personal identity perspective highlights the impact that individual values and personal characteristics like gender, race, religion, and economic status can have on lawyers, but identity does not operate in isolation from a social and organizational context. Thus, our own interpretation uses the concept of communities of practice as a way of locating the multiple sources of collegial control that impinge on the work of divorce lawyers and that grow out of personal identities, workplace settings, and professional ideology.

Studying Legal Practice

For a variety of reasons, divorce law is an excellent arena in which to explore issues of legal professionalism in practice. The arena of divorce law provides an opportunity to explore links between the macrolevel analysis of large-scale changes in the profession and the microlevel examination of decisions that lawyers make each day. As the American legal profession as a whole experiences increased specialization, economic competition, and growth in law firm size, we can see the implications for legal practice of shifts in divorce work from sole and general practitioners to specialists in small firms. As more women enter law and begin to dominate the family law bar, we can examine whether—and how—gender influences the construction of communities of practice and the meaning of legal professionalism. In divorce practice as well we can see some of the implications of the changing content of the law and the character of legal institutions, since divorce work is altered by no-fault laws, changing concepts of equity, and widespread use of mediation. Divorce law also permits us to examine the variable relationships between lawyers and clients, since divorce clients vary substantially in the intensity and character of their demands and their ability to underwrite them financially.

The practice of divorce law occurs in fairly small, localized settings. Despite the significant recent work by Landon (1990), Seron (1996), and Van Hoy (1997) and the earlier work of Carlin (1962), O'Gorman (1963), and Handler (1967), we still know strikingly little, according to Freidson, about the "modest and ubiquitous settings of individual or small firms who serve individual clients in community or otherwise ordinary locales" (1994: 70). We will examine just such locales by investigating sole practitioners and lawyers in small practices in New England. Unlike their more widely celebrated professional peers in large, corporate law firms, many lawyers in private practice in the United States—60 percent in 1991—still practice by themselves or in firms of five persons or fewer (Curran and Carson 1994: 7–8). Although of lower prestige within the legal profession, these sole and small firm practitioners fall closer to the nineteenth-century ideal of the independent professional (Kronman 1993) than do corporate lawyers in large firms.

At the same time, some scholars have argued that sole and small firm practitioners may be most vulnerable to pressures for ethical lapses (Carlin 1966; Auerbach 1976), although these pressures may be countered by a tightly knit, homogenous bar in a small city (Handler 1967). There is also evidence to suggest that divorce lawyers face disproportionately high numbers of formal complaints about unethical practice (Davis 1991; Trevethick 1995). Thus, the work of divorce lawyers outside large urban areas provides a particularly interesting site for the examination of professionalism in practice. The difficulties these attorneys face in managing to "act professionally" should help to reveal the character and depth of the day-to-day challenges to professional ideals and lead us to a clearer understanding of the variable meanings of professionalism in practice.

The detailed picture of divorce lawyers' work that emerges from our analysis reflects in part the special characteristics of the law and social organization of two small, largely rural New England states. But we think that the challenges these practitioners identify and their struggles to deal with them will resonate with most divorce lawyers and indeed with many lawyers in small-firm or solo practices. These challenges include questions about the nature of lawyers' expertise, the independence of lawyers' judgment, the meaning of advocacy, the place of public service within the private profession of law, and the problem of finding satisfaction in legal work.

Our research draws on lengthy interviews with 163 Maine and New Hampshire divorce lawyers and on a sample of nearly 7,000 divorce cases from court dockets in the two states over a nine-year period (including a sample of docket cases for the lawyers we interviewed). The appendix provides a detailed explanation of our research sites and methods. In this book we rely heavily on the interviews to give voice to the ways in which lawyers understand and make the choices that constitute their work. They speak in many different voices, however, because lawyers vary substantially in how they respond to the dilemmas of practice. The variations in their responses stem from the individual values and socially constructed identities that lawyers bring to their work, the institutional context created by local courts and state law, and crucial aspects of their work settings—their degree of specialization, the economic resources of their clients, and the nature of their work organizations. These key factors, working through communities of practice, help to produce the varieties of professionalism in practice.

Organization of the Book

In chapter 2 we introduce readers to divorce law practice through portraits of five very different divorce lawyers. These lawyers work under varying conditions but nonetheless face many common issues and decisions in their practices. Their stories show the importance of personal and professional identities for constituting the major arenas of judgment in legal practice and for defining versions of legal professionalism. This chapter also permits us to present some of the complexity represented in whole persons that may be obscured by the variable-by-variable analysis of later chapters. Chapter 3 presents complementary views of professional identity, by examining the collective and collegial context for law practice. In it we describe multiple, overlapping professional communities of practice that simultaneously help shape and are shaped by the conduct and values of individual attorneys. Such communities include the bar as a whole, the family law bar, specialists (and nonspecialists) in family law, geographic communities of practice, and the communities of individual law firms.

Each of the next five chapters shows the influence of these communities by addressing a particular area of judgment or choice faced by individuals in legal practice. Chapter 4 demonstrates the limited relevance of technical legal knowledge to the work of divorce law and explores lawyers' struggles to define the boundaries of their expertise. Chapter 5 explores how lawyers manage client demands yet also assert their professional independence. Chapter 6 portrays one of the central expectations of the formal role of attorneys—the expectation that they will act as advocates for their clients—and examines how divorce lawyers define advocacy in practice.

The crucial conflicts between self-interest and client service are considered in chapter 7, which shows how client resources and the organizational setting of practice affect lawyers' daily struggles to set and collect fees and serve their clients' interests. In chapter 8 we draw together many of these themes in focusing on how individual lawyers understand their roles as professionals and find satisfaction in their work.

Throughout these five chapters we demonstrate how and in which situations the particular ideas, norms, and choices of lawyers are linked to individual communities of practice. Thus, we show where the economic self-interest of divorce lawyers responds to the resources of their clienteles, but also where it is resisted by lawyers' adherence to professional rules or personal commitments to service. We show how membership in a law firm produces different incentives for lawyers than those experienced in sole practice, especially with regard to fee collection. Throughout this analysis, the gender of the attorney and degree of specialization in family law emerge as related and important factors in understanding the variability in lawyers' conceptions of their professional roles and in shaping the norms of communities of practice. Client resources—the amount of justice that clients can afford—play a crucial role in shaping the nature of lawyer advocacy, the extent of client-counseling, and the degree of client autonomy. Formal legal rules and procedures and professional conduct rules also emerge as key influences on lawyers' understandings of their roles and on particular kinds of decisions.

Finally, in chapter 9 we link findings such as these on client resources, specialization, gender, and organization of practice from our microlevel analysis to broader changes in the legal profession to suggest how collegial standards have been transformed as a result of changes in law and legal institutions, and in the economics, organizational structure, and demography of the profession. We also argue for an analytic focus on collegial identity, organization, and control of work through communities of practice as a way to understand how norms operate in the choices lawyers make. We then sketch ideas for a theory of collegial control and identify several unanswered research questions, as well as some comparative research strategies. In conclusion, we explore the usefulness of thinking about communities of practice and collegial control of work for debates about professionalism within the bar.

2

THE MANY FACES OF PROFESSIONALISM IN DIVORCE PRACTICE

Well, there's the new yuppie type woman divorce lawyer.
And there's the old-timers, like myself, that's trying to get it
through as easily and quietly as possible. And then there are
the in-betweens from the big firms that have richer people.
—George Elder, a Maine divorce lawyer

Divorce lawyers vary in their understandings of professionalism in divorce practice. Some of these differences are shaped by the nature of their practices. Some derive from individual variations in character and values, while others are rooted in gender roles, age, and experience, and still others in the organization of their law firms. Specialists often understand their roles in divorce cases differently than do general practice lawyers. Unlike sole practitioners who do divorce work, lawyers employed by law firms face demands to be attentive to the interests of partners and to firm policies. Attorneys whose clients have few resources find themselves pressed to structure and limit their time in ways that lawyers with well-to-do clients do not. Women appear somewhat more likely than men to see special personal meaning in divorce practice.

The myriad faces of professionalism that we found in our study complicate Sarat and Felstiner's (1995) portrait of a more homogeneous sample of divorce lawyers, while reinforcing their picture of divorce work as "different from most other areas of legal practice" (1995: 151). Their focus on the lawyer-client relationship and their small sample size did not permit them to identify crucial differences among attorneys and clients. A small number of clients cannot "stand for Everyclient, and their lawyers for Everylawyer" (Chambers 1997: 221). Legal specialization, law firm organization, clientele differences, and individual lawyer identities such as their gender matter in the ways that attorneys conceptualize their responsibilities and engage in their daily work. The diversity in practice that we introduce in this chapter thus extends Sarat and Felstiner's description of divorce lawyering and more generally challenges the organized bar's unitary approach to professionalism.

Yet the different versions of professionalism in divorce practice also reflect shared professional ideologies and similarities in the demands of work. Thus, while recognizing variation, we explore the commonalities among lawyers with differing practices that result from similarities in client expectations and the legal and institutional settings of divorce work. Virtually all divorce lawyers experience the common challenges of identifying, acquiring, and applying relevant expertise; forging working relationships with clients; providing effective representation of client interests; generating sufficient income to remain economically viable; and finding satisfaction in their work. These common challenges organize our examination of variability among lawyers in the chapters that follow.

Throughout this book, we select from interviews with individual attorneys to illuminate these common themes of professionalism in practice and to examine differences in ways that divorce attorneys deal with them. In this chapter, however, we take a different approach. Here, we introduce five attorneys and present in considerable detail the descriptions they have provided of themselves and their divorce work. We do so first because it is important to establish the empirical underpinnings of our analysis. While we began our study with an interest in identifying similarities and differences among lawyers, it was not until the interviews were completed that we fully understood just what we had been looking for. It was our respondents, in other words, who helped clarify for us the themes and issues that lie at the heart of this analysis. But the nature of the research enterprise often requires that respondents' stories, opinions, observations, and arguments be reduced to usable pieces of data. As those data are disassembled and reassembled, the voices of the individuals who provided them too often become faint and disembodied. Recognizing the inevitability of this process, we wanted to begin this analysis where we began the research itself: with a group of living, breathing human beings speaking for and about themselves—though, admittedly, not without frequent interruptions.[1]

In focusing on these five lawyers, we do not intend to present them either as types or as typical. Indeed, it is probably safe to say that each is absolutely unique in his or her particular combination of qualities and characteristics. In his seminal work on matrimonial lawyers, O'Gorman developed a typology of role orientations, distinguishing those attorneys oriented toward solving problems, helping people, or earning a living (1963: 120–132). In addition, he classified attorneys in terms of their role definitions—primarily as advocates or as counselors (132–145). Kressel also distinguished between counselors and advocates among the divorce specialists that he studied (1985: 138–153). These distinctions reflect significant variations in the ways that lawyers define their roles in relation to clients, and we will draw from these efforts as we propose our own typology of role orientations in chapter 8. But these useful analytic typologies lose the complexity of variation found in a finer-grained look at individual divorce lawyers.

Why five lawyers, then, and why *these* five? After surveying the entire set of interviews, we were able to identify the factors that appeared to account for the most important variations in professionalism in practice—at least among divorce lawyers in New Hampshire and Maine: gender, specialization, type of clientele, and type of practice. The task then was to select a small number of respondents who revealed in their interviews enough variation around these characteristics to illustrate a range of approaches to common issues of professionalism in divorce practice. Thus, we present this particular quintet of divorce lawyers.

George Elder: Old-Time Practitioner

After over 30 years of practice, George Elder[2] now finds himself the senior partner of a small firm located in an old Victorian house on a tree-lined street in the city where he grew up. His current caseload of roughly 60 divorces constitutes about half of his open case files, and he describes his clients as representing a cross-section of the population. Although Elder's billing rate of $125 per hour might discourage clients of modest means, he regularly waives or reduces retainers and says that he often neglects to record every hour he works for clients. As a consequence, Elder reports that he rarely bills more than 20 hours in a case and completes at least a third of his divorce cases in ten billable hours or less. His clients thus range across income groups but remain concentrated in the working class with which he identifies.

George Elder's disdain for the changes he has seen in law practice resonates throughout his interview. Escalating costs, greater preoccupation with procedural matters, and increased formality among lawyers top his list of complaints. His view remains that of a self-described "old-timer," committed to serving the working people he came from and placing great value on his own integrity.

> I think I can sell myself to a jury. They look at me, and they'll say, "This guy's not lying" or "he's truthful." And people take me, and

they'll say, "He might be rough, but dammit, he's fair." And that to me is my asset. I'm not one of those bookworms or these geniuses. Far from that. But I think I can talk with people, and people will respect me, and I keep my word.

For George Elder, the heart of the practice of law lies not in bookish knowledge of the law and legal procedures but rather in personal qualities and human relationships. He rails against contemporary law practice that relies too heavily on formal discovery and results in "too much motions, too much waste of time." Indeed, to represent clients with limited resources at the rates that he charges requires him to be especially attentive to limiting the number of hours he puts in on each case.

Women attorneys represent to Elder the newer breed of lawyers who are responsible for the paperwork and attention to detail that he most dislikes.

> Women lawyers are harder to deal with than men lawyers. I don't know what they're trying to prove. . . . But I find that women lawyers are a little bit more meticulous about little things—whether [a divorcing party] should get the TV or the VCR. Men don't fool around with that.

Unlike many other attorneys who insist that the parties themselves divide their personal property and set visitation schedules, Elder feels it is his responsibility to take a part in doing so. But unlike these "women lawyers," he devotes far less attention to these details than to other aspects of the divorce.

In his relationship with clients, Elder sees himself as in charge of running the case, although he allows the client to set the direction. Unlike most of his peers, he expresses a willingness to take on a client who is out to punish the other party, even though he thinks it wasteful and harmful to do so. As he puts it, "I'll tell them that if you're hiring me as a hired killer, it's no good. I'll do it, but it'll cost you money for nothing because in a divorce there is no winner. Nobody wins in a divorce." At the same time, Elder insists that he do the work of advocacy, even in negotiation. He explains to his clients that they should not speak to their spouses, that he—as the lawyer in charge—will handle all the negotiations. Such views about negotiation may reflect both George Elder's sense of professional self and an old-world paternalism toward women clients whom he sees as often too weak to negotiate for themselves. In fact, he believes that he has a reputation for being a "woman's lawyer," though it is a characterization he resists. Ironically, Elder's reputation as an advocate for women and his concern about women's disempowerment resembles that of some modern-day advocates who are acutely sensitive to gender inequalities and power disparities. He also joins some of them in decrying the abandonment of fault-based divorces and the emergence of the notion of a 50–50 split in resources. Indeed, he empathizes with his female clients in their forties and fifties whose husbands "have picked themselves up . . . young chicks and, well, to me, they should pay for that." However, Elder's paternalistic sense that his professional role requires that he be in charge of the divorce process distinguishes him from some feminist lawyers who view client participation as a central goal in their work.

Another important aspect of Elder's self-identity as a lawyer is his reputation for being a tough advocate who does not fear going to court. As he explains, "You'll find a lot of lawyers, they don't like to go to court. They're just scared of court. Well, this is one thing I'm not. You want to go to court, let's go to court." His willingness to try his cases reflects not only Elder's love of oral argument but also his commitment to strong advocacy, a commitment that shapes the way he approaches negotiation.

> They know that I can flare, and I . . . you want a battle, you're gonna get a battle. You want to play ball, we'll play ball. If you want the facts, I'll give you the facts. . . . I mean I treat them [other lawyers] the way I would want to be treated. If I have an attorney that comes in full force, like . . . , I'd cut her down, and I'd shoot her down, and I would very seldom settle with her. She's got that aggressive arrogance with me. You don't want any compassion or anything. Just be arrogant with me and, bastard, you're going to get it all the way. You're not going to scare me with your arrogance. If you come in slowly, and even if [your position] is way out, I'll say, [Let's talk."]

While presenting himself as an old-fashioned, rough-hewn court advocate for the weak, Elder also shows the compassion he feels so many bottom line–motivated lawyers lack. He believes that he must be more open to listening and providing emotional support in divorce cases than in the rest of his practice—more open, in fact, than he feels comfortable with. Indeed, he rates "being a sensitive listener to clients" as the most important in a list of lawyer skills.

> You've got to be a little bit more sympathetic, you've got to be able to listen longer, you cannot be curt, and you can't be too rough with them. They're in a stress position. You've got to go along with them. It takes sometimes three or four meetings before you can start saying, "No, you can't do that." The first meeting you almost just gotta be like a psychiatrist. You just listen, listen, listen and you just can't be like a cop and say, "No, you can't do that. Yes, you can do that." That's enough for them to start crying and lose [control]. You've gotta be a very, very good listener the first meeting.

Although George Elder responds, at least initially, to the emotional needs of his clients, he sees his role primarily as producing legal outcomes for them. Thus, he evaluates his own success in divorce cases in terms of whether he "got shafted or not" by the legal results achieved, not in terms of the client's adjustment to new life circumstances.

Although Elder wants to continue to serve working people as he did in the past, he finds it harder to do so because of the increasing procedural demands imposed by courts and opposing counsel and the escalating costs of operating a law firm.

The cost of a law firm to operate is so high now that, when I was just with another lawyer, you could have a client and you could give him free advice and you could be very friendly, and I built up my clients like this. Today, you're almost like a computer, like a machine. Somebody calls, you have to put it down. Somebody does this, you have to put it down. I feel as if, [if I were a client] I'd say, "You can't even say hello to this guy, you've got to pay him?" That intimate feeling is gone, and it bothers me. I'm from the old school. You know, a guy sees me, he comes in for a few minutes, I didn't bother [to bill him]. Forget it, you know? Now it's hard to say that, and I'm getting reprimanded by my other lawyers. They say, "We know you're doing it."

Yet, even in the face of pressures to give priority to the firm's bottom line, Elder retains a deep sympathy for the difficulties low-income people face in paying legal bills: "Oh my god, it's terrible. I feel sorry for these people." As a consequence, he says, "I lead with my heart," offering his services at no or low cost to needy clients:

How can you say, "Get out of here, you haven't got any money?" The lawyer is being pictured as a grotesque individual who's only out for the buck. I don't like that and, sometimes if I don't take the case, I even tell them what to do. Now believe me, I'm not trying to be a do-gooder and all that, and I'm not trying to run for office. That's my makeup. I feel sorry. I come from working people, and sometimes, I've seen my secretary look at me, and I'll say, "Get her in here." Somehow, I'll take the case and forget the bill. We're supposed to help people.

Elder's old-fashioned view of service gets in the way of the modern imperatives of running a law practice in businesslike fashion. Because of his seniority and his relative financial comfort, he can afford to continue at least some of his traditional commitment to helping people in need. But each year, the pressures mount against that practice.

Elder thus defines legal professionalism in terms of personal integrity and human understanding, not in terms of technical legal skill. The lawyer-client relationship combines elements of the hired gun and the pater familias. He allows the client to set the goals, even if he disagrees with them, but he does not cede any responsibility to the client in doing the work of the case. For Elder, law practice means helping people, with a good income following naturally from that effort, but not driving it. Half of Elder's practice is devoted to divorce not because he identifies particularly with family law, but rather because divorce cases provide an important means of helping people.

How does Elder compare with the other 162 lawyers that we interviewed? All but three of the 37 lawyers in our sample with 20 or more years of experience in law practice are men. These older attorneys are twice as likely as the younger lawyers (43 percent to 21 percent) to have a general practice. In many ways Elder represents the 42 experienced general practitioners in our sample who are mostly men (83 percent) and disproportionately have working-class clienteles. Like most of these general practitioners, Elder sees his role largely in terms of his legal craft—that is, his ability to attain favorable legal outcomes for clients. George Elder's identity seems linked to the community of general practitioners rather than to the "new breed" of divorce specialists among whom he might be counted by the volume of his divorce work. Most of these specialists,[3] in fact, turn out to be women (57 percent) and generally are younger than Elder as well. We meet one of them next in the person of Andrea Wright.

Andrea Wright: Feminist Divorce Specialist

Andrea Wright maintains with her partners a practice devoted almost exclusively to family law. Billing at an hourly rate of $125 and requiring a retainer of $1,500, she effectively limits her practice to a middle- and upper-class clientele. Those clients find themselves at home in the comfortable furnishings of Wright's office, located in a spacious and well-appointed downtown building in a small urban center. She estimates that at any given time she has about 60 open divorce files. Her middle-class clients can generally afford the time she puts in on cases, which is rarely less than 10 billable hours and in half or more of her divorce cases over 20 hours.

As a committed family practitioner and a feminist, Andrea Wright maintains a primary interest in counseling clients, especially women. She says that women often select a woman lawyer, and indeed wives constitute the bulk of her clientele. Wright understands her central responsibility not in terms of obtaining legal outcomes for clients but rather as assisting them to adjust in the long run to a new social role and a new set of economic challenges. As she says, "I see my primary responsibility is getting them off to a new start. Turning their lives around so that they are done emotionally and legally with one part of their life in order to get along with the rest." As a result, Wright judges her own success in a divorce case not with regard to winning or losing but rather in terms of her clients' growth and adjustment. She explains that she assesses "the perspective that my client takes out when we are done at the end of the relationship. Whether my clients were able to see this experience as something that has been helpful in the context of their lives." In particular, she views her work as "restructuring a family," a task that she differentiates sharply from problem-solving that focuses only on the short-term legal issues. In Wright's words, "The two people that are getting a divorce are going to have a relationship one way or the other for the rest of their lives, generally speaking. And so I see my job as restructuring that family with a view to the long-term as well as the short."

Consistent with her emphasis on the long-term, Wright places value on reaching agreements that are fair to both parties rather than trying to get as much as possible for one side. She believes that "it is in my client's interest that the other person not leave the marriage feeling soaked. If you create a situation where there is long-term resentment, you'll pay." In a variety of ways, then, Wright serves as a counselor to her clients, although she tells them "that I am not a counselor" and that it would be "a lot cheaper for them to find a counselor." But she goes on to say of her typical client: "If she wants to counsel with me that is fine. I think I am pretty good at it." Helping clients to come to terms with the divorce and to make plans for a new life is a meaningful part of her job as a divorce lawyer.

Given her commitment to counseling, it is perhaps surprising that Wright reports that she has a reputation as "a real pushy broad litigator kind of person." She finds her reputation ironic because litigation is what she likes least about her practice. In fact, she professes to find the adversarial system incompatible with her personal values.

> Because litigation is stylized war, and I don't think of myself as a warrior. It is a lot of bravado and one-upmanship, and it doesn't have the goal of finding the truth, finding a fair result. A goal of winning goes against the grain for me. It is a real ethical dilemma in many ways. And participating in the system doesn't feel ethical.

At the same time that Andrea Wright disavows a taste for litigation, she believes that she has earned her reputation, at least in part, by pioneering the use of interrogatories in the divorce process.

> When I started, I started doing interrogatories, and I had so many lawyers call me up and swear at me that it was unbelievable. It was like interrogatories are not part of divorce practice. [Another female lawyer] and I sort of developed interrogatories, sending them back and forth. Those interrogatories have spread, and I see my own interrogatories a lot. Although obviously people have added—now it is just part of the whole practice.

In her approach to divorce work, which she started doing in the late 1970s, Wright mirrors the views of many of the "new breed" of specialists serving middle- and upper-income clienteles. She contrasts her style with that of general practitioners like George Elder who see divorce cases as mostly emotional in content, requiring less legal intervention than other cases.

> The older lawyers . . . did not take divorces as their "bread and butter" and it was never seen as a field with any prestige or any substance or any money or anything that they would want to have anything to do with. They did it because they had to. They are real hard to deal with because they think that I am a Rambo because I think that there are lots of things that need to be dealt with in a divorce.

Wright's view, which she shares with many other specialists who serve upper-income clients, is that divorce should be taken as seriously as other areas of civil law practice. Accomplishing this goal means applying all the tools of civil litigation, including formal discovery and motion practice, to family law. By taking the lead in that effort, Wright appears to have distanced herself even further from the community of general practice lawyers of which George Elder is a part. However, as chapter 3 will show, over the years a new community of family law specialists has grown up around Wright and other—mostly female—lawyers pioneering in this field. Indeed, Wright has been active in state legislative and appellate arenas to strengthen the legal rights of wives in divorce and to reform family law procedures.

Despite her reputation as an aggressive advocate, Wright resists clients who want to beat up on the other party. Such an approach treats the divorce process as warfare, and she resists serving as someone else's warrior. When faced with such a client, Wright sees that it is her role to move them away from such a position.

> I try to do a lot of work with the client in terms of what is motivating them, where the hook is. This guy can't unhook until you do. And some clients are just intractable. They can't move. And if they don't follow my advice. . . . I had a lady a couple of months ago who was using visitation just unbelievably to jerk her husband around. She was a battered woman, and he was a real cad. Boy, was she provocative! And if he didn't bring the check the day she wanted it, she would deny visitation. I told her explicitly that you can't do that, and she left me a note saying, "I did it." I wrote her a letter saying, "Find yourself a new lawyer." It's not worth it, being involved in that stuff.

Thus, unlike Elder, Wright refuses to be a hired gun and readily turns away clients who resist her counseling and advice.

Given her views of her role as a divorce attorney, it is not surprising that Wright acknowledges but deemphasizes technical legal knowledge in talking about her specialization. "Actual family law is real simple," she explains, but then goes on to outline the other areas of law, finance, and psychology that she believes are essential. Her view of the necessity of broad knowledge across areas of law accords with that of many other divorce specialists, as does her primary emphasis on the financial issues of divorces among parties with significant assets. So too does her attention to other sorts of expertise outside the law—especially in psychological theory and research—that can presumably aid lawyers in undertaking a counseling role to aid clients in adjusting to the new conditions of life after divorce.

Given the character of her practice, Wright finds that she and her partner can afford to shape their fees, within limits, to the economic resources of clients—but only after joint consultation. She describes, for example,

> one client who has been so hard-hit by life that we just don't have it in us to charge her very much. But mostly we just look at income and assets. There are some people who can just do the retainer and that's it. There are some people who can't do the retainer—they can bring us a $1000 and that is it. We try very much to work with our clients on the finances. We set up payment plans if people can't come up with the lump sum up front.

At the same time, Wright acknowledges that her retainer "does a lot of screening." In addition, she and her partner each try to carry at any time one pro bono case referred by the bar association.

Wright reflects on her reputation for "bitchiness" and finds in it a positive message about her capacity to assist clients with things that are important to them.

> I think there is a certain amount of sexism in the view that women lawyers are Rambos in the divorce law. . . . And it is because I care about the details, that I don't let them slide. There is a kind of ethic [among lawyers] that divorce is not important. You get a settlement and you get out of there. And I am sitting there saying, "No, this *is* important. It is important to my client, and it is important to this negotiation." People come to me because I have such a reputation of being such a bitch, and pushy, and all that. And I think it is because of the detail. I want specific and careful [divorce agreements] if we are going to do it. And I will fight for the details.

In spite of her dislike of the adversarial system, Wright finds satisfaction in combining her knowledge of human emotions and relationships with her knowledge of relevant bodies of law to assist clients, especially women, in rebuilding their lives. For her, advocacy and counseling are not mutually exclusive but part of the same commitment to helping clients cope with divorce. Professionalism for her resides primarily in the effectiveness of that help, not in the exercise of the legal craft or in her reputation among her peers.

In this approach to divorce work Wright resembles many of her colleagues among family law specialists who also emphasize client adjustment rather than legal outcomes. Two-thirds of those lawyers in our sample who specialize most in divorce (75 percent or more of their practices) are women, although some of the men with such practices would mirror Wright's attitudes. Unlike those divorce lawyers such as George Elder with lower concentrations of divorce cases, the most specialized family law practitioners also frequently (82 percent of the time) have clients who are concentrated in the upper middle and middle classes. The ability of clients to pay for substantial attorney time allows the attentiveness to detail that characterizes Wright's practice and those of many of her specialized colleagues. Henry Genrus, whom we meet next, has adapted his practice to very different economic circumstances.

Henry Genrus: Low-Cost Practice for the Low-Income Client

Henry Genrus works as a sole practitioner, directing his practice toward an urban, low-income clientele by pricing his services at the unusually low hourly rate of $45 per hour. For an uncontested divorce, he charges a flat fee of $150 (without children) or $165 (with children) plus costs.

"That's a simple [divorce]," he explains, "uncontested, no mediation, no arguments, no motions pending. Just do the paperwork." Genrus estimates that half or more of his cases require less than 10 hours of his time, and he can recall only a handful of cases over 10 years that required 20 or more hours. Located on the edge of the downtown area, his modest storefront office, with files stacked everywhere, reflects the heavy volume this practice generates. A busy secretary/paralegal screens cases and does preliminary interviews in a neat but spare reception area.

The character of Genrus's practice reflects his conception of his professional role and commitment:

> The goal, sort of, or the vision of [my office] is to provide legal services for those that don't qualify for [free legal services] and yet really may not have money, the kind of money that's necessary to go to most other lawyers. And to take smaller, more routine types of cases that can be handled without a lot of research and time-consuming sorts of things. More routine sorts of things. So that the overhead can be kept down, and prices can be kept down. So, we do a lot of domestic relations, whether that's divorce, or custody or child support. Some minor criminal things, drunk driving, shoplifting, that sort of stuff. Bankruptcies.

According to Genrus, domestic relations cases constitute at least 70 percent of his 200 or more open files.

Although he generally feels successful in offering an important service to lower-income clients, Genrus finds that the demands of keeping up with a high-volume practice weigh heavily on him.

> It's sometimes real frustrating. I mean, you work real hard, you don't make a lot of money. Sometimes you don't do a very good job—you're real busy, you forget things, screw something up. You know you can do a good job for a client, but you think you could have done better. I mean, just because you're doing it for less, if you're not doing the job, then you really aren't doing them a favor. So, that goes back and forth. Some days you feel pretty good, other days . . .

Indeed, Genrus agonizes about how much good he really is doing, balancing his own self-critical assessments of the quality of service against its low cost and accessibility. As a consequence of the difficulties of keeping up with 150 or so divorce cases, he concedes that both he and his clients might be better off if he had fewer active files.

> Well, I think it would be healthier for me and for the clients if I decreased it some, maybe charged a little more, or something. And wasn't quite so on the edge here as far as getting things done. Risking doing sloppy work. . . . I mean, I've got some cases that are seriously neglected here. And I keep promising people I'll get to it.

Given his very low charges for services, however, Genrus cannot easily reduce volume without affecting his modest income. In fact, much of what he does in his practice reflects his need to minimize demands on his time and to maximize cash flow.

By designing his practice explicitly to serve lower-income clients, Genrus believes that he "gives at the office" daily, and thus he can neither afford nor finds it necessary to donate his service to clients through formal or informal pro bono service. His fees are so low that he cannot afford to discount them further for clients who are unable to pay his rates. Collecting fees up front has a particular urgency for him.

> I try to get it in advance, I mean, before we go to court for the final time so that it doesn't become a problem. Not only because I want to get paid, but the administrative hassle of sending out bills and keeping track of all that is just more hassle than I need. So, the deal is you pay before we finish. Sometimes that gets away from you.

Billing itself creates overhead that he must minimize, so collecting fees up front both ensures that he receives the modest fees he charges and helps control costs.

Genrus must also find ways to control his time investment in each case. To that end, he tries to screen new clients to make certain that their divorces are really not contested. This means that the clients Genrus accepts must be realistic about what they can obtain. Generally, he believes that clients come to him with limited and realistic expectations.

> They know that I'm not a magician, and I just can't get them stuff. And a lot of them don't necessarily ask for that. I mean, many of them don't . . . they didn't want to get divorced, and they just want to be reasonable and fair, and they're not expecting to "win" or to "get" something. So, you know, they expect that I'm going to do the job, and that I'm available, and that I'm not going to charge them a fortune, and the job will get done.

For the few clients who seem unreasonable and want to wreak havoc on their spouses, Genrus provides strong counsel and may even send them to another lawyer.

> I will try to subtly twist them away from that. If it really gets obvious and hard, I will just plain out and say that. "This is domestic relations. You've got to let that issue go and get on with this thing." You know, try to be right up front with them about it. If they are still into that, I may tell them to go elsewhere, that I'm here to help them get a fair settlement. You want revenge, you go pay $150 an hour for it.

While preferring negotiation to trial and seeing trial as a "failure of the system" to reach a fair settlement, Genrus also notes the need to avoid a reputation as a lawyer who cannot function in a courtroom. At the same time, most of his work involves settling cases, and he has become skilled in managing the process so that it involves as little of his time as possible. He encourages a majority of his clients to do as much of the negotiating as they can, something he feels generally that they can do.

> There's not a lot of property to deal with. The child support issue, you know, we plug the formula in, and they do a little talking about that.

You know, other than dividing up the TV's and you know, a lot of the visitation is, "Yeah, we're working that out. That's okay. We don't even want to put in a schedule, just a reasonable visitation." So, they handle most of that. They just tell me, "This is what we've agreed to."

When a lawyer represents the other party in a divorce, Genrus prefers to let her make the first offer, largely because it means that she will then do much of the paperwork necessary for crafting a settlement.

It's just easier. I mean, let them. If they do a good job, they've gathered all the information together. They've got the lists of property, they've got the pensions, or whatever the issues are and the type of car, the year, just all that logistical homework that might be a pain in the neck, time consuming. They've got it all in a nice, neat little package. We might not like anything that they suggested, but at least we know; we have a piece of paper to work from. And I can just send that on to my client and say, "What do you think of this?" And then we can come back and say, "Well, we like this and this and this, but we don't like that." Rather than try to create that, which is time consuming. It takes a certain amount of effort to sit down with your client and put that kind of a package together. So, just from a lawyer's laziness standpoint or work efficiency, it's easier for me to respond, especially if the other side does a good job of presenting the issues and their position.

Similarly, given the nature of his practice, negotiating in person makes much more sense than the time-consuming drafting and exchange of letters with client consultations at each stage.

Like other lawyers, Genrus struggles with the demands on his time presented by the emotional needs of his divorce clients. He must balance these against his own need to get on with the many other cases he has underway, as well as his clients' incapacity to pay him to listen. Nonetheless, Genrus does spend some time allowing clients to express their feelings, both because he understands the client's desire to be heard and because listening may help him do his job as legal counsel.

I try to listen for two reasons, to a point. One, because you may pick up information through listening that is important to the divorce or to what you're trying to accomplish for your client. And, two, because you've got to establish a rapport with them, and they may need that, and if that's what they need, you try to provide some of that. But at the same time, there's a real limit to that. I mean, once you think you understand what it is they want and where they're coming from, a continuation of that . . . I'm not trained for that. And they need to see a social worker. I mean, I try not to say, "I don't have time to listen to you," I mean, sometimes I'm better at that than others. Some days I'm patient, and some days I'm busy.

In responding to his clients' emotional expressions as in managing their expectations and negotiations, this divorce lawyer is constrained by the nature of his high-volume practice and the limited resources of his clients.

Ultimately, Henry Genrus views himself as an effective and efficient problem-solver and enjoys that aspect of his work much more than the rough-and-tumble of adversarial struggle.

> Well, I guess I feel most comfortable in the domestic relations area. You know, I mean, usually you can work it out and I like the idea that it's not a commercial kind of thing. I like sort of the attitude, you've got a problem here, let's figure out how to make this thing work.

At the same time, there are hints that Genrus regards "real divorce lawyers" as a breed apart from himself. In noting that occasionally clients have left him to go to another lawyer, he observes that some clients "realize the case is getting a little more complicated than what they want and maybe they'd better go hire [an expensive specialist]. Hire a real lawyer or something." The sense that he is not himself a "real lawyer" also echoes through his comments about the relative unimportance of knowing the law in his practice.

> Well, I mean, the type of cases I handle are simpler types of cases, so there's a lot of divorce law that I don't know, but I don't handle those kind of cases. For the kind of cases I handle, I know what I'm doing. But if you're talking about international stuff, I mean, custody disputes that go across international borders, where there's conflict of interest, conflict of jurisdictions between the states, I don't get involved in that stuff. Rarely, but almost never. If there's a heavy-duty accounting problem about the valuation of a business, I don't see those kinds of cases, generally. I mean, real heavy duty tax consequences. There's a lot of high-powered divorce lawyers that deal with that all the time, and if I were given some sort of an exam, I would fail that miserably.

There may be in these comments an echo of the prestige hierarchy of the legal profession that says, in effect, that "real law" involves property and monied people, not the poor. That view helps to create Genrus's anxiety over whether he is really a professional.

By engaging in a low-income practice, he has placed himself at the margins of his profession. He finds it difficult to reconcile his personal commitment to the work he has chosen with the ideology of legal professionalism. Yet, more than most attorneys, Genrus lives out the commitment to access to legal counsel that remains a central tenet of the organized bar and codes of professional responsibility. He has developed strategies to deliver competent service at a low cost, but he is torn between recognizing what he has accomplished and what he cannot do given the circumstances of his practice. The very features of his practice that make it affordable also make him vulnerable to classic problems of neglect or malpractice. Given the rules against unauthorized practice of law, Henry may be safe from competition from paralegals and others, but not from the nagging sense that he lacks the expertise that presumably is a hallmark of professionalism.

Genrus is not unique in our sample of divorce lawyers. Four or five other attorneys have practices similar in many ways to his, but his challenges in representing lower-income clients are more widely shared by the 42 percent of our lawyer sample who rely largely on working-class clients or a mix of working-and middle-class clients. For these attorneys, as for Genrus, heavy caseloads and resource constraints significantly influence the amount of time that can be billed to clients. Because he is a sole practitioner (like 28 percent of the attorneys in our sample), the selection of clients and the character of his practice are completely in Genrus's hands. Almost three-quarters of these sole practitioners are men, but, unlike Genrus, 70 percent devote less than half of their work to divorce. These sole practitioners do not face the same constraints on choices to protect the firm's interests that George Elder experienced when he wanted to help low-income people. Lawyers in larger firms and with higher billing rates generally work under a very different set of circumstances, as we shall see by examining Edgar Prosper's divorce practice.

Edgar Prosper and the Divorces of the Rich

Located in a spacious and attractively remodeled old brick mill, Edgar Prosper's firm includes 16 attorneys, numerous paralegals, and clerical staff. The expensive furnishings testify to an economically successful practice. A flexible retainer of about $10,000, a personal billing rate of $200 per hour, and a typical legal bill for a divorce of around $100,000 make clear that Prosper's is no typical divorce practice. The firm itself does varied civil work, including some divorce. About 35 percent of Prosper's practice consists of domestic relations cases, and he estimates that he currently represents about 15 divorce clients.

> My practice generally is a business-oriented practice. I'm sort of the general counsel to a lot of smaller, some medium-sized businesses, smaller businesses, two million and under, medium-sized, two to 20 million, that's my frame of reference. I also, as a result of that, these same clients get into domestic relations situations very heavily, and the type of divorce work that I do today is very much akin to a corporate dissolution. I get involved in more of the larger money divorces.

Given the resources of his clients, Edgar Prosper does not worry much about collecting fees. His pro bono work is formally defined, and he undertakes it in another area of law rather than in domestic relations.

With the kind of clientele that he has, Prosper devotes considerable time to each case. He estimates that most of his cases take over 100 billable hours and often involve other, more junior attorneys in the firm.

> Even if it's going to be an agreement, just going through the financials, accounting records, tax records and appraisals and verification of what the assets really are, because there's a major malpractice situation on the hit parade. We just brought two of those cases against other law-

yers who really failed. One client received a settlement based on her husband being worth five million, and it turned out he was worth about 27 million. The lawyer didn't do any financial investigation at all and had her settle the case.

Ethical obligations, legal liabilities, client needs, and client ability to pay all press toward investments of time in Prosper's divorce practice that dwarf the billable hours typical in most divorces. Unlike many of his colleagues who must constantly take stock of their clients' capacity to afford their time, Prosper can do whatever it takes, confident that his clients can pay his fees.

At the same time that Prosper finds interest and challenge in presiding over the dissolution of marriages of the wealthy, he expresses distaste for the emotional components of the practice. He comments, "I find it easier to represent the man in most instances, particularly if they're business or professional people." He then explains why. "They get over the emotionalism of the divorce much quicker in most instances." Perhaps influenced by the fact that a majority of his clients are men, Prosper finds parallels between the practice of divorce law and corporate work. He concludes that the emotional state of divorce clients resembles that of corporate officials in the midst of a corporate break-up: "There's an emotional overlay involved in every divorce case. I do a lot of shareholder litigation, corporate dissolutions, and there's the same emotionalism there. The only thing is there aren't kids involved, but the same degree of emotional upheaval and distrust." As a result, he would prefer to delegate the emotional matters to an outside expert, rather than deal with them himself.

> I like to try to get my clients going to a competent counselor that I can talk with. Inevitably at some point in the divorce, unless you're trained, if you listened to a conversation you would swear the client was terribly angry at you and a lot of lawyers can't discern the distinction. They're really not angry at you, they're just angry. And if I have them going to a good counselor, I'm able to send messages through the counselor that make the whole process much easier.

From this perspective, the emotional turmoil of the client is problematic not because it disrupts the life of that person and makes their future adjustment difficult. Rather, the problem is the disruption of a working lawyer-client relationship that Prosper tries to manage carefully.

> I try to explain to them that it's costing them $200 an hour for me to listen to their emotional upheavals, and they can do much better with a professional for 90 bucks an hour or 100 bucks an hour. A lot of them still want to go through their drill with me, so they do, just so long as they're aware that's what we're doing.

Prosper thus employs legal bills as a means to control the emotional outpouring of clients, although their capacity to pay the price may limit the effectiveness of this tactic.

Instead of becoming absorbed in his client's emotional turmoil, Prosper sees his professional role as bringing reason to a difficult situation. To do this he must establish independence from the client. As a result, he is careful to limit the kind of relationship he establishes with clients.

> One of the worst things you can do is become the friend and confidant of your client because at that point you stop being a professional counselor and you become just that, the friend and confidant and you become so emotionally involved in the case that you'll find it impossible to let go of it and settle it in an objective fashion. Plus your client will regard you in a much different light and tend to become very demanding and almost abusive of your time. And people in need, need somebody's ear. And if you exhibit a willingness to give it to them, they'll take it all. Let the client understand that you're not hired to be a professional confidant or buddy or social worker.

Not only does Prosper carefully limit the scope of his relationship with his clients, but he also actively tries to diminish the emotionality of clients and bring reason to their analysis of their own circumstances.

> I spend a lot of time trying to diffuse what I call the nonsense or the bullshit, and I will be very firm with my client that this is not a matter of spite, and I have a whole pitch I give to them, like, particularly if there are children, I say, "Look, the two of you are getting divorced, but you're still going to remain the parents of the children and in order to be an effective parent you have to have an ability to communicate with your ex-wife or ex-husband. And if the children really are as important to you as you tell me they are, then you will start acting in that fashion because there's no way you can be an effective parent and not communicate with the other parent. And your kids need both of you. And so I don't want to hear all that nonsense."

His bluntness with clients about being reasonable toward their spouses reflects a broader concern for the importance of future relationships between parents and between parents and children. Prosper's views are similar in some ways to those of Andrea Wright, who also focused on the need for fairness in the divorce process and on restructuring the family.

Prosper sees his corporate and divorce work as interconnected, not only in terms of the client base but also through approaches to practice. Legal professionalism in his view involves legal skill and knowledge. It also means a capacity for cool, rational judgments that will assist clients in making business and personal decisions. Emotions may be part and parcel of divorce, but they are not the business of lawyers, who instead deal with money matters and establishing workable long-term financial relationships between former spouses. The work that Prosper does as counsel to corporations helps to shape his approach to divorce. Thus, his client counseling style resembles that of Melissa Newton who, as we shall see, comes to divorce work from insurance defense.

A handful of other lawyers in our sample combine business and divorce practices, and two or three of these represent well-to-do clients in a small but steady stream of divorce cases with high-stakes property issues. Like Prosper, their perceptions of their relationships to clients and of their roles in representing them usually reflect their work in business law. As nonspecialists, their commitment to divorce law differs sharply from that of specialists and is generally akin to the approach of generalists who see divorce work as an essential part of their practices. On the other hand, Prosper shares with many of the specialists an ability to devote a considerable number of hours to a case because his clients can afford substantial bills. In fact, 61 percent of the lawyers in our sample with upper-middle-class clients concentrate at least half of their work in divorce, and 48 percent of them devote three-quarters or more of their practice to divorce. Prosper also works in a firm large enough to provide ample resources and support for the administrative side of law practice. However, as a senior partner in such a firm, he differs from Melissa Newton who exemplifies the younger generation of law firm associates, many of whom are women.

Melissa Newton: Law Firm Associate

With a law degree only four years old, Melissa Newton has already learned a great deal about law practice as an associate in an 11-person firm, located in a sleek new office building in an urban center. Working in a business law practice concentrating on insurance defense, she reports devoting only about 10 percent of her work to family law and estimates that currently she represents seven divorce clients in a caseload of just under 100 cases. She draws largely working-and lower-middle-class clients who may have to stretch to afford the $1,000 retainer and an hourly rate that Newton thinks is "70 or 75 dollars, something like that." Working in a medium-sized firm, especially as an associate, she has little contact with or control over the billing process.

The practice of divorce law attracted Newton because she wanted some diversity in her work. She also believes that compassionate lawyers are needed to help people at their most vulnerable.

> The reason I got into it was we have a big family and a lot of divorces. And I saw them being very dissatisfied with their counsel, and I just said, "That's awful, I would never do that." And I kind of felt a commitment. I guess some people see it as a way to make money. I don't think I ever want to have a sole divorce practice. I'd rather be able to take cases that I felt compelled to take and give it my all and have a good attitude about it than just say, "Oh, here's another divorce."

Newton's commitment to family law is reinforced by the opportunity that it provides to have personal contact with clients and to feel that she has made a difference in someone's life.

> Some cases can be very anonymous. Especially in worker's compensation, you may never meet those whom you represent, the employer

or the insured. It could all be done by phone. But [in divorce law] I get to know them and get to see their interests. I had a case that I just concluded, the one I went to trial on, and when I saw this individual come in, you could see that he was depressed and as we progressed through the process he started to come back to life a little bit. In the end when we absolutely won this case, he was just a new man and I could see that that was what he was. He kind of had the twinkle in his eye back. And so when I saw him, it really made the crappy cases worthwhile to see I did make an impact on someone.

Like George Elder, Melissa Newton finds that her compassion on occasion prompts her to ignore a client's limited resources in responding to his difficulties. Unlike Elder, however, she does not have the seniority to overcome the firm's resistance to giving away her time. Her firm, like many others, has tried to set policies and to routinize retainer and billing procedures in order to reduce the likelihood of unpaid bills.

The retainer is $1000, and the way it works is, the first $500 is actively used, the second $500 is held, and once the first $500 is used up, we request a second $500. And that's a new policy, probably in part generated because of me being too darn nice. But we find that clients are also less willing to fork up money once the [lawyer-client] relationship has begun, and we've been left with a big deficit. And I say [to potential clients], "Feel free to call around. That's what I've got to get, and I'd love to help you, but I can't help you if you can't pay that."

Firm policies also prevent Newton from discounting her fees for needy clients without a formal firm decision. She does, however, carry a couple of formal pro bono referrals at a time and confesses that she does not record every phone call on her time sheet for billing when she thinks the client cannot afford it.

Unlike sole practitioners and some small firm lawyers, Melissa Newton's firm has a steady flow of clients and does not need to accept every client who appears in its waiting room. The absence of such economic pressures makes it possible for Newton to screen clients based on criteria other than their ability to pay a retainer.

I feel that I can refuse a case if I want to. There's no pressure on me yet that I've heard about or perceived to take every case that comes along. And only one other lawyer in our firm does domestic law, and we kind of agree on this, that if you can't work with someone, there's so many emotional issues involved and these people are emotional when you deal with them, that if you can't really empathize with them, then they're gonna be unhappy with you and you're gonna be unhappy with them. So generally, if I feel that I can't work with someone, I'll say "I'm not in a position to help you right now, but let me give you names of some people."

For some lawyers, such screening is a luxury they cannot afford because the uncertainty of their client base makes it essential to take almost any prospective client. In such practices, lawyers must choose between strong client management and simply doing what each client wants.

The clients Newton least wants to take are those who want to get back at their spouses through the legal process.

> One woman called me up on the phone and she said, "I really want someone who's gung ho now. I really want someone who's gonna go in there and nail him." And I said, "Well, maybe you don't want me because that's not my style. I prefer to be low key and assess what's going on. You know, maybe you want a man. Maybe you want some big guy to go beat up on your husband, but that's not me." And it was interesting because she said, "No, no, I really like you, I think I want you." I said, "I don't think I want you." But that's how I would handle it.

Although Newton reports that she really enjoys "the flashier parts of legal work," like trying a recent divorce case, she views herself as committed generally to reaching fair settlements. At times she wonders a little about that approach.

> Maybe that's a problem because I'm not a scrappy one. I guess I don't have the attitude in every divorce that I'm gonna nail the other one. I want, especially if there are kids involved, to get a fair result. I try to talk clients into something that's fair, and if they want everything, I'll say, "Yeah. I'll fight for everything but I don't think that you're being realistic."

Of course, her willingness to "fight for everything" depends on the client's ability and willingness to pay the price, something that few of Henry Genrus's clients, for example, can afford to do.

Newton contrasts her style of representation with that of divorce specialists whom she sees as "scrappy. I get the impression of them being scrappy, nickel-and-dime, kind of tenacious. That's not my approach to it." By this, she means that specialists tend to resist compromising on what Melissa views as small differences, something she has become accustomed to doing with business clients in the rest of her practice. In this regard, her perception of specialists resembles that of George Elder. Melissa Newton also shares with Elder and with Andrea Wright a view that men and women differ significantly as divorce clients. Men appeal to her as clients because they are "more realistic" and less emotional than women are and thus easier to represent.

Helping clients understand their rights has become more important to Newton than listening to their emotional outpourings. Asked to rate on a one-to-five scale the importance of "being a sensitive listener to the client," she observes that "when I started I would have said that's absolutely essential, but I think that it can make it difficult if you're perceived as too personal, so probably a three or a four." Lawyers should instead be objective and resist identifying with clients and taking on their emotions. Unfortunately, in her view, many other divorce attorneys become too closely identified with their clients. As a result, she limits communications with opposing counsel to letters.

> I guess it's the pettiness of the clients, and I detest that. And many of these lawyers become the petty client. They call me up and they whine at me and I say, "Don't whine at me. Tell me objectively, 'Oh, my client did this.' " Because I'll just whine right back, and I think that's just so unbecoming, to assume the characteristics of your client.

In her brief experience as a lawyer, Newton says she has learned to distance herself from her clients and to see independent and objective judgment as central to her role as a professional.

Maintaining independence as an attorney requires learning techniques for controlling clients, especially when they "expect the world" of a lawyer, as Newton believes is often the case. Billing proves an important mechanism for achieving this goal by imposing costs on what she views as inappropriate conduct. In response to one client who dropped in weekly at the office and phoned on other occasions, Newton altered her practice of not billing for every minute of time. This man's behavior shifted—probably, she thinks, because "he started reading his bills." Pro bono clients thus pose a special challenge because without a bill to pay, they can impose demands on the lawyer and choose courses of action without being restrained by the costs.

> Definitely, they don't understand the value of a dollar. I firmly believe that they should be charged something, and I think we can. I sort of found out later on with this one case I had that we can charge disbursements [costs]. And I think that's a good thing because they come to respect your time more which I think paying clients, if they don't at first, when they get their bill for every telephone call they've made to you, they learn to respect your time more. Often with pro bono cases you can never do enough. You can never do it right.

Client management is a central issue for Newton, perhaps because of her relative inexperience, her easy-going manner, and her gender. Her clients might demand too much of her time or ignore her advice. Through experience, however, and with the structure and support of the law firm policy, she is discovering techniques to handle clients effectively, while still providing the kind of caring and careful representation she values.

Melissa Newton was drawn to divorce law to help people deal effectively with a traumatic period in their lives. Her experience with both business and divorce clients has taught her ways to deliver on that goal without listening endlessly to emotional outpourings and to cut off potential clients whom she might find hard to manage. Her junior status and her loyalty to her firm are teaching her more about the importance of restraining informal pro bono work through disciplined collection of fees up front and more careful—though still not complete—recording of her time on each case. Law firms teach those lessons particularly well, while sole practitioners like Henry Genrus struggle to learn them on their own.

In our sample of divorce lawyers, 70 percent of the law firm associates are women, while women constitute only 27 percent of partners and of sole practitioners. But the hard lessons of practice that Newton is learning are shared by men and women equally. Her relatively low billing rates and frequent representation of working-class clients distinguish Newton's divorce practice from those of most of her larger firm peers. In our sample of lawyers, firm size is directly related to the resources of clients—80 percent of the lawyers in the larger firms like Newton's report largely upper-middle and middle-class clients, compared with only 39 percent of sole practitioners and 60 percent of those in firms of two to five persons. Thus, neither Newton's nor Edgar Prosper's larger firm practices are typical in their clienteles, but each reflects the resources and constraints characteristic of practice in larger firms.

Conclusion: Arenas for Judgment

Divorce law practice has many faces, but divorce attorneys share common arenas for discretionary judgment, even if their decisions vary. These arenas are the sites where professionalism is both variably enacted and contested. For divorce lawyers these arenas of judgment include five that will be the focus of chapters 4 through 8: determining the meaning of expertise; choosing how to reconcile control *by* clients and control *of* clients; deciding how to balance contention and cooperation in relations with other lawyers and parties; learning how to serve clients and the public while making a living; and finding meaning and reward in the work of divorce law. These arenas of judgment—expert knowledge, independence, advocacy, public service, and career commitment and reward—relate closely to the central elements of the professional model developed by Freidson (1994). In each arena lawyers engage in a common struggle to make reasonable judgments. They do so, however, with reference to various conditions of practice—especially specialization, law firm organization, and client resources—and to different personal values and to perspectives shaped by such characteristics as gender. These conditions, characteristics, and values both challenge professionalism and help to define it in practice.

A central but seldom acknowledged aspect of professional work is the struggle to deal with conflicting demands and expectations that arise in everyday practice. In his examination of "the reflective practitioner," Schon (1983) highlights the necessity of imaginatively solving substantive problems. In Schon's view, the most effective practitioners are distinguished by their creativity and thoughtfulness in the open-ended enterprise of problem solving in contrast with their less effective peers who can only apply technical knowledge in formulaic ways. Schon's analysis would have us focus on how lawyers think about and employ the law to meet the needs of their clients. But beyond the substantive challenges of the law, attorneys face problems of practice—for example, how to relate to clients, how to deal with opponents, how to manage multiple cases simultaneously, how to make money. These problems of practice, much more than the substantive issues of law, constitute the crucial arenas where professionalism is enacted.

Formal codes of professional responsibility implicitly recognize these arenas of judgment and make multiple and sometimes conflicting demands on lawyers. Ultimately, the task of judgment falls to attorneys in their everyday work. Professional practice in this sense involves the accumulated strategies and rationales for making decisions and taking action in the face of these conflicts and in the context of collegial expectations and evaluations of one's conduct. The five lawyers we just met demonstrate the varying character of these strategies and rationales in the particular arenas of judgment that we study in this book.

What are the boundaries of a lawyer's expertise? Although none of the five lawyers views divorce law itself as a technically complex body of knowledge, each has a sense of a special expertise and a reference group that reinforces that sense. Andrea Wright—heavily specialized in divorce work—regards knowledge of several fields of law, and of the psychology of family relationships, as central to her practice. The capacity of her clients to pay for that expertise helps make it possible for her to develop that knowledge. Henry Genrus, also a family law specialist, worries that what he does is not *real* law, since his practice requires little technical legal knowledge. His stock-in-trade, however, lies in knowing how to provide legal assistance at an extraordinarily low price to clients in need. In sharp contrast, Edgar Prosper relies more on his knowledge of business law than on any expertise in divorce law to deal with complex property issues. Unlike Andrea Wright, neither he nor Melissa Newton nor George Elder attaches any value to expanding the definition of expertise to include psychology or family dynamics.

To what extent should lawyers permit their clients to determine the ends and means of divorce representation? Relationships with clients pose similar problems for each of these five lawyers as they attempt to strike a sometimes tenuous balance between providing independent advice and accepting direction from the client. Each lawyer reports having had challenging clients who made unreasonable demands or had inflated expectations about possible outcomes. Andrea Wright, Henry Genrus, and Melissa Newton place a premium on screening out difficult clients at the start. Since George Elder and Edgar Prosper do less prescreening, they often have to try to educate their clients. Both Elder and Newton, however, indicate that they would continue to represent clients who want unattainable goals, while Andrea Wright and Henry Genrus, for different reasons, say they are more likely to part ways with difficult clients. Melissa Newton emphasizes the need for lawyers to distance themselves from their client's emotions and might criticize Andrea Wright for failing to do so.

What does advocacy for clients in divorce cases consist of and what are its limits? All five of these divorce lawyers understand their professional role to be that of an advisor on the substance and procedure of divorce and of an advocate where necessary. But differences in the resources of their clients and in their interpretations of the nature of appropriate advocacy lead to substantial variations in the amounts of time devoted to cases and in the use of informal or formal procedures. Those lawyers with clients of limited means tend to prefer informal settlement processes, with minimal reliance on the tools of formal litigation. Henry Genrus tries to take only uncontested cases and is content to act largely as scribe, encouraging his clients and the other lawyers to do as much of the work as possible. George Elder wants his clients to do very little. He manages to get the work done for his largely working-class clients through tough but not nit-picking negotiation and by frequently discounting his bills. Andrea Wright utilizes the techniques of civil litigation to ferret out information and is a tough negotiator in working through the details of divorce. She devotes many more hours to her cases than Henry Genrus and George Elder do, and her clients generally can pay for them. For both Melissa Newton and Edgar Prosper, advocacy is shaped by the deal making they have learned in representing corporate clients. Both lean heavily on unreasonable clients to compromise and prefer splitting the difference to what one calls the "nickel-and-dime" approach of lawyers like Andrea Wright.

How do lawyers provide a public service while making a living? Each of these five lawyers recognizes a commitment to service as part of his or her professional identity, but they differ substantially in their ways of translating that commitment into action. Having built a service component into the very structure of his low-cost practice, Henry Genrus struggles to collect payment for every hour of his time up front and cannot afford to take formal pro bono referrals. George Elder believes that lawyers should help people, and he often takes advantage of his senior status in a profitable firm to do so by heavily discounting his fees. Melissa Newton started down Elder's path, but, like Elder, has experienced pressure from the firm to rein in her generosity. Because of her junior status in the firm and her own desire to protect herself from client demands, Newton imposes self-restraint on her desire to help much more than Elder does. However, like Elder, she continues to take formal pro bono referrals. Andrea Wright also accepts such referrals as part of her highly specialized practice and can afford on occasion to discount fees for especially needy clients. With the most lucrative practice of the five, Edgar Prosper chooses to contribute his time and business expertise to assist elderly clients facing insurance or business fraud.

How do lawyers find personal meaning in their work and what nonmonetary rewards do they derive from practice? Because they see their roles so differently, these five lawyers find varying rewards in their work. Andrea Wright stands out among the five in evaluating her work in relation to her client's overall emotional and social adjustment to divorce and its aftermath, rather than in terms of the attainment of a legal outcome. Melissa Newton too is pleased to see "people get on with their lives" but takes no personal credit for it: "that probably has nothing to do with me, though, but more the personalities involved." Instead, her definition of success focuses on whether both she and her client are satisfied with the legal outcome. Edgar Prosper and Henry Genrus each emphasize aspects of outcome appropriate to their particular clienteles. For Prosper, a divorce is successful "if the parties can go about their lives in a reasonable fashion with something close to the equivalency of their past lifestyle." In contrast, Henry Genrus derives satisfaction simply from helping the divorcing parties move from contention to agreement over issues like visitation. George Elder evaluates success in a divorce case more in defensive terms: not being "shafted" by the outcome and not being reported by his client to the bar. Clearly, the extrinsic rewards of practice vary considerably as well, from the modest income eked out by Henry Genrus to the very comfortable living achieved by Edgar Prosper.

Thus, we can see in these five lawyers' accounts of their professional lives the five arenas of judgment that are our focus in this book and the forces at work that help to shape and constrain the judgments that lawyers make in these arenas. Certainly, individuals have considerable room to make choices reflecting their own personal preferences. But judgments are also socially patterned, reflecting both client resources and similar work settings. Practice decisions never occur in complete isolation but always in some sense reflect the observation of and interaction with colleagues with whom attorneys share communities of practice, the focus of our next chapter.

3

COMMUNITIES OF PRACTICE

The lawyers that I deal with on divorce work ... we usually
know one another. We've had other cases together. We both
tend to view the case similarly. We're gonna be advocates for
our clients, but we will obviously talk to one another and try
to effectuate a satisfactory result without a lot of discord and
difficulty.

> —a New Hampshire divorce lawyer

Lawyers inhabit layered and overlapping communities of practice that
help to constitute the multiple meanings of legal professionalism. In
the eyes of some theorists and many bar leaders and law teachers, the
legal profession as a whole provides the community that defines professional norms and shapes the conduct of practitioners. Yet, such claims
have been challenged by those who view the decisions of lawyers as
reflective of personal identities or as shaped by their work settings and
clients instead. In this chapter we try to draw these different perspectives
together to trace a more complex and differentiated view of collegial com-

munities of practice. These communities provide the context for the construction of varying versions of professionalism in practice.

For divorce lawyers, the most inclusive but distant community of practice is the legal community at large that shares similar professional socialization and, through formal structures, presumably defines a set of normative boundaries for conduct. Fairly remote connections to the larger professional community are reinforced through the daily work of divorce lawyers that highlights the boundaries between lawyers and non-lawyers and gives some practical meaning to the otherwise distant codes of professional responsibility. Much less inclusive and more fluid communities of practice include those of local courts and those of divorce specialists as compared with general practitioners and large firm lawyers. Competing with these for some attorneys are the smaller communities defined by law firms that can provide immediate and intense connections to professional peers.[1]

Lawyers help to construct these communities of practice and belong to several simultaneously. Each provides distinctive and sometimes inconsistent influences on the ways that individual attorneys understand and carry out their work. In addition, they provide a rough cognitive map for locating other lawyers and predicting and explaining at least some of their conduct. Thus, the work lives and identities of lawyers both shape and are shaped by their communities of practice.

The Legal Community

In the course of most divorce practices, lawyers find constant reminders of their bonds to other attorneys. The common language and ideology of legal education and the formal organization of the bar, with its codes of professional responsibility and discipline systems, provide meaningful reference points that repeatedly draw lawyers' attention to their general professional identities and their differences from nonprofessionals. Indeed, lawyers appear to be the only occupational group to have coined a new word—*nonlawyer*—to divide the world between insiders and outsiders.[2] In their conceptions of themselves and their reflections on their own behavior, attorneys seem to take seriously this larger, loosely connected legal community. The identity of "lawyer" and membership in the general community of lawyers matter for divorce attorneys as they act out their professional roles in the context of both informal and formal norms.

Informal Norms: The Language and Etiquette of Law Practice

The old story about the single lawyer in town who had no business until a second attorney also hung out a shingle tells much about a distinctive feature of this profession. In adversarial matters at least, lawyers require an attorney on the other side to act out their professional role. Much of legal practice and the ideology that supports it depends on interactions between lawyers who share a language and understanding of rules and roles. The common assumptions at the foundation of legal practice may become invisible to experienced attorneys because they can typically be taken for granted in dealing with other lawyers. However, when they must contend with nonlawyers, especially in litigation or negotiation, divorce attorneys discover—through the absence of peers—just how much they depend on the common ideology, language, and norms of the legal profession.

In Maine and New Hampshire, and probably in many other states, a great many divorces—50 percent of Maine divorces and 47 percent of New Hampshire divorces—involve only *one* attorney, not two.[3] Many of these are relatively simple, legally uncontested cases, in which the parties either have or wish to work out an agreement but enlist the assistance of an attorney to put it into formal terms. Employing only one lawyer obviously saves considerable money, an especially important consideration when resources are limited. As a consequence, divorce lawyers with working-class clients face unrepresented parties on the other side more often than do attorneys with upper-middle-class clients.[4] Nonetheless, virtually all lawyers who do divorces find themselves at least occasionally with an unrepresented party on the other side.

Unrepresented parties pose at least two sorts of problems to an opposing lawyer. If they are cooperative in seeking a settlement, they pose a challenge to the professional prohibition against representing adverse parties. If unrepresented parties are not cooperative, they undercut the assumptions of partnership and shared expertise that underlie adversarial proceedings and the negotiation that occurs in their shadow. In this section we will examine the ways in which unrepresented adversarial opponents help to reinforce recognition of professional community and norms. In the next section we will look at the special problems of professional responsibility created by cooperative *pro se* opponents.

The adversary system presumes advocates of equal skill, making use of court procedures and sophisticated knowledge of law to advance their clients' interests (Schwartz 1978). Negotiation in the adversarial context requires similar rough equality among advocates. When they find themselves with opposing counsel, therefore, lawyers not only are comfortable using their knowledge and advocacy skills but also feel obliged to do so to ensure a fair process for their own clients. Permission to utilize one's legal skill and knowledge aggressively collapses, however, without the presence of a trained advocate on the other side. An unrepresented opponent can render such skills irrelevant or even counterproductive and can make lawyers feel hesitant to deploy them. At the same time, such situations implicitly highlight the general identification of lawyers with other attorneys.

Unschooled and unsocialized in the law, unrepresented parties cannot predict legal outcomes, may misunderstand legal procedures, and do not know the peculiar "etiquette" of litigation and negotiation. As one lawyer noted, "Whenever you've got a *pro se* person on the other side, you sort of almost expect the worst." Another described the biggest problem with an unrepresented spouse: "the person is really unconscious of the meaning of these things which lawyers are very familiar with." A third attorney explained:

> I always get nervous when I have a *pro se* person because I almost feel—I mean, I know I'm only representing one party, my client, and I have to represent that client—but it's like sometimes I feel there's a fine line between taking advantage of somebody that's not represented, and yet not representing my client as well.

When lawyers deal with unrepresented opponents, they share the tacit understanding that much of what they do as advisors and as advocates presupposes a lawyer on the other side. Most obviously, unrepresented parties' lack of basic legal knowledge poses a special problem in the rare cases that go to court. Often, the result is not to give an advantage to the lawyer but rather to render the attorney's professional skills useless. A judge may take up the burden of ensuring fair treatment for unrepresented parties with the result, in the eyes of some lawyers, that unrepresented parties can "get away with murder."[5]

> When one side doesn't have an attorney, it's very difficult for the judge not to become the other side's attorney because the judge wants to make sure that all constitutional protections are afforded the *pro se*, and will ask the questions on cross-examination that the *pro se* would not have asked.

By leaning over backward to even the odds, judges may actually tip the balance in favor of the unrepresented litigant.

Lawyers also generally report exercising self-restraint in undertaking court proceedings that have no legal merit, but unrepresented parties have no such constraints. One attorney expressed frustration with this: "Some *pro se* litigants do everything wrong and wind up costing you and your client a fortune—frivolous motions filed, not showing up, having no sense of any kind of reasonable result indication. They have no one telling them that they are out of line." Occasionally, this may produce a rather comic, if frustrating, situation:

> I can think of a custody case that I've got going, and the man filed a writ of habeas corpus, which is what's generally used to get somebody out of prison. And it was just impossible to respond to. It was very artfully written. I'm sure he took it right out of a form book.

The unpredictability of *pro se* opponents contrasts with the relative predictability of opposing lawyers who know the rules of the process and do not want to appear foolish before either their peers or the court.

Lawyers can also play out their roles as legal professionals more easily in negotiation when they face an attorney on the other side. When the negotiating partner is *pro se*, lawyers cannot rely on judicial intervention to even the balance between parties.[6] That means that lawyers must themselves worry about how to behave in order to represent their own clients effectively while being "fair." As one attorney put it, "I don't want to upset them by trying to use my legal knowledge to intimidate them or anything, so I'm very careful about that negotiation." By definition, negotiation requires the participation of two or more parties. The techniques that normally lead to case settlement assume a nominal opponent who in truth must be a negotiating partner, ideally adhering to the norm of divorce practice for "reasonableness" that we describe later in this chapter. Lawyers often set boundaries on clients' expectations and try to defuse their emotionalism, but unrepresented parties can easily be "unreasonable" and "emotional." In any case, because *pro se* parties do not participate in the professional community, they are not prepared to play the game according to its special rules.

By examining the special problems that unrepresented parties pose for divorce attorneys, we can see more clearly the easily taken-for-granted norms and expectations built into the broad community of lawyers. Lawyers learn to play by a certain set of rules that define relationships and limit expectations—and, to some degree, make the game of law predictable. The rules govern private exchanges between lawyers in negotiation and conduct in court. When someone joins the game without knowing the rules, however, the game itself collapses. Without the structure of the rules and the sense of expertise and control that comes from knowing its routines, lawyers can find themselves uncertain and uncomfortable. In the most general sense, then, lawyers share broadly with their colleagues an identity as lawyers and some assumptions about the adversarial game, its rules, and the etiquette of playing it. Nothing brings the existence of this shared community of lawyers more clearly into focus than trying to deal with a party on the other side of a divorce who represents himself. Because *pro se* parties are so common, divorce practice reinforces the otherwise distant sense of professional community by emphasizing the borders between lawyers and nonlawyers.

Formal Norms of Professional Conduct

Shared membership in the legal community matters not only because of the reciprocal character of lawyering and the common understandings about how one plays the adversarial game. It also matters because lawyers recognize—although differently and perhaps selectively—that they share a code of professional conduct[7] to which they should attend because it is right to do so and because they might get in trouble if they do not. As divorce lawyers make decisions about their relationships to clients, conduct with other parties and attorneys, and behavior in court, the formal codes of professional responsibility serve as reference points, especially in the few instances where they are relatively unambiguous.

In many instances, however, the rules fail to resolve and may even mask the difficult judgments that lawyers must make in their practices.

The lawyers we interviewed described themselves as constrained in their representation of clients by their "own personal guidelines and ethical guidelines." Clients' demands that lawyers behave in ways that could be interpreted as "unethical" led some lawyers to threaten withdrawal from representation. Thus, for many divorce lawyers, the larger professional community appears to provide a source of both identity and esteem, where reputation matters and professional sanction hurts.

Codes of professional conduct also matter because lawyers wish to avoid the embarrassment, anxiety, and substantial investment of time and effort that result from having a formal grievance complaint filed against them. Both Maine and New Hampshire have formal disciplinary procedures to handle complaints against lawyers, although their personnel and processes differ.[8] For divorce lawyers, the complaint process itself may be the punishment because exoneration is common.[9] This concern about grievances has strong empirical foundation because divorce cases lead the list of case types in producing complaints against attorneys in both Maine and New Hampshire (Davis 1991:226; Trevethick 1995: 18). Many lawyers recognize this likelihood and practice defensively[10] in order to reduce the likelihood that complaints will be lodged against them. The particular character of divorce law practice places special pressures on lawyers to be attentive to such problems as dual representation, neglect, unclear fee arrangements, parting with nonpaying clients, the meaning of "zealous advocacy," and second thoughts by clients who settle for less than they might. However, codes of professional responsibility provide only limited guidance in most of these cases because of their generality and mutual inconsistency[11] and because attorneys have uneven knowledge and understanding of them (Abel 1989: 143).

In the context of ambiguity and confusion about the nature of the formal rules guiding their conduct as professionals, divorce lawyers appear to pay particular heed to a relatively clear rule, such as the one prohibiting representation of opposing parties in litigation.[12] This rule takes on special importance in divorce cases because divorcing couples may ask a lawyer to draft a divorce agreement or only one spouse may hire an attorney, leaving the other unrepresented and potentially reliant on the "opposing" lawyer for advice. The attorneys we interviewed indicated that it was not uncommon for lawyers to have couples come in together to request legal assistance in obtaining an uncontested divorce.

> They say, "We have worked out everything, and we want you to represent us." And that is very definitely a "no-no." Sometimes I will say, "I can't talk to either one of you now because you both have been in here." I might on occasion do that but in a few instances I have said to the person who has made the phone call and set up the appointment, I say, "This person is my client." [And to the other spouse,] "I cannot represent you because I can't represent both of you."

You have to tell them, "Look, I can only represent one of you. As long as Joe understands that I am representing Sally. Decide right now who it is." If they say Sally, then that's who it is. We have a form letter, in fact, that we send out to all *pro se* opponents. "If you have any questions at all about it, see a lawyer, review it with a lawyer before you sign. We represent Sally and only Sally."

Although not explicitly referencing the operative codes of professional responsibility, these and other attorneys saw the rule against dual representation as binding on them and tried to conform accordingly.

Such clear prohibitions appear to be the exception in codes of professional responsibility, however. More commonly, the rules provide conflicting expectations, appear ambiguous in application, or are misunderstood. Ultimately, the task of giving them concrete meaning falls to attorneys in their everyday work, often in part through conversations with peers. The work context—especially the complexity of the perceived legal issues such as property division, and the capacity of clients to pay lawyers for negotiation time—appears to help shape the interpretation of these rules. This does not mean that work context wins out over professional norms, however. Instead, the real and perceived demands of the work itself help to define lawyers' senses of their professional responsibilities.

In sum, formal rules of professional conduct clearly do not determine the behavior of divorce lawyers in their everyday practices. Nonetheless, the rules matter both in their aggregate as a representation of a collective sense of professional responsibility and in their specific guidance—when they provide it—about how to behave under certain circumstances. Given the frequent ambiguity and inconsistency of such rules—themes that we develop elsewhere in the book—it should not be surprising that knowledge, interpretation, and understanding of them vary individually and collectively in response to the demands and incentives of the workplace. But the fact of variability does not deny the simultaneous reality of a loose but meaningful professional community of lawyers with both formal and informal norms. That variability underscores the importance of further examination of the characteristics of the work setting and the other communities of practice that help give meaning and guidance to lawyers as they construct professionalism in practice.

Communities of Divorce Lawyers

Lawyers who find themselves regularly interacting with each other on different sides of divorce cases constitute a community of practice. Not all lawyers do divorce work although surprisingly many do it occasionally. For example, in our samples of divorce cases from docket records between 1984 and 1988, 45 percent of the names listed as attorneys of record in New Hampshire and 39 percent of the names in Maine had only one case sampled in any court. Another 21 percent of the lawyers in the New Hampshire dockets and 16 percent of names in Maine had only two cases. This suggests that large numbers of lawyers only do an occasional divorce. In New Hampshire, the 20 percent of divorce lawyers who did the most divorces handled 56 percent of the total representations in our sample, while in Maine they handled 65 percent of the cases.[13] The large group of attorneys who occasionally represent divorce clients works at the margins of the community of divorce practice. The general community of divorce lawyers is itself further divided between those specialists and lawyers whose practice is more general or, like Melissa Newton's, is concentrated in another specialty. In the next section we will first consider the general community of divorce lawyers and then the finer gradations within it. As we examine these communities, we will see more clearly how important they are in providing reference points for the crucial judgments of lawyers.

The General Community of Divorce Practice: The Norm of the Reasonable Lawyer

The general community of divorce practice stems from shared interest, experience, and knowledge about divorce law and from repeated contact and reputation. In this community, lawyers depend on one another as negotiating and litigating partners and develop common expectations that serve to regularize behavior, rendering it more predictable and their work more manageable. The common norm of a "reasonable lawyer" defines both typical and expected behavior within the community of divorce practice. One-third of the attorneys we interviewed explicitly used the terms "reasonable" or "unreasonable" to characterize "types of divorce lawyers," and many more invoked the concept of reasonableness elsewhere in the interview or used another adjective like "realistic," "rational," or "practical" to distinguish among divorce attorneys.[14]

The notion of the reasonable lawyer provides guidance to attorneys who must negotiate the abstract and conflicting demands of their professional role in the context of the special characteristics of divorce law. How does zealous advocacy get balanced with the need for professional independence and objectivity? How much should lawyers guide their clients and how much should they be guided by them? How can lawyers manage to serve clients with modest resources in the context of a time-consuming and expensive adversary process? Such questions are raised indirectly but not necessarily answered through the codes of professional responsibility. The informal practice-based norms of the reasonable lawyer, however, give a somewhat clearer, although still incomplete, operating definition of what it means to be a responsible professional in divorce practice.

A reasonable lawyer first and foremost knows divorce law, understands the range of likely outcomes and the criteria for them, and accepts the consequent reality that divorce cases generally should be settled. She willingly cooperates in negotiation because she knows the law of divorce well enough to understand that it does not lend itself to win-lose outcomes.

> You just need to be rational, and you've got to be reasonable and know what the law is, so you can advise your client what the law is and then, in my opinion, there's no divorce that should go through on a contested basis, unless someone is being unreasonable.

Furthermore, she recognizes likely and acceptable outcomes of divorce cases and thus can be counted on to counsel acceptance of a settlement close to the typical result. As one attorney said, "I think the lawyers who practice for any length of time in the family law area know that it's kind of like a bell-shaped curve, that most results fall in a fairly narrow range of percentiles." Another lawyer put it this way:

> There's for the most part a group of attorneys who pretty much have the same expectations of what's going to happen and what you're going to get in a divorce. You're going to start on a 50–50 split on the equity, you may go here on one, there on another, alimony's going to be in this range, that kind of thing.

Reasonableness thus requires experience and knowledge in divorce practice that help to diminish the likelihood of demands or offers that fall outside of the range of acceptability.

Being willing to settle does not mean that reasonable lawyers are pushovers, however. As one lawyer put it, "I'm not saying they roll over by any stretch of the imagination, but they're realistic." While advocating for the client's interests, the reasonable lawyer knows that not all issues in a divorce have equal weight. A lawyer commented, "you have to be a bulldog at times and other times you have to be a poodle too. Sometimes you've got to understand that this isn't worth fighting over." Another attorney explained: "Obviously, you have to rely on your own best judgment of what battles are worth fighting and what battles are not, and how far to fight them. And there are some lawyers in town who take zealous advocacy to a new high." Thus, the reasonable lawyer separates important from unimportant issues and demonstrates good judgment and common sense in evaluating a case. As we shall see in the next section, however, specialists and general practice lawyers differ substantially in their views of what distinguishes large from small issues.

Second, reasonable divorce lawyers remain objective and refuse to take on the client's emotions and anger as their own. By contrast, lawyers who become overly identified with the client's position lose their professional independence and become "knights on white horses who tell their clients what they want to hear."

> There are lawyers who adopt immediately their client's idiosyncrasies and deal through the whole case with the other lawyer and other party like they're Saddam Hussein and get very upset at the other lawyer and very upset at the other party and take a completely subjective partisan view of the situation.

Well, there are those who are the soul of reason and well-skilled, such as I. There are the others who seem to become emotionally involved with their clients and their client's cause, and that gets in the way of negotiating a reasonable resolution.

The reasonable lawyer recognizes that he should not take on his client's cause as his own personal battle and that he should maintain a generally dispassionate and independent view of the case, the client, and the outcome.

This independence of judgment and refusal to invest their own emotions in the case help reasonable lawyers to maintain "control" over their clients. Rather than letting clients "call the shots," reasonable lawyers "set their client's expectations." Indeed, 31 percent of lawyers we interviewed specifically mentioned the issue of client control as a major dimension of variation among divorce attorneys. It is not enough for the reasonable lawyer herself to know the law, the system, and "what a case is worth." She must clearly work to teach her clients these lessons, or, at least, to distance herself from unreasonable client demands. As one lawyer explained: "The worst thing you want is a weak lawyer on the other side. He's going to waste your time. He'll do what his client tells him to do instead of telling his client what to do." Another lawyer similarly noted:

> There are some types who are, I guess I would characterize them as total advocates who don't strive for the fair resolution. They strive for, they'll go for just exactly what their client wants, even though it may be unreasonable, and they don't seem to be willing to bring their client around.

The reasonable lawyer rejects the "hired gun" role and instead guides the client firmly to want or at least to accept the kinds of outcomes that are likely.

Third, reasonable divorce lawyers demonstrate honesty, integrity, and openness in their relationships with other lawyers. These qualities are part of the professional "etiquette" discussed by Freidson (1994: 203), a set of norms that members create to define professional working relations with each other. One aspect of this etiquette is that lawyers are not to let disagreements over case outcomes turn into personal animosity. Another aspect is honesty and keeping your word in discussions with your peers. As one attorney put it, "Reasonable people are not going to play games, are not going to try to hide anything, are going to try to be straightforward." Finally, the norm of reasonableness means that lawyers are to share information with one another rather than forcing opposing counsel to use the court to obtain it. That is, to be reasonable means "that you don't make it difficult to get information that I am perfectly entitled to, and otherwise I am going to have to go to court to get it, and it is going to cost everyone time and money, and I am going to get it anyway."

In sum, many attorneys who regularly practice divorce law share common conceptions of reasonable conduct. The portrait of the reasonable divorce lawyer shows a tough-minded advocate committed to settlement as the best resolution in divorce (but willing to go to trial if necessary), knowledgeable about the law and likely legal outcomes, objective and independent in judgment, and willing to guide the client to a fair outcome. Collegiality does not get in the way of advancing the client's interests, but neither does thoughtless advocacy undermine the working relationships necessary within the community. Judgment and balance prevail in this view of the consummate, reasonable professional.

In contrast, "unreasonable" lawyers have been given nicknames by their colleagues that reflect a lack of judgment and balance: "Rambo," "hired gun," "gunslinger," "loose cannon," "jerk," "shoe-banger," "mouthpiece," "asshole," "shark," "pitbull," "mad dog," and "son of a bitch."[15] These lawyers exacerbate rather than reduce conflict, rely heavily and inappropriately on the tools of litigation, and see negotiation as another battleground rather than a place for reasonable accommodation. These are the attorneys "who simply cannot walk by a fire without throwing some gasoline on it, whether they are in a divorce case or anything else." The gasoline consists of outrageous demands in settlement negotiation, vituperative comments and personal antagonism, dishonesty and unreliability, and overreliance on civil litigation techniques of discovery and motion practice.

Those who violate the norm of the reasonable divorce lawyer may do so because they are outsiders to that community, sharing neither its standards nor its bonds of reciprocity.

> And then maybe the last category is the litigator who has more of a personal injury-type practice. Divorces come along every now and then. They take them, they haven't a clue as to what's been happening in the practice of family law. They think it's an automobile accident case and they treat it that way.

Although the greatest contrasts in practice may be between those inside and those outside the community of divorce practice, not all insiders share or live up to the same standards of reasonableness. Lawyers within this community quickly earn reputations and labels among their peers when they violate the norms. But no other efforts appear to be made to change their behavior.

Even the norm of the reasonable lawyer proves too general to apply perfectly to different practice settings within divorce law, however. The general community of divorce practice is itself divided into family law specialists and general practice attorneys (or other specialists) who interpret somewhat differently this ideal. These interpretations reflect the overlapping effects of specialization of practice, social class of clients, and gender of the attorney.

Divorce Specialists and General Practice Lawyers

Some lawyers regularly represent divorce clients as part of a broader general practice or in addition to their specialized work in other areas. A few attorneys concentrate their work largely or entirely in the area of divorce. Divorce specialization appears to have grown and changed considerably during the last 30 years, as we discuss in chapter 9. Nationally and locally, family law has taken on new importance and gained new status. Specialization has also divided the community of divorce law practice into divorce specialists and general practice lawyers.

A substantial number of lawyers in both Maine and New Hampshire concentrate their practices in divorce law. Among the divorce lawyers we selected for study, for example, 36 percent reported that half or more of their caseload consisted of divorce cases, and 20 percent indicated that divorce constituted three-quarters or more of their work. Concentration of practice in divorce law relates strongly both to the sex of the lawyers doing the work and the social class of the clients. Women appear disproportionately as divorce specialists while men appear disproportionately as general practice lawyers. In our sample of lawyers women constituted 33 percent overall, but 67 percent of the lawyers with practices involving three-quarters or more divorce cases. At the same time, those attorneys who specialized most heavily in divorce were almost four times as likely (48 percent) as those with a lower proportion of divorce clients (13 percent) to report their clienteles to be largely upper middle class. Thus, when specialists and nonspecialists meet in a divorce case, the opposition is likely to be across gender and clientele-class lines as well. It is not surprising, therefore, that the conceptions that general practice lawyers and specialists have of one another often intersect with views of gender and differences in the social class of their clients.

Specialists and general practice lawyers share a commitment to reasonableness but tend to understand its meaning differently. From the perspective of many general practice lawyers, the advent of specialization in divorce has brought with it far more formality, difficulty, and expense in resolving divorce cases. Their views echoed those of George Elder whom we met in chapter 2:

> It becomes very difficult now to deal in divorce cases because there has I think developed in New Hampshire a cadre of attorneys who specialize in divorce work, and they make it very difficult to settle a lot of divorce cases that I find frankly are nickel and dime divorces cases and that normally ten years ago or five years ago were able to be settled. And you simply can't settle them. They always end up going to trial with lots of pretrial discovery and interrogatories. In the old days—I am old enough to say "in the old days"—we would get letters from attorneys and telephone calls and you get: "This is what my client has." And now you get interrogatories.

The use by divorce specialists of standard litigation techniques to ferret out information and to attend to detail in divorce cases comes as a shock to general practice lawyers.

> There are a group of lawyers, a small group of lawyers who would make a federal case of every divorce. They're going to have depositions and they're going to have extensive interrogatories, and they're going to want to hire expert accountants to go in and look even though you and I can get within two or three percent sitting down here discussing it.

Many of these generalists, accustomed to an "old-boy network" that dealt informally with a wide array of matters, believed that divorces should be moved along expeditiously; small issues should not be exaggerated. In this view, divorce cases resemble the contract or real estate cases that generalists deal with every day. For one such lawyer, the archetypal unreasonable lawyer was one "who makes a mountain out of molehills. They're very common in divorces. I don't understand this, where you spend five hours negotiating a $1,200 matter, which has just cost the two clients combined more than $1,200. You know? It's insane." Generalists thus define reasonableness in terms of efficiency and informality: "We're almost by definition, we have to have this lawyer-negotiator [approach] because we have a lot of conflicting demands on our time and other cases, most other civil cases particularly. I mean, you function effectively only if you can move things along."

The understanding of reasonableness that prevails among general practitioners reflects the exigencies of their work and the resources of their clients. It is striking to note the similarity of views about the reasonable lawyer between these men in general practice and Melissa Newton, whose divorce work with working-class clients is part of a practice largely devoted to insurance defense. Common experience with clients of limited resources and a practice of negotiation and deal-making bring lawyers of differing backgrounds to share similar views of their roles. Notions of professionalism are grounded in the experiences of practice.

By contrast, divorce specialists generally see themselves as far more serious about divorce work than those who merely "dabble" in it. They are committed to a broad understanding of the legal intricacies of property division, the difficulties and risks of the legal process, the psychological dynamics of divorce, and the importance of divorce to the parties who struggle through it. Specialists also know one another and prefer to deal with one another in divorce cases.

> You have a category of attorneys who spend most of their time doing domestic law who tend to be for the most part sensitive to the issues, sensitive to the imperfections and the system, and they really try to make the process work as best they can for the client. Those are the best people to work with.

I think the categories would be those who are sensitive to the needs of families and those who are not—those who approach a family law case with that same sort of killer instinct that you have for other types of cases, and those who do not, and I find that the family law lawyers who have been at it longest and have the best reputations and do the best work fall into the sensitive category. Those are attorneys who realize that we are not practicing the same sort of law when we're doing a family law case that we are in a personal injury case or other types of hired gun litigation.

Specialists thus tend to see themselves as especially serious about divorce cases and committed to adapting the adversarial legal process to deal with them. They see differences between themselves and other lawyers and identify strongly with a community of divorce specialists.

Specialists sometimes disparage general practice lawyers who, in their view, do not care about what matters to divorce clients and who generally behave with insensitivity to the special character of divorce work.

I tend to call this group, with some exceptions, the ham and eggers. By and large I don't like to see them on the other side of a case. A lot of these people do not work a file the way a divorce file should be worked. They resist a legitimate request by the other attorney because they're time-consuming. I'll have ongoing problems with discovery from these types of attorneys. They will not respond to a legitimate and reasonable request for information, which means you have to either file a motion, get them in court and tell the judge that they have to do it, or they've got to find some alternate means to get the information. I prefer working with [divorce specialists]. I prefer it because I know what I'm dealing with. I know that as far as the broad rules that they'll be supplied with, there's an air of professional courtesy that will exist between myself and the other attorney and that makes the thing go smoother and probably results in a better outcome for both parties.

While generalists see the specialists as too formal and too attentive to detail in divorces, specialists see generalists as too cavalier in their approach to family law and thus resistant to legitimate efforts to treat it seriously by applying the tools of civil litigation to divorce cases. Both identify "unreasonable" lawyers but translate the notion into quite different expectations about how the "divorce law game" is to be played.

These differences in part reflect class variation in clients. General practice lawyers with working- and middle-class clients must be especially attentive to case costs and billing hours because they typically cannot expect to collect fees for more than 10 or so hours of work on a case. Attorneys with upper-middle-class clients, however, generally expect to bill for at least twice as much time. The tasks they must undertake also vary. Lawyers with more prosperous clients handle more complex property issues—for example, valuing businesses or professional practices— and have come to rely on the tools of formal discovery to facilitate these tasks. Notions of reasonableness thus evolve from the perceived necessities of practice. Professionalism is constructed differently under these varying work conditions.

The meaning of professionalism appears also to be influenced by personal identities, especially the gender of attorneys in divorce practice. Family law specialists are disproportionately women, while generalists are disproportionately men. Perceptions of the relationship of gender to the style of practice thus get wrapped up with the differences in the styles of specialists and generalists. We heard long-time general practice lawyers talking about

> the new yuppie female lawyer. . . . They put out a file for a simple divorce case—you wind up with a file that looks like this. [Q: That file is almost two inches thick.] That's right. And their demands are outrageous and unreasonable and an abomination. They start off by sending you a statement of how they think the case should be settled, and you hardly get through it without throwing up. It's so unfair. You know what I mean? It's absolutely a monument to their ignorance to be able to think that any lawyer worth his salt would go along with any such a goddamn deal as that. You know what I mean? That's the problem I've had with them.

> Maybe that's a broad statement but some of the more aggressive ones that I have dealt with I would say they have been women. I think that they have manifested less willingness to try to resolve this thing and to try to work out the differences and reach a settlement.

These comments came from men with general practices that involved largely working-class clients or a mixed middle- and working-class client base. Their negative views of the style of women in practice reflected the same complaints that they directed at specialists, with perhaps the added difficulty they felt in working with women lawyers who were relative newcomers to the legal community.

For many women attorneys, particularly specialists in family law, divorce cases have special meaning. In advocating aggressively for their clients, female specialists in divorce distinguish themselves from men in general practice who, they believe, treat divorce cases with insufficient seriousness and fail to bring to them the same vigorous advocacy they employ in other cases. A female attorney observed:

> I find that oftentimes, men attorneys are not doing a lot of divorce work. They usually give it all to the new or younger associates. Men attorneys don't understand why, if I'm doing 60 percent of my business as divorce work, I really care about this just like they care about the real estate closing or the contract deal. They would tend to think of that as being very hard-nosed and very strident as opposed to just being incredibly aggressive or prepared for your client. So I find that, oftentimes, men attorneys are very willing to reach a compromise that in business would be fine. I would be lying to you if I said it wasn't a fine deal. But because it involves visitation or life insurance, or it involves. . . . If she's paying $95 a week in day care, and he's giving her $95 a

week in child support, and I think I can make an argument why she should get $110 a week, then they think that's too pushy. That's too aggressive. In business, it would be. In business, with $15 a week—give me a break. Nobody's going to fight over that. But in a divorce situation, I think it makes a huge difference in their lives. Both for the men and women. . . . Women take the divorce work a lot more seriously than men do.

That women may take divorce cases "more seriously" than men could both result in and from the fact that the female lawyers we interviewed represented women as clients in 72 percent of their docketed divorce cases, while male lawyers represented women in 54 percent of their cases. Many women attorneys may find they identify especially strongly with the plight of their female clients and want to acknowledge that connection through care and attentiveness in dealing with the case.[16]

Male lawyers appear more highly differentiated than female attorneys in their views about divorce cases and divorce law practice. Men who specialize in divorce may also share the attentiveness to detail and sensitivity to client involvement that women attorneys generally see themselves as having, regardless of specialization. As one woman lawyer said,

The women I see as pretty similar. I don't see the men as pretty similar. I think the difference would be in some attorneys' approach in terms of making decisions for the client, in being the major decision-maker as opposed to involving the client in that process. I know of some attorneys who will make a lot of decisions for the client, and the client gives up that control and that power, and it's just a perpetuation of what that client's gone through all her life.

The women and men who specialize in divorce work perceive themselves as approaching divorce cases more seriously and with greater attentiveness to client needs—especially for participation in decision-making—than those men who take on divorce cases as part of a more general practice of law. Their views of reasonableness give more weight to client autonomy and empowerment and to careful use of formal legal processes than do those of general practice lawyers. This interpretation of professional norms reflects their own commitment to divorce work as "real law," as well as a feminist sensibility, and the greater capacity of their clients to pay for the time required to engage clients extensively and to forego some informal shortcuts. Resources of clients and the lawyer's gender thus interact with specialization to differentiate more particularized communities of practice where the norm of reasonableness takes on finer shadings.

Law Firms as Communities of Practice

In its analysis of lawyer professionalism, the ABA's Commission on Professionalism distinguishes sharply between solo or small firm lawyers and those in larger firms. In the latter, the Commission insisted, "the responsibility of easing the transition into practice should rest on the shoulders of those firms" (1986: 22). In particular, larger firms should help new attorneys deal with the practical and ethical issues of law practice. Kelly's (1994) and Lee's (1999) research on the widely variant cultures of law firms also points to the power of collegial expectations grounded in the workplace to influence the behavior of lawyers. These views call our attention to the importance of large law firms as communities of practice.

Our study focuses on solo and small firm lawyers, however. Twenty-eight percent of the attorneys in our sample practiced alone, while 53 percent were in firms ranging in size from two to five. Only 12 percent worked in firms of 10 or more lawyers. Given the likely impact of individual personalities in a small firm, it is more difficult to view them as having the same powerful and persistent cultures of practice that may shape the individual conduct of attorneys in large firms. But there was evidence in our study that certain aspects of even small firms mattered, especially as they overlapped with and reinforced other communities of practice.[17]

Firm cultures should be viewed as different from but connected with the pressures and expectations that law firms may generate about efficiency and contributing to the bottom line. In chapter 7, we argue that the membership in a partnership or firm can change the professional and moral calculus for attorneys. For example, joining in practice with other lawyers creates a set of financial obligations that at times compete with responsibilities to clients. Although sole practitioners have to worry about overhead costs and paying employees, partners and associates in law firms have obligations to colleagues to follow policy and "keep up their end of the partnership." To give away one's time as a sole practitioner is a personal sacrifice, but in a law firm it means giving away someone else's livelihood too. In this context, variations in law firm cultures about professional roles and responsibilities may relate to expectations and policies about which cases to take on, how to deal with clients of limited resources, and when to accept formal pro bono work.

Geographic Communities of Practice

Geographic boundaries also define communities of practice based on shared institutions, procedures, rules, and bar membership, as well as on repeated interactions and common experiences in the same courts. These communities appear in our study both at the state and local levels. Lawyers within a state constitute a distant community of practice in that they operate under the same legal, bar, and court rules. Since lawyers are licensed to practice within particular states, the state community of practice has relatively clear boundaries, but it may be limited in its day-to-day relevance to lawyers' behavior. Although they obviously are not in regular contact with one another, lawyers in a state community of practice share a reputational network, bar organizations and activities, a professional disciplinary process, and legal rules and procedures. Together, these produce a common identity as a Maine or a New Hampshire lawyer.[18]

Important institutional and legal differences across state boundaries reinforce these communities of practice and influence lawyers' definitions of appropriate professional conduct. For example, at the time of our study, Maine had had five years of experience with mandatory divorce mediation in contested cases with minor children, while New Hampshire attorneys had had little exposure to public or private mediation. In addition, New Hampshire allowed fault to be considered in property distribution whereas Maine did not. These institutional and legal differences appeared to influence the ways that divorce lawyers defined and understood their obligations in divorce cases. For example, the divorce law community in Maine seemed to be less committed to adversarial advocacy than were their counterparts in New Hampshire. Maine lawyers were significantly more likely to respond that their negotiating goal in divorce was a "fair settlement for both parties," whereas New Hampshire lawyers were twice as likely as those in Maine to select as their goal, "getting the most for the client"[19] (McEwen, Mather, and Maiman 1994: 179). The presence of mandatory mediation in Maine appears to have strengthened an already strong norm in family law practice that encouraged attention to the interests of both parties in divorce, while the continuing legal framework for fault may have promoted greater contention in New Hampshire cases.

Additional evidence for greater legal contest in New Hampshire divorces comes from docket data on adversarial motions.[20] In New Hampshire, the average total frequency of such motions per case grew from 1980 to 1988, but in Maine, it fell significantly during that time period (which coincided with the advent of mandatory mediation). That is, adversarial motions in New Hampshire increased from 0.77 per case in 1980 to 1.06 in 1988, while they decreased in Maine from 1.14 in 1980 to 0.92 in 1988. The drop in formal legal contention in Maine appears to be associated with the introduction of mediation. With a changed institutional framework for divorce, Maine lawyers came to rely less on adversarial legal procedures for representing their clients' interests.

Lawyers in Maine were also significantly less likely than those in New Hampshire to emphasize client control as an important distinction among divorce lawyers, that is, to distinguish between reasonable lawyers who controlled their clients and hired guns who did not.[21] Mediation in Maine may help account for this difference. By teaching reality to clients, mediators reinforced the lessons of the lawyers (McEwen, Mather and Maiman 1994: 163–168). The Maine attorneys we interviewed made this point over and over in different ways:

> Probably one of the biggest things is mediation puts the client in touch with reality in some instances. Where I'm not successful in driving

home the point that the client is being unreasonable, where the client suspects that I don't have his or her interests at heart. You can say to a client, "You can't get that," and go to mediation. The mediation takes place, and this and that, and it shows that it's not only my ideas. Then I can come out and say, "Well, I told you." It gives them a second opinion.

Because many cases went to mediation, the common "reality-testing" experience could even out the differences among lawyers in their willingness to encourage their clients to be "reasonable," strengthening the hands of those attorneys least comfortable or willing to take on that role.

Similarly, and more powerfully, local communities of practice emerge around regular interactions in the context of a particular court or set of courts.[22] As one attorney described the significance of these interactions: "A thing that really helps the lawyer is knowing his court, the clerks, and the mediators, and things like that, so you're a lot more comfortable. It may not give you any edge, but it certainly doesn't hurt." Such local identities become clearest when they are missing—when lawyers go to distant courts where they find that they know no one. A local community of practice defines the home environment for lawyers, and as such it appears comfortably familiar to them.

> I have a good working relationship with a lot of attorneys in the neighboring county and generally when I go down there, if there's an attorney on the other side, it's somebody I've been dealing with. [But in places where] I have no idea who they are, they don't know who I am, there's less cordiality and tendency to sit down and chit-chat with someone.

In the context of these local identities, some distant courts develop reputations for being different and difficult. As one attorney described trying cases in a neighboring county, "Well, you get your visa and you go into York County." The sense that there are insiders and outsiders is a fundamental part of communities of practice. An urban divorce lawyer commented about crossing the border into a nearby county: "It's just that they get to knowing who the neighbors are, and we are smart-aleck whipper-snappers from Portland and think we can run the thing. You know, that's sort of their attitude."

The existence of local communities of practice is confirmed by the commonly shared stereotypes of other local communities. For example, attorneys who practiced in small communities or rural areas characterized lawyering in the cities as far more "litigious" or "adversarial" than in their hometown bars. These lawyers preferred to work locally, where lawyers had learned to accommodate one another informally in the context of their professional advocacy.

> I find that I'm very happy practicing here because most of the lawyers, including the hard noses, are people you can get along with. And you can sit down and talk and you can say things without it being shoved

down your throat. Go to Portland and it's a different ballgame, all barracudas.

Up north, it's a lot less formal than it is down south, for example, and you don't very often see interrogatories sent out in divorces. You would if the party was just in the dark and had no clue what was going on, but generally you don't. You call me up and you say, "Could you send me the last couple of years' tax returns?" And I say, "Sure," and I go to the client, and I get the last couple of years' tax returns.

These perceived differences may have something to do with lack of familiarity and the absence of bonds of reciprocity in the larger communities. But it also proves to be generally consistent with evidence about the distribution of contested motions in divorce cases across courts—evidence showing considerable variation from one court to another, even within the same state.[23]

Cross-county differences in local legal communities reflect a complex mix of forces that differentiate the collective experiences of divorce practice. Southern Maine and southern New Hampshire have more wealth than northern sections of the states, and it is in these areas where most of the divorce specialists—serving mainly higher-income clients—have their practices.[24] Their concentrated presence within the divorce bar affects the tenor of practice and shapes ideas of reasonable professional conduct. Courts in the southern parts of Maine and New Hampshire also have more participation from Boston area attorneys. A New Hampshire marital master (a lawyer designated by the state to handle family law cases) characterized differences in the ways divorce lawyers practiced around the state: "There is the basic North/South difference. In the southern part of the state you really feel the influence of the Massachusetts lawyers." Several New Hampshire lawyers echoed this view of a distinctive style of divorce practice "closer to Boston." Massachusetts lawyers "tend to paper far more than they do up here," and they are "more the overlitigation" type.

Judges, marital masters, and even court clerks also influence local legal communities through their patterns of decision making and preferred ways of handling cases. For example, in New Hampshire, scheduling practices for pretrial conferences for divorce cases differed quite a bit from county to county. Where one county court mandated the hearings "in all divorce cases that are contested," another county "rarely if ever has them," according to one marital master. Other masters pointed to differences among themselves in how hard they typically pushed parties to reach agreements, in how tightly they controlled the pace and evidence in contested hearings, or in how formally they ran their courtrooms. Local court practices regarding issues such as these helped constitute lawyers' understandings of appropriate and expected professional conduct.

Further evidence of distinctive patterns of practice in local legal communities in Maine comes from court records of case filings and from lawyers' self-reports about participation in mediation sessions. The highest rate of filing divorce actions in Superior (as opposed to District) Court occurs in Maine's Cumberland County, with 13 percent of divorces filed there in 1989 to 1990, compared with a rate of less than 4 percent in the rest of the state. Lawyers in the more northern Penobscot County had developed different expectations about their role in mediation than had attorneys in other parts of the state. Lawyers there reported requesting mediation later than attorneys elsewhere (only 13 percent requested mediation when the case was filed, compared with 45 percent of attorneys in the other three Maine counties we examined). Furthermore, lawyers in this northern county attended mediation sessions much less often (48 percent) than did attorneys elsewhere in Maine (89 percent). These differences in practice ultimately reflect locally evolved conceptions of the nature of the professional role and responsibilities of attorneys.

Conclusion

According to Webster's dictionary, one meaning of "community" is "a social, religious, occupational or other group sharing common characteristics or interests." In this chapter we have emphasized the "common characteristics or interests" shared by the many communities of lawyers who do divorce work. More important than the simple description, however, is our analysis of how communities of practice help define individual lawyers' understandings of their professional roles and obligations and in so doing assert limited collegial influence over many of their discretionary decisions. The meaning to practitioners of these overlapping communities—of the bar as a whole, of divorce practitioners, of specialists, of law firms, or of local courts—grows largely from the character of the work environment. To the degree that they connect to the day-to-day work and decisions of lawyers, these communities of practice become useful reference points for them. Such communities thus play a central role in framing and defining differing versions of professionalism by translating the general and often contradictory professional identities and norms into guiding principles for daily application.[25]

The "profession of law" provides divorce practitioners with a very general sense of community, through common language, informal norms, and formal rules. The tacit understandings about roles shared by the larger professional community are made more meaningful in divorce practice by the frequent encounters between lawyers and nonlawyers acting *pro se*. The profession's formal norms—especially those few that are relatively unambiguous—are also made relevant to practitioners by the possibility of facing a grievance complaint. But despite their relevance in practice, neither the informal understandings nor the formal norms of the legal community as a whole provide lawyers much guidance in making the many discretionary judgments that are central to the practice of divorce law. However, other practice-based communities, reflecting more closely the structure and demands of court procedures and the local characteristics of clients and legal practices, enclose lawyers more tightly and provide clearer, more particularized norms and expectations about what it means to act "professionally."

The norm of the reasonable lawyer, for example, guides divorce attorneys in defining the appropriate level of advocacy and the role of representative of the client. It also helps lawyers find the balance between thoroughness in preparation and affordable representation. The general norm of reasonableness thus calls for good judgment in responding to the conflicting demands of practice. As we have seen, however, the meaning of reasonableness varies with the location and kind of divorce practice. Other, even more particularized, communities of practice emerge out of the circumstances of practice and provide collegial reference points for individual lawyers in making day-to-day decisions.

These fluid and overlapping communities of practice serve to differentiate lawyers by specialization, class of clientele, and gender, as well as by state and by court within states. Each division involves an emphasis on somewhat different aspects of the lawyer's role, but together they reflect responses to the common challenges of divorce practice identified in chapter 2. For example, all lawyers must make judgments about how involved they should be with clients. But those with lower-income clients must assume that their clients cannot afford protracted proceedings or long hours of counseling and must define their professional responsibilities accordingly. Since the use of formal discovery makes little sense when property holdings are small, lawyers learn to share information informally in order to save their clients' and their own time. The community of general practice lawyers thus has evolved a view of divorce work that generally resolves the question of how much time to spend with clients in favor of minimizing that time. But such limited involvement makes less sense for the community of specialized attorneys representing upper-middle-class clients. Some of these clients are legally entitled to large and potentially hidden assets, and most have the resources to pay lawyers to use the formal legal process fully, as well as to provide them a forum for discussion of their concerns about the divorce. More particularized communities of practice thus provide differing reference points for divorce lawyers about crucial shared judgments.

Communities of practice represent and reinforce collegiality. Collegiality itself works both to enforce and to constrain control of the behavior of individual lawyers. On the one hand, these communities share standards of conduct and enforce them. The capacity to sanction conduct is limited, however. Aside from the rarely invoked powers to suspend or disbar that are now reserved for courts, professional peers employ reputational sanctions—ranging from a formal public reprimand by a grievance panel to an informal label as a "Rambo." On the positive side, lawyers earn reputations as good and honest professionals both from judges and other attorneys. Such collegiality, however, also supports "a reluctance to judge [that] is sustained by an even greater unwillingness to confront apparently erring colleagues, let alone to take any action to otherwise correct them in the interest of the well-being of clients" (Freidson 1994: 204). Indeed, the common pattern among the divorce lawyers we interviewed was to condemn from a distance those who violated the informal norms of practice but not to confront them openly or to seek ways to change their conduct. In fact, no clear or effective mechanisms exist to support such interventions, even when an attorney's behavior appears to impose costs on her own clients, on the other lawyers she faces, and on those lawyers' clients. Typically, these violations of informal norms of reasonableness do not constitute breaches of formal codes of professional responsibility but rather a lack of judgment in resolving the central issues of practice—for example, letting clients make all the decisions or being an unremitting partisan. In this context, formal mechanisms of control are irrelevant and informal mechanisms weak.

Despite their weak enforcement mechanisms, communities of practice matter in defining professionalism and shaping conduct. Lawyers look to them as useful reference points in making the many judgments that divorce work demands. Such communities help to guide choices and to legitimate them. They are readily available to lawyers through the interactions with peers that occur naturally in divorce practice. Conformity to their norms presumably makes practice easier and reduces the anxiety that would come from chronic uncertainty about how to act. But the norms of communities of practice do not determine practice by any means. Individuals still vary substantially in the ways that they perceive their roles. The interplay between communities of practice, conditions of work, and lawyers' personal identities becomes clearer as we examine five central areas of judgment in the following chapters.

4

THE BOUNDARIES OF EXPERTISE

Divorce is relatively cut and dried in terms of what the law is. I have the Maine laws, I have a treatise. If I'm not sure of an answer, I look it up.

—a Maine divorce lawyer

The concept of expertise has always been central to debates about the meaning of professionalism. For the functionalists who pioneered the sociological study of professions, it was the professional's expertise— the mastery of a body of knowledge of value to society—that both justified and necessitated self-regulation of professional behavior to ensure that it served the public interest (Parsons 1939; Goode 1957). To varying degrees, the more recent scholars of the professions have been less willing than their predecessors to accept at face value the idea that professionals actually possess distinctive expertise (Larson 1977; Abel 1989; Kritzer 1998b). Even the skeptics agree, however, that the sine qua non for the success of an occupational group seeking to establish itself as a profession is the capacity to persuade the public to accept its claims to special knowledge.

Following Larson (1977), Freidson calls this process of persuasion the "professional market project," through which workers establish a "secure jurisdiction in the social division of labor" (1994: 202). If this endeavor is successful, it is followed by a "professional maintenance project" that aims at sustaining the workers' status and privilege by institutionalizing their formal knowledge through standardized training and credentialing. Thus, Freidson calls expertise the "least common denominator of professions" (1994: 157).

Similarly, Abbott's (1988) historical analysis of the "system of professions" demonstrates how some occupational groups have achieved their professional status by successfully asserting "jurisdiction" over a given area of work by persuading the public (or the government) of their special competence to do it. Once these jurisdictional claims are established, Abbott contends, they are maintained by individual practitioners whose "work is tied directly to a system of knowledge that formalizes the skills on which this work proceeds" (1988: 52).

For lawyers in divorce practice, identifying the "system of knowledge" that gives them their professional status proves difficult—for the lawyers themselves, as well as for the researcher.[1] Attorneys handling divorce cases face particular obstacles in asserting claims of special expertise. For one thing, they know that many divorces occur without legal help at all and recognize the limited demands for technical legal knowledge and skill in much that they do.[2] For another, they know from experience what some research tells us—that the legal profession as a whole holds divorce lawyers in a poor light, rating the matrimonial field as low in terms of intellectual challenge.[3] Consequently, attorneys practicing in this area must struggle to overcome both the popular perceptions and those of their peers that they lack special knowledge.

The skills of family law that lawyers described to us during our interviews do not generally lie in technical expertise or formal knowledge but resemble instead the skills of Schon's (1983) "reflective practitioner." The reflective practitioner builds knowledge for solving real-world problems through self-conscious examination of the experiences of practice. Or, as Dingwall (1976) puts it, lawyers—like other professionals—"accomplish profession" through their everyday activities in practice.

At the same time, law is often cited, along with medicine and engineering, as an occupational field whose professional market project has been particularly successful at staking a claim to expertise and to the status and privilege that accompany it. Within the legal profession, elaborate structures—law school accreditation, bar examinations, licensing, mandatory continuing education, formal codes of conduct, and disciplinary bodies—reinforce both legal expertise and the *idea* of legal expertise. Because of the notable breadth of its claims to expertise, the bar has been subject to frequent attacks on its jurisdictional flanks by other work groups. For example, Abbott describes how in the early twentieth century American lawyers suffered the loss of their monopoly over title and collections work, leaving them with only "an advisory jurisdiction" in these areas (1988: 273). More recently, lawyers have fought with accountants over whether some of the financial services offered by accounting firms constitute the unauthorized practice of law (Gibeaut and Podgers 1998). Divorce lawyers presumably are especially vulnerable to such "attacks" because it is difficult to claim their skills as either esoteric or exclusive.

In this chapter, we first discuss the particular skills that divorce lawyers claim as their own, and the ways in which these skills grow from the experience of dealing with cases, rather than from formal technical training. Then we see how these perceptions of legal skills and their boundaries from other arenas of expertise play out in potential interprofessional competition between divorce lawyers and mediators. In the final section, we explore variations in the ways that lawyers articulate their primary professional skills and mark the boundaries of their skills and roles as lawyers. These variations turn out to be linked to particular communities of divorce practice—attorneys representing high-or low-income clients, specialists or nonspecialists, and women compared with men. Within these communities we find groups of lawyers defining boundaries of professional expertise and constructing its meaning in ways that suggest some developing *intra*professional competition in divorce practice.[4]

Defining Lawyers' Expertise in Divorce Practice

The nature and boundary of professional expertise are defined through the "acts of professional work" (Abbott 1988: 35) that our research addresses. We sought to understand the ways that divorce lawyers constructed their own versions of expertise in their day-to-day practices in part by asking our respondents to rate on a scale of one ("not important") to five ("essential") six skills that a divorce attorney might utilize.[5] Although the list of skills is basic, it does provide a benchmark for establishing how divorce lawyers rank order them and for comparing the ratings by different communities of practice. Two-thirds of our lawyers expanded on their ratings, and we draw on those explanatory comments, along with their responses to several related questions, to explore what lawyers in divorce practice believe to be their special expertise.

Table 4.1 reports the mean scores that lawyers gave to each of these six skills. As these data show, there was a consensus within the divorce lawyer community on the two most important skills: the ability to listen sensitively to clients and to effectively negotiate problems.[6] The lawyers we studied, like other personal plight lawyers in solo or small practices (Seron 1996), perceived their expertise to lie more in the area of interpersonal communication and negotiation than in technical legal knowledge. One of our lawyers said, "that is a good list" and commented perceptively, "It is interesting because what it makes me think about in that list is how much of that really you depend on experience. Except for the first one, which is just knowledge of the law, just about everything else

Table 4.1 Lawyers' Ratings of Importance of Skills in
Day-to-Day Practice of Divorce Law, on a Scale of 1
(Not Important) to 5 (Essential)

Skill	Mean Rating
Being a Sensitive Listener to Client	4.30 (n = 157)
Being a Skillful Negotiator	4.27 (n = 157)
Being Expert in Divorce Law	3.97 (n = 157)
Being a Skillful Litigator	3.68 (n = 157)
Knowing the Judges	3.50 (n = 155)
Knowing the Other Lawyers	3.25 (n = 156)

I think really comes with doing a lot of divorces."[7] This perspective on professional expertise emphasizes that the most salient professional knowledge is acquired largely through experience.

Listening to Clients

When lawyers rated "being a sensitive listener to the client" as the most important skill in divorce law practice, they had several distinct versions of "sensitive listening" in mind. For some, the skill of listening to clients was essential because it furthered the instrumental purpose of eliciting information for the construction of the technical legal case. Listening to clients mattered, in other words, "in order to get everything I need out" or "to get at the bottom of the divorce . . . [to know] how solid their position is on various issues." Recognizing the potential for emotions to block information gathering, as well as the need for adequate information for effective legal representation, some lawyers stressed the skill of listening for the information it revealed.[8] As one explained, "You have to be skillful in picking out items. You have got to make damn sure you are listening to those things." Gathering this information required *careful* listening to clients, but not necessarily "sensitive" listening in the sense of having a good bedside manner. As another explained, "If you are saying, 'Does that imply being compassionate to the client so they think you are listening, so that they feel better?' I don't know. If it's being a good listener so that you hear, you receive what the client is telling you so that you can use that in your negotiation or your litigation, that is very important." A third lawyer noted wryly that "you don't have to listen sensitively about property."

Another reason to listen was to build a close and trusting relationship with clients, to strengthen their faith in their lawyer. "You need to let your clients know that you understand their problems . . . that they are placing their trust in you and you are going to do everything that you can to get everything that they need." Good listening skills thus helped to define and strengthen the lawyer's role as fiduciary for the client, a critical part of professional responsibility, regardless of whether any information was gleaned through the listening process. As one lawyer said bluntly, listening is essential because "if you don't have that, you won't have clients."[9]

The third way of understanding sensitive listening to clients was as a means of providing emotional support and help for them during the painful process of divorce. Sensitive listening allowed lawyers to befriend and assist clients in solving their problems and moving on with their lives. As one lawyer said, "There's a lot of emotional stuff going on, and I really like to become friends with my clients." Another explained, "Going through my own divorce gave me a great deal of empathy for what my clients have to go through, and when somebody cries in my office, I know how much it hurts." By listening to their clients and responding sympathetically, these lawyers could, as Ellmann (1993) suggests, apply Gilligan's (1982) ethic of care as they enacted their professional role. "Divorce requires the attorney," one lawyer said, "to be not only a legal technician [but] a generic problem-solver helping people cope, sort of handholding."

This version of listening thus differed significantly from the first two, which served the more narrow conception of the lawyer as a legal advocate who needs to know the facts and have the trust of the client. One attorney described this latter view as follows: "You've got to wear two hats. You've got to be a counselor as well as an attorney and the counselor being more of a personal counselor than a legal counselor." This more expansive view of "professionally legitimate problems" (Abbott 1988: 41)[10] and expertise blurs the line between "legal and nonlegal" issues that many attorneys wished to draw.[11] Those lawyers who held this broader view of professional responsibility and expertise—about a quarter of the lawyers we interviewed[12]—generally saw their personal counseling skills as arising from practical experience, although a few sought out new training and collaboration with psychologists and family counselors.

More commonly, however, the lawyers that we interviewed insisted on distinguishing between what they perceived to be legal and nonlegal issues in a case and frequently diverted the latter by referring clients to professional counseling.[13] This boundary of professional expertise—between divorce lawyers as experts in certain kinds of problems and counselors as experts in other areas—was constructed in lawyers' offices through discussions between attorneys and their clients. Although most lawyers knew they could not be too rigid or unsympathetic to their clients' concerns without calling into question their allegiance to clients, they worried that they lacked the qualifications and patience to give appropriate advice or to justify the time (and therefore money) required to do so.

Divorce lawyers who reported that they strongly discouraged clients from discussing emotional issues insisted that a conceptual boundary line separated the legal from the nonlegal sides of a case, and that an attorney's expertise did not extend to personal matters. They defined their professional role in terms of "helping with legal rights" or educating clients "as to what the law says, as to what I would predict a court would do." They were not there "to either judge my client's personal decisions or to assist them in making a personal decision." Although two-thirds of the lawyers who drew such lines acknowledged that they had to tolerate emotional content in the initial conference ("It's expected at the outset") or even through the first several meetings, they tended to believe that the skillful divorce lawyer guides the client to shift away from the personal issues to the legal ones that should preoccupy the attorney.

The attorneys we interviewed thus positioned themselves across a broad continuum, ranging from those who felt they should counsel their clients about their personal problems to those who tried to confine discussions with clients to the legal issues. Thus, lawyers varied in the ways that they understood their own expertise and roles.

Negotiating Effectively

The data reported in Table 4.1 show "being a skillful negotiator" in a virtual tie with "being a sensitive listener to the client" for importance in the day-to-day practice of divorce law. As attorneys explained their numerical ratings, however, they suggested that negotiation, much like listening to clients, involves very little technical training and is instead something that lawyers learn as they engage in and reflect on their practices. Indeed, as one attorney said, skill in negotiation is "absolutely essential [because] that's 95 percent of what a divorce lawyer does." For the lawyers we talked with, negotiation skills were of a rough-and-ready sort, beginning with "being prepared," and continuing with being practical, listening well, and communicating clearly.[14] In other words, lawyers' skill at negotiation in divorce had multiple meanings, but each of these rather generic qualities was gained through experience, not formal legal training.

Understanding the ability to negotiate as uniquely a lawyer's skill was made more difficult by the fact that often clients wanted to engage in negotiation themselves, and in some instances attorneys preferred them to do so. We questioned attorneys about how they viewed the client's role in negotiation.[15] Fifty-five percent indicated that they encouraged clients to negotiate, 33 percent said that they permitted client negotiation, and 12 percent reported that they actively discouraged clients from negotiating on their own. Thus, a substantial majority of divorce lawyers, whether out of conviction, necessity, or both, saw a part for their clients to play in the process of negotiating a divorce.

In discussing the value of client participation in the negotiation process, lawyers repeatedly referred to two sorts of issues where such participation was quite consistent with the lawyer's own professional role as a "skillful negotiator." These concerned arrangements for children's visitation schedules with the noncustodial parent and division of the couple's personal property and household items.

Many lawyers claimed that there was a particular advantage to having the divorcing parties make their own visitation agreements because such settlements were more realistic, workable, and long-lasting than anything the lawyers might work out. They emphasized the importance to divorcing parties of being able to reach agreements on the details of joint parenting. Some also commented that they regarded this type of negotiation as useful preparation for the couple's post-divorce relationship. For example,

> I'm involved in a legal process which only lasts a number of months to get them to a divorce. They are then going to have a number of years when they are going to have to deal with that other person in order to try to keep involved in the child's life. So we try to encourage them to talk about visitation.

It was appropriate for clients to be involved in visitation issues because they would continue to demand the divorcing parties' attention long after the lawyer has moved out of their lives.

But underlying the respondents' concerns with efficacy was also the earlier noted distinction between legal and nonlegal issues, between issues where they felt they could be helpful as lawyers and those they could not be. Arrangements for visitation, for example, are almost infinitely variable and are not dictated by any real legal rules. The general principles of shared parental rights and responsibilities (in Maine) and joint legal custody (in New Hampshire) have nothing to say about whether a child should be picked up on Friday afternoon or Saturday morning, or whether the children should visit the noncustodial parent for one month or two during the summer. Thus, most lawyers believed that they had nothing special to contribute to such discussions. As one attorney asserted:

> On certain issues the clients can come to agreements independently of the lawyers. Let's say it's visitation rights. I mean, what does the lawyer care in the long run about visitation? If they're happy with what they've worked out on visitation, then go with it! Who's to say it's not good for them?

Encouraging their clients to take responsibility for negotiating child visitation arrangements thus made good sense not only because it served the clients' long-term interests, but also because it relieved lawyers of responsibility for dealing with these nonlegal issues.

The lawyers' willingness to encourage client-to-client negotiation applied as well to the task of dividing the couple's personal property (often categorized generically as "pots and pans"). Like the arrangements for children's visitation, the disposition of household furnishings cannot easily be resolved by applying legal rules. Even the principle of equitable distribution is of little value in determining who should get the Tupperware, coffee mugs, lawn furniture, or James Taylor albums—just a few of the many items that lawyers mentioned in describing their disdain for becoming involved with division of the couple's effects that too often involved petty squabbles over "stupid" issues.

> I tell [the client], "You decide who gets the steak knives and the cups.
> If I have got to decide that, we're in deep trouble." And I encourage
> that. I almost never get into that. I've got one going right now where
> I'm arguing over two cats, and that's really bad, let me tell you. And
> I had one I'll never forget. What did we argue over? I think it was a
> set of stainless steel flatware. Oh, it was terrible. That was the entire
> divorce, a stupid set of stainless steel flatware.

In the course of their daily practices, therefore, lawyers had to struggle to define the boundaries of their own special expertise as negotiators in deciding whether and when to permit or encourage client involvement. The somewhat arbitrary distinction between legal and nonlegal issues provided a convenient and commonly used dividing line that helped to define the attorney's role and responsibilities. Cost considerations provided another reason for leaving such disputes for clients to resolve, since the value of items in dispute is usually less than the cost of the lawyer's time. As one attorney reported saying to a client, "Look you're paying me more than the stupid property is worth." For most divorce lawyers, there was simply no reason to waste their negotiating skills or time on such matters. Leaving them for clients to deal with did not threaten the lawyer's expertise in negotiation; rather, it preserved that expertise for what they saw to be more appropriate and important subjects—those with higher price tags and requiring more legal knowledge such as ownership of pensions and real property or alimony issues.

The professional knowledge associated with "being a skillful negotiator" on selected matters, however, also included the capacity to evaluate the clients' ability to advocate for themselves. Lawyers reported certain circumstances under which they would not permit their clients to discuss settlement terms with their spouses. These would include situations in which one spouse was intimidated by the other, where physical abuse had occurred during the marriage, where the parties' bargaining skills clearly were unequal, and where there was excessive hostility. Thus, it was not only the nature of the issues that determined the boundaries of professional expertise but also the lawyers' assessments of their clients' competence to defend their interests in negotiation. Such assessments could thus help to expand or contract attorneys' senses of their own responsibilities in divorce cases.

Expertise in Divorce Law, Litigation, and Local Knowledge of Judges and Lawyers

"Being expert in the law of divorce" ranked a fairly distant third among the six skills rated by our respondents and reported in Table 4.1. This rating tells us something about the relative lack of importance that practitioners ascribed to knowing the "black letter" of divorce law. Legal expertise clearly mattered in practice and thus the skill was rated "very important." But why was it not rated higher? The most straightforward explanation for considering substantive legal expertise to be less than essential in divorce work is that, as several respondents put it, "there just isn't much law" governing divorce, and what exists is "not that complicated." According to this view, any reasonably competent lawyer knows enough law already to handle divorce cases as part of a general practice. And when a more difficult question of divorce law does arise, the answer is not hard to find. As one lawyer explained, "That's why they have law libraries." Or as another said, "As long as you have the skills to look it up, you don't need to have everything right at your fingertips." A third lawyer noted that "anyone can become an expert in any area of the law, in other words, of knowing the law. And divorce law can probably be one of the easier ones." More than one respondent mentioned the standard treatise on their state's domestic relations law as the "one book" that was essential for the divorce lawyer to own.

By contrast, the few lawyers who rated "being expert in divorce law" as essential in day-to-day practice emphasized the constantly changing nature of the field and the need to stay abreast of new cases, statutes, and legal rules.

> You certainly have to be thoroughly familiar with the statutes. There aren't that many of them, but they are constantly updated so you have to read everything that comes in. The child support guidelines and the things that go into that are constantly changing so you always have to be alert to those changes. New cases are coming out every week from the Supreme Court. You should be reading all of those domestic cases, because that's what changes the law.

These lawyers saw much greater complexity in family law and more material to master than the great majority of their colleagues.

Although technical legal expertise is supposed to be central to the professional identities of lawyers, it was not seen that way by most of our respondents. A wide range of perceptions across different groups of lawyers also emerged in the ratings of three other skills related to legal training and advocacy—skill as litigators, knowledge of the judges, and knowledge of other lawyers.

Lawyers' ratings of "being a skillful litigator" placed it fourth in importance on our list, but as with the rating of technical legal expertise, there was wide variation in responses here. The most common reason given for the relative lack of importance of litigation skill was that so few divorce cases are tried. "If it comes down to that, it's [litigation skill] important but most of them don't." Several lawyers explicitly compared the small role played by litigation versus the necessity of being able to deal effectively with clients. For example, one of them noted: "That is not as important, although I certainly came to divorce work because I had the litigation skills, but so much of this practice is client dealings, and I would say 90 percent of the cases end up being settled by the parties and their lawyers."

The lawyers who rated this item relatively highly emphasized the need for effective courtroom presentation and the ability to clearly present one's case to a judge. And since court hearings are different in family law—with special rules of evidence and procedures—some lawyers said they could not simply transfer the ordinary litigation techniques of a jury trial to a family law case. One had to know the specific procedures of the marital courts and the proper way to present one's case to a judge or marital master in chambers. Consequently, as one concluded, "you don't need to be an F. Lee Bailey or somebody like that."

For many lawyers, litigation skills were considered relatively low in importance because negotiated settlements were seen as the preferred outcome in divorce cases—for both the clients and their children. From this perspective, then, several attorneys emphasized that the goal in marital practice is to *avoid* litigation, so "by the time you litigate in a sense it's almost a failure." Or as another one said, "Most cases don't get litigated so, in the cases that go to trial, it's essential. But not many of them go to trial if you're doing your job." "Doing your job," then, meant acting according to the norms of the reasonable lawyer and settling cases by negotiation. But this exact point led some lawyers to express another way of thinking about litigation skill. These attorneys emphasized the *linkage* between negotiation and litigation, noting, for example, that "if you are a better litigator, that gives you an advantage in the negotiations, an unspoken advantage," or that "the stronger the litigator that you are, the greater the respect somebody else has for you, so then the better the negotiator you are."

If litigation skills were not seen as vitally important elements of the professional expertise of divorce lawyers, it is not surprising that "knowing the judges" was viewed as relatively low in importance as well. On the one hand, judicial interpretations of statutes and case law in each local court establish the backdrop for settlement, and, indeed, it was divorce law that provided the arena for Mnookin and Kornhauser's (1979) examination of "bargaining in the shadow of the law." On the other hand, if much of the law is relatively straightforward and few cases get tried, it is understandable that the lawyers we interviewed saw knowledge of the judges as less important than other skills. This item also showed the greatest variation out of the six skills in responses from our lawyers. While some lawyers largely discounted the role of the judge because of the frequency of settlement and attorneys' inability to control who the judge was, others thought it crucial. Lawyers who gave credence to this item explained that by knowing individual judges, they could shape a court presentation to avoid issues that might irritate them or construct arguments to appeal to their predilections. But such stories of biases were frequently contradicted by other lawyers who insisted that judges are evenhanded in deciding divorce cases. Thus, divorce lawyers had different views of the value of this form of local professional knowledge as an aspect of their expertise.

Another aspect of local professional knowledge—knowing the other lawyers—was rated lower still, but its average rating suggests that it was still seen as an "important" skill in day-to-day practice. Since law is a social process as well as an intellectual one, knowing one's colleagues presumably makes work easier, and—according to our lawyers—more effective. For one thing, lawyers said that they could more easily anticipate the course of a divorce case if they knew the lawyer on the other side, being familiar with his or her particular work style and preferences. An experienced attorney could predict the timing and cost of a case, depending on the identity of an opposing lawyer and thus better advise their clients.

Knowing the other lawyers helped in day-to-day practice because it signaled the kind of communication and negotiation one might have. "There are some of us that see each other all the time, and we can cut through a lot of the verbal jousting and get down to business," one attorney explained. Can a lawyer pick up the phone and speak informally with the other lawyer? Or must everything be done in writing because of lack of trust or knowledge about the other side? Those are the kinds of questions that lawyers must answer, and the answers come through experience. As one attorney said, "Of course, with a 'snake' it is always in writing. There aren't any phone conversations." Lawyers said they adapted to each other's approaches by shifting the form of communication, changing offers given in negotiation, or changing the interpretation of offers received from opposing counsel. On the other hand, these tended to be seen only as marginal differences that eased practice or made it more comfortable.

The crucial skills in day-to-day divorce practice remained those of listening to clients and negotiating with opposing lawyers. Neither of these skills is taught formally to most lawyers, and neither is confined to them. Thus, what appear most important to divorce attorneys are skills that are difficult to claim exclusively as within their professional sphere. This would seem to make divorce lawyers especially sensitive and vulnerable to competition from nonlawyers such as mediators.

Divorce Lawyers and Mediators—Case Studies of Interprofessional Competition

The introduction of no-fault divorce in the 1970s was accompanied (and to some extent fueled) by questions about the roles that lawyers had played in the traditional adversarial divorce process (Jacob 1988). Indeed, to the extent that changes in law diminished the role of the courtroom in divorce, it challenged the hegemony of lawyers who had exclusive rights to practice in courts. Later, the increasing use of divorce mediation brought new self-styled experts into the arena, sparking battles over control of divorce work between the organized bar and organizations representing social work and mental health professionals (Fineman 1991). Divorce lawyers in the states of Maine and New Hampshire illustrate two different responses to the competition presented by the new threat to lawyers' hegemony posed by mediation and help to elaborate our understanding of how divorce lawyers define the boundaries of professional expertise.

When Maine adopted mandatory divorce mediation in 1984 for all contested cases involving minor children, no turf war developed over the control of divorce work, despite considerable initial skepticism and even resistance by some lawyers. From the very beginning, Maine's version of divorce mediation accommodated, welcomed, and as a practical matter often required attorney involvement. The key characteristics of the Maine experience were that *all* of the issues in a divorce were on the table for mediation—finances and property, as well as child custody and visitation; that lawyers were not discouraged from attending mediation; and that the mediators were initially almost exclusively nonlawyers who served the courts for token pay rather than competing with lawyers in the private market for clients. Because property issues were at stake in mediation—issues that lawyers see to be centrally within their province as experts—attorneys in Maine were especially likely to attend mediation sessions. There they could use their knowledge of marital property law on behalf of their clients, confident that they would not be challenged by mediators on such points. But they also discovered that mediation sessions could facilitate their work as attorneys more generally, and thus they gradually embraced the process (McEwen, Mather, and Maiman 1994).[16]

By contrast, divorce lawyers in New Hampshire expressed reservations about the few, largely private mediation practices that were just beginning when we did our study. Although generally supportive of the *idea* of mediation, they worried that widespread use might sacrifice clients' legal rights or harm disadvantaged parties in divorce because they presumed that mediation precluded lawyer involvement and thus deprived parties of legal advice, advocacy, and expertise. Indeed, the small number of private New Hampshire mediators also defined the process as a distinct alternative to the legal system, not as the complement to and extension of the court process that mediation offered in Maine. Lawyers' participation in mediation was discouraged, and lawyers were formally prohibited by New Hampshire bar rules from acting as mediators themselves.[17] New Hampshire attorneys also had limited experience with mediation.[18] Hence, many divorce lawyers in the state initially responded to this new process of dispute resolution by defending their expertise as protectors of the legal rights of clients.

The New Hampshire lawyers we interviewed emphasized that they knew "the law" but that mediators did not. "People go into mediation not knowing what their rights are," as one lawyer said, and this could cause a serious problem. Or, as another explained her concern with mediation, "If the parties go in there without lawyers, there is a great possibility that somebody is not getting what they deserve in a divorce." At the same time, most New Hampshire lawyers did see a positive role for divorce mediation in dealing with certain issues, specifically, division of personal property, setting visitation schedules, and occasionally resolving disputes over child custody. As one lawyer put it: "I only send people to mediation in two cases. I will not send them there to do any major property. I only send them for personal property—which I've already told you I don't give a damn about—and I do it for visitation schedules." According to another:

> There are things that I can do as a lawyer, but that I think can be done better by the mediation process. That mostly involves custody and visitation, issues, things surrounding the children. When are they going to camp? Who's going to pay for it? Lawyers hate that stuff. "Do I have to sit there and go through every week of the year with you?"

These differing responses to mediation in Maine and New Hampshire reflected common views of legal expertise—lawyers' command over legal rules and the ability to apply those rules to what they saw as important legal problems (real property, not personal property or visitation), and the ability to advocate for their clients to protect their rights. In Maine, where the mediation process was organized and understood to preserve that turf for lawyers, attorneys were willing to cede—or share—other knowledge claims (skill at helping people divide personal property or set up visitation or at facilitating the expression of clients' emotions) to the mediators. In New Hampshire, however, the early structure of private divorce mediation brought lawyers and mediators into apparent competition, with the consequence that attorneys were reluctant to accept mediation, except where it was confined to the nonlegal issues that many saw as outside of their area of expertise.[19]

Communities of Practice and the Boundaries of Professional Expertise

In our analysis thus far, we have described the overall view of the community of divorce practitioners. However, there was considerable variation among attorneys in the content of what they saw to be their special expertise, and we found certain skills to be linked to the characteristics of lawyer's practices and their personal identities. The income status of divorce clients, the degree of specialization in divorce, and the lawyer's gender all influence their understandings of both the degree and the kind of expertise one must possess to be a competent practitioner of divorce law. These understandings of the nature of professional expertise are products of the lawyers' individual experiences of and reflections about their work and of their ongoing relations with peers in communities of practice. Through interactions with their peers and as they responded to the daily challenges of practice, lawyers gave concrete meaning and priority to the skills that constitute their understanding of professional expertise.

For Richer and for Poorer Clients

Lawyers who worked with clienteles of different resources varied in what they understood their roles to be and the expertise required to do their work. These differences in perception were further reinforced through interaction with like-minded lawyers handling clients of similar means—or especially in the case of lawyers for the working class, facing unrepresented spouses on the other side. Attorneys with working-class clients learned through experience that they could not make a living by extensive negotiation, formal discovery and motions, and lengthy trials because their clients simply could not pay the bills. Those with higher-income clients generally worked in different communities of practice, in which lawyers spent more time on cases and devoted themselves to carefully crafting settlements, negotiating extensively, and litigating if necessary.

Lawyers with clients of limited means rated negotiation skill as considerably less important than did their counterparts with middle- or upper-middle-class clients, in part because they less often dealt with divisions of real property.[20] "Negotiation is not an important tool in divorce," said one attorney, because "my practice tends to be the lower-middle class and you don't have a lot of marital property." The divorce cases understood to require the most substantial negotiation by lawyers were those in which significant financial assets are at stake. In addition, the capacity of clients to pay for lawyer time to negotiate other aspects of a divorce was clearly related to their resources.

When one thinks of "legal negotiation" in divorce, the typical image is of two lawyers bargaining over the case. But "the reality is that two-attorney representation characterizes a small proportion of the divorcing population" (Pearson 1993: 281). In about one-half of the divorces undertaken by lawyers in our study—and especially in those cases involving lower- or middle-class couples—the lawyer was *not* facing an attorney on the other side but rather an unrepresented spouse. Negotiating for a client against a *pro se* spouse involved a very different kind of approach, one not generally viewed by lawyers as part of their professional skill set, as noted in chapter 3. Thus, the meaning and importance of negotiation skill as one aspect of professional expertise were shaped both by the nature of the work and by the communities of practice that reflected these work patterns.

The resources of clients not only helped to shape lawyers' views of the importance of their own expertise as negotiators, but also created pressures both for and against encouraging clients to take a hand in negotiating the divorce. On the one hand, lawyers whose clients had limited resources felt the pressure to have them take on some of the negotiation in order to save lawyer time. By contrast, attorneys with affluent clients were more likely to report *discouraging* client participation in negotiation. Fully one-quarter of the lawyers with affluent clienteles reported that they did so compared with only 9 percent of lawyers with middle- or working-class clients.[21] It is understandable that this position would be concentrated among divorce lawyers whose clients had more assets, and where the lawyers perceived the law to be more complex and their own expertise more crucial to fair resolution. On the other hand, lawyers with middle- and upper-middle-class divorce clients appeared more likely to experience pressure from their clients to participate in settlement negotiations to permit them to retain power over their lives. As one lawyer observed:

> And I also think—this gets more to the sophisticated person going through the process—there's a real issue of self-direction, of control. Some people don't like to just turn it over to an attorney and just hope that the terms come out right, and all those kinds of things. They just want to be able to be there and take control of their own lives in the legal process and know what the other side is saying directly, instead of having to go through three other people in the process.

In these instances, lawyers had to balance their own sense of professional expertise with these client needs and share the work of negotiation accordingly. Thus, lawyer roles regarding negotiation varied significantly with client resources and influenced the ways that attorneys understood the boundaries of their expertise.

Perceptions of the importance of litigation skill as a crucial component of professional expertise mirrored the significant differences in understandings of negotiation skills according to class of clientele. With larger and more complex stakes at issue and more resources from clients to underwrite the costs of lawyer time, it is not surprising that lawyers with middle- and upper-middle-class clients would view litigation skill as a central part of the expertise they brought to representing clients.[22] By comparison, lawyers representing working-class clienteles tended to rate skill at litigation as less important, commenting, for example, that "it doesn't come up that often." When it did arise, the issues tended to be simpler, and as one such attorney said, "divorce litigation probably requires less skill than other types of trial work partly because it's become more standardized by virtue of statutory law and case law."

Thus, the boundaries and nature of professional expertise needed to resolve divorce cases—whether by negotiation or litigation—were influenced by the resources of clients. As lawyers geared their professional service toward one client group or another, as they faced the different demands of cases involving little property versus substantial property, and as they regularly interacted with lawyers representing similar clients or faced negotiation with an unrepresented spouse, they came to define and value skill at negotiation and at litigation in different ways.[23]

Lawyers with different levels of specialization in divorce made different claims about the nature of their professional knowledge, a variation that was linked to the kinds of cases they handled. For the many specialists who chose family law practice rather than having it thrust on them, expertise was tied up with professional identities. Table 4.2 portrays the direct relationship between level of specialization and the perceived importance of "being an expert in divorce law."[24] This relationship reflects not only the level of personal investment in the work, but also the tendency for specialization to relate to the resources and needs of clients. Clients with fairly "simple" divorces—especially ones where there is little or no property to divide—were less likely to be insistent on seeking a specialist as counsel. Since fewer of the cases that came to nonspecialists[25] required detailed knowledge of divorce law, those attorneys did not see it as having the same value as did the specialists.

Indeed, many of the nonspecialists that we interviewed contended that the nature of their cases made the complete corpus of family law rules and case law irrelevant to their practices. In the words of one general practitioner, "It's [knowledge of the law] not that important. First of all, you have to understand it's not hard to be an expert at a level that is appropriate for the cases that I handle." Lawyers whose livelihoods did not depend on divorce cases, and those who handled only simple divorces, did not have the time or need to stay abreast of divorce law, using treatises and reference to the statutes as necessary for exceptional cases. "Is worker's comp benefits considered marital property?" asked one attorney rhetorically. "I can't remember because every time I look it up, it's in one ear and out the other. That's what the books are there for, to remember."

Divorce specialists were aware of and could be infuriated by the nonspecialists' incomplete knowledge of divorce law and the casual dismissal of its importance. It was bad enough, they said, that so many lawyers do not know the law they claim to be practicing. What is worse is that they either do not recognize their ignorance or do not care to rectify it.

Table 4.2 Lawyers' Mean Scores for Importance of "Being an Expert in Divorce Law" by Degree of Specialization in Divorce

Specialization	Mean Rating
More than 75 Percent Divorce	4.35 (n = 30)
50 to 74 Percent Divorce	4.10 (n = 25)
25 to 49 Percent Divorce	3.87 (n = 52)
Less than 25 Percent Divorce	3.80 (n = 50)

$F = 2.33$ with 3 and 152 d.f. (n = 156); $p = .08$

I can see lawyers who just don't keep up. Especially if they're in the situation of not doing it full-time. For instance, I don't want to do criminal [work] because I would feel like maybe I'm malpracticing because I can't keep up with it. There are so many people now, with the changes in the [child] support guidelines, they don't know what's happening and they're not doing it the appropriate way.

Not surprisingly, most specialists depicted the field of divorce law in markedly different terms from the nonspecialists. Where nonspecialists saw only a limited and static body of law relating to divorce, specialists described a rapidly changing, increasingly complicated field. Specialists were likely to challenge vigorously the assertion that there is simply not that much divorce law to be learned.

I've had some cases with attorneys who have excellent reputations but don't do divorces very often, and I think, particularly in Maine, there's been so many changes in the last few years that if it's not something you do on a regular basis, I think your client's at a real disadvantage.

These divorce specialists also tended not to think of "divorce law" as a single discrete field, but rather as an area of practice that encompasses many kinds of law. They spoke of complicated tax questions and real estate law, and some also pointed to relevant nonlegal bodies of knowledge as essential to their practice. Divorce specialist Andrea Wright, for example, elaborated on her observation that "actual family law is real simple":

[But] you need to know a lot of different areas of law in order to constantly represent a lot of different clients. You need to understand corporate law and corporations and finance in order to represent [a client] where there is a business involved. You need to understand a lot about finance. You need to understand a lot of psychology, a lot of family systems dynamics, child development.

Another lawyer whose practice consisted almost entirely of family law provided a similarly expansive list of the areas of knowledge necessary for effective divorce law practice:

You need an understanding of the broad principles of child rearing and psychology. You have to be knowledgeable about tax law, some knowledge about pension law, and you have to know how to read a balance sheet. And you have to understand the principles of an appraisal for business and real estate. You have to know something about alcoholism. You have to know something about the psychology of an abused victim.

Specialists then were likely to put relatively greater store in a broadly defined range of knowledge that required far more than the familiarity with the basic rules and procedures of divorce that general practice attorneys found sufficient.

The different degrees of importance that specialists and nonspecialists ascribed to divorce law expertise were a reflection of its significance in their practices. The specialist presented herself to divorce clients, many of them with relatively substantial assets, as someone whose superior knowledge of divorce law would serve the clients' interests. This superior knowledge was what justified her fees, which were likely to be higher than those of nonspecialists. The divorce specialist was much more likely than the nonspecialist to attend workshops and read journals that kept her informed about new developments in divorce law and to discuss those developments with colleagues who shared similar interests and commitments. Thus, the importance that the specialist attached to "being expert in divorce law" (as well as in litigation) reflected the considerable economic and psychological investment that she and her like-minded colleagues had made in that expertise. In ways that were not true for the lawyer whose divorce caseload was only part of a more general practice, the specialists' conception of what it meant to be a professional divorce lawyer embraced substantive mastery of a multifaceted, complex, and dynamic body of knowledge.

These perceptions of what one needs to know and to do to be an effective divorce lawyer are usually constructed in and reinforced by the overlapping communities of practice in which a lawyer situates herself. When divorce specialists exchanged written interrogatories, when they prepared memos citing relevant case law, and even when they compared notes at workshops and seminars, they were reinforcing each other's belief in the importance of keeping a close eye on the client's case and knowing the law of divorce. On the other hand, when generalists discussed over the telephone what each thought a case was worth and then agreed to settle it by "splitting the difference," they were fortifying their mutual conviction that there was little to be gained by contest in divorce and that the law itself was "no big deal." Both versions of what constitutes divorce expertise made good sense in the context of the lawyers' respective divorce practices, and in the normal course of things neither the specialist nor the generalist had much reason to assert—much less examine—his position. On the relatively infrequent occasions when these two competing versions of expertise collided—when the specialist and the generalist represented opposing parties in a divorce—the difficulties that followed only served to further reinforce the low opinion that each had of the other's approach.

Gender, Lawyer Roles, and Expertise

We have seen that the nature of lawyers' practices shapes their views of professional expertise. But it is also the case that individual characteristics of attorneys help to define the roles that they perceive for themselves and their understanding of the requisite expertise for doing their work. In our research we found evidence that women lawyers tended to bring a different orientation to their roles and their expertise as divorce lawyers than did men. These data are consistent with the conclusions of Jack and Jack (1989), who report finding a somewhat greater "care orientation" (Gilligan 1982) in women lawyers. And they support Menkel-Meadow's hypothesis that "because of the affective and emotional work that women have been socialized to do, feminist lawyers may demonstrate greater sensitivity to client relations" (1989: 316).

Among Maine and New Hampshire divorce lawyers, we found a significant difference between the importance that men and women lawyers placed on "sensitive listening to clients." Women attorneys rated this skill on average at 4.54, in contrast to a 4.18 mean rating by the men.[26] There was also more consensus among women respondents on the importance of listening to clients, in contrast to a wider range of responses of the men to this question,[27] thus supporting the idea that women lawyers may share a more common view of the divorce lawyer role than do men lawyers.

In lawyers' comments about the importance of the skill of sensitive listening, there were also hints of a gender difference in the understanding of lawyer roles, client demands, and the meaning of listening skills. One woman, for example, articulated the emotional, affective reasons for listening: "I enjoy counseling my clients through a divorce the best. I think a lot of women seek a woman lawyer. I think that my own interest is in women's issues. And my style is that I attend to much more than just the law in a divorce." This perspective was shared by some of the men lawyers who specialized in divorce as well, but women (particularly the specialists) tended to express it more frequently.

In this view, handling divorce cases requires particular sensitivity, recognizing the client not only as an assemblage of facts and figures about marital finances but also as a fragile human being in need of help through the divorce. The lawyer's responsibility, from this perspective, was to try and attend to all the needs of clients rather than focusing only on the financial ones. A woman lawyer explained:

> The other thing that I think women will do—at least the women lawyers that I know—they have a real keen sense of what sort of resources [there are] within the community . . . so that the total needs of the client are better met. I think women attorneys are much more attentive to their clients. And this is, you know, a gross generalization, but I think that it's true.

In making this generalization, she refers to other women lawyers as if they constitute a community of practice in which views of how divorce work should be carried out are shared and distinguished from what is viewed as the traditional (male) way of handling divorce. Not all women held this perspective, of course, but for those who did, there was a clear sense that they were doing something different, trying to carve out a niche for themselves in providing a new and distinct kind of professional service in divorce. And this shared perspective helped to establish and sustain a community of practice among women divorce attorneys that reinforced that view.[28]

There are a number of ways to think about these gender differences in divorce attorneys' understandings of their roles and skills. Perhaps women simply care more about listening than men do, whether as the result of socialization, psychological factors, or male dominance that allows women to listen but not speak (MacKinnon 1987). Hotel and Brockman (1994) found that women divorce lawyers in Canada were more likely than men to describe themselves as good listeners and empathetic with clients, a view that is consistent with what our lawyers reported about their values in divorce practice.

It may also be that some women *select* divorce law practices because of the nature of the work and the opportunities there to forge personal bonds with their clients. That is, the attorneys who choose to practice in this area, rather than in tax law or corporate litigation, place particular value on human emotions, personal communication, and social relationships. We know that women attorneys in our sample were disproportionately specialists; women were also more likely than men to be content with their current proportion of divorce cases, instead of seeking to decrease their divorce work.[29] Clearly, the views of specialists and of women practitioners are mutually reinforcing. From this perspective, women's personal identities may be subtly redefining or adapting their professional identities.

A third way of thinking about this variation by gender lies in the expectations of clients about the service they will receive from their attorneys. Wilkins (1998) makes this point about expectations of lawyers in the context of racial identity when he suggests that even if black lawyers *could* somehow check their race at the door, they can never escape the fact that their clients and other lawyers will always see them as black. The same is true for gender. Clients of female lawyers may expect them to listen more to their troubles and to be more nurturing, and women lawyers in turn may come to place greater value on this aspect of their service. This dynamic could be intensified by the fact that women lawyers represent a disproportionate number of women as divorce clients. In a sociolinguistic study, Bogoch (1997) found female clients to show less deference to female lawyers and more often to seek cooperation and solidarity in conversations with their lawyers.

This latter dynamic, however, appears to complicate the relationship between gender and views of divorce lawyer roles. In answers to our question about how lawyers respond to clients who insist on talking about their personal or emotional issues, we found that women appeared to be slightly less likely than men to report that they encouraged their clients to discuss their emotional problems.[30] Some female lawyers expressed a conflict over whether such listening and provision of emotional support detracted from their being a "real lawyer," a role conflict found in other research on women in the legal profession (Jack and Jack 1989; Hotel and Brockman 1994; Bogoch 1997; Sommerlad and Sanderson 1998). One female attorney explained her ambivalence quite thoughtfully:

> I think a "sensitive listener" connotes someone who is empathetic, who is more emotional, and I think if you are a sensitive listener you're

going to encourage that person to come to you to be sensitive. And I think that it is especially important when you are a woman practicing in the marital area. Whether you are representing men or women, women are perceived as the nurturants, the "we'll make it all better" kind of people. I am not a man so I can't say that doesn't occur with male attorneys as well, but I feel that when conversations get to that point, where somebody is just constantly looking for that kind of support, I'll cut those conversations short. I don't feel that it is necessarily a good trait to be a sensitive listener.

Not wanting to be stereotyped as a nurturing female, this lawyer worked hard to dispel that image and to assert what she saw as the emotional distance of professional authority. She was wary of being pressured into a relationship with her clients that would compromise her own sense of expertise.

Sorting out the effect of gender identity on professional roles and perceptions of expertise is a complex task, for the lawyers themselves as well as for scholars. The ways that lawyers listen to clients are influenced by personal inclinations, formal legal training about professional roles, stereotyping, and client expectations. Another influence comes from the intersection of attorneys' professional and personal lives. In her study of solo and small firm lawyers, Seron (1996) did *not* find gender differences in lawyers' views of their work with clients. But the differences that did emerge, Seron argued, "are in the degree of access to the overtime that permits balancing the demands of continual calls from clients with the realities of paperwork" (1996: 126). That is, because of the time constraints on women divorce lawyers due to greater family demands, they may work harder to place strict boundaries on the time and attention they give their clients.

Conclusion

Divorce lawyers face the daunting task of persuading their colleagues in the bar, their clients, the general public, and themselves that they are indeed professionals with particular expertise. This process of persuasion rests, as Abbott (1988) suggests, on lawyers' asserting special claims to knowledge (albeit socially constructed knowledge) so that they can maintain control over the market for their services, on the one hand, and establish professional authority in relation to their clients, on the other.

How do divorce lawyers' knowledge claims relate to the project of establishing jurisdiction over their service and authority over their clients? The answer lies in both the narratives of *inter-* and *intra*professional competition related in this chapter. The introduction of divorce mediation challenged lawyers in divorce practice to assert more clearly what it is that they can provide clients that mediators cannot. The response, at least from Maine and New Hampshire attorneys, was to insist on the necessity for their expertise in protecting clients' legal rights, in reviewing any agreements involving finances or significant property, and in protecting clients who are unable to participate in mediation on an equal basis with their spouses. Other issues, however, lawyers felt could more readily be ceded to mediators. In both states, lawyers explained that they thought divorce mediation was very helpful for resolving issues over child visitation and over division of personal property and in giving room for parties to vent emotions. This potential competition with mediators could be resolved from the perspective of divorce lawyers by allocating to mediation the tasks that most of them liked the *least* and saw as the furthest removed from their professional roles and expertise as attorneys. This sort of resolution, which we saw at the level of daily practice, has been most common nationally in the outcomes of broader political struggles over statutes that typically require mediation only on custody and visitation issues while preserving resolution of property matters for attorneys (McEwen, Rogers, and Maiman 1995: 1362). At the same time, it is important to note that the Maine experience suggests that broader accommodations can be reached between divorce lawyers and mediators, when their roles are not structured or perceived in competitive terms.

Intraprofessional competition among divorce lawyers who aim, consciously or not, for different segments of the market rests on a similar dynamic. Clearly, specialists competed directly with general practice lawyers for clients. These specialists, who included a large proportion of women lawyers, distinguished themselves by claiming special expertise in divorce. Their claims rested on a broadened vision of special knowledge that extended beyond the basic features of divorce law to include tax and estate law and psychological perspectives. They also depended on a different understanding of the professional role of counsel in divorce cases, one that employed the techniques of civil litigation such as interrogatories and motions, attended to detail in negotiating agreements, and may have provided the kind of emotional counseling and support to clients that was less common in more traditional legal practice.

Not only were the specialists trying to attract clients, but they were also working quite consciously to increase their prestige within the bar. Shamir calls this "indirect" competition—an "open struggle for influence and prestige within the professional hierarchy" (1995: 127). For example, their use of civil litigation techniques may not only persuade clients that these are lawyers who will fight hard for them in the courtroom, like "real" lawyers do, but also persuade their colleagues in the bar that their work is more similar to other, higher prestige areas of civil law. Similarly, as we will note in chapter 8, the transformation of divorce into family law and its closer connection to the "helping professions" are symbolic efforts to improve the image of the work and broaden its knowledge base.

In one sense, these struggles to define and redefine the boundaries of expertise for and among divorce lawyers focus on efforts to secure market control in the face of competition (Abbott 1988). In another sense, however, these struggles reflect efforts to adapt the knowledge systems of divorce practice to changes in the broader society as well as to shifts in the legal process itself (Halliday 1987; Shamir 1995: 123). The efforts of many female divorce specialists to take divorce seriously and to redefine what it means to represent divorce clients can be viewed as significant attempts to adapt the law in action to social changes in family structure, the position of women in society, and the recognition of emotion as part of human life. In a more recent work, Halliday argues that "the politics of lawyers must be taken seriously. The nature of those politics helps define, either negatively or positively, a professional identity that balances lawyers' economic and clientilistic behavior with their action on behalf of primarily noneconomic causes" (1999: 1010). The ways in which the boundaries of expertise in divorce law are defined reflect at least in part lawyers' politics and responses to change, issues that we return to at the conclusion of this book.

5

MAINTAINING CONTROL OVER CLIENTS

Some attorneys are very resolution-minded . . . to try to keep the clients friends if they can, particularly if there are children involved, to try to minimize the areas of dispute, to try to control their clients, to try to keep them from driving each other crazy during the process.

Some attorneys are strictly advocates of their clients. They don't care if the case settles. Their client gave them a position and gave them their marching orders, and they're out there to try to achieve that . . . and will even represent their clients in unreasonable positions.

—a New Hampshire divorce lawyer

The degree to which members of an occupational group enjoy independence in decision making is equally important as expertise as a criterion of professionalism. Independence is complicated, however, for professions that provide service to paying clients or customers. Professional advice may collide with the equally important principle of client and consumer autonomy—the idea that clients should be able to accept or reject the professional's guidance. The primacy of this latter principle is well recognized by official professional canons of both medicine and law. But in rejecting the professional's advice, the client is in some sense rejecting the professional's—and the profession's—authority. Therefore, a central challenge of professional practice is not only to make judgments and give advice but also to persuade clients to accept these as their own.

In legal practice this challenge plays out in the complex relationship between lawyer and client over participation in the case and control over decision making. The lawyer quoted at the beginning of the chapter describes two different resolutions of this challenge in divorce practice. Some attorneys devote considerable time to persuading their clients to accept advice and direction. Others do not, serving as more passive agents of their clients' wishes. These two roles in legal practice reflect competing visions of legal professionalism. In this chapter we explore how and why divorce lawyers respond to the competing goals of independent professional judgment and client self-determination. This chapter shows somewhat greater uniformity in lawyers' conceptualizations of their professional roles than we saw in chapter 4. Most attorneys revealed that they worked to set their clients' expectations, to educate and persuade clients of what they—the legal experts—have learned about the realities of divorce and its consequences, and about what the legal rules will permit. Attorneys described various techniques of education and persuasion they used to influence client decision making. They also had significant power to define the very relationship between lawyer and client—whether to accept a client's case, how much to charge, how quickly to move the case, and whether to part ways with a client who resisted too much.

Agent for Client or Independent Advisor?

Professional standards and norms are not fixed but rather are socially constructed and evolve over time (Paterson 1996). The professional role of the lawyer in relation to the client illustrates this change well. "From the beginning, professional standards evinced an ambivalence between client orientation and a desire to maintain independent judgment" (Zacharias 1995: 1315). Lawyers have always been expected both to serve the client *and* to render independent advice, but the normative emphasis on one or the other role has shifted with political and social contexts and for different clienteles. An earlier vision of lawyers as proud and vigorous advocates of client demands may now be disparaged by the familiar phrase "hired gun" (Auerbach 1976; Gordon 1988; Zacharias 1995).

Professional standards today permit lawyers to follow *either* vision in practice, the hired gun or the independent advisor role. The Model Rules of Professional Conduct prescribe that "a lawyer shall exercise independent professional judgment and render candid advice," [1] and further state that a lawyer may withdraw from representation if "a client insists upon pursuing an objective that the lawyer considers repugnant or imprudent."[2] But at the same time, the Model Rules endorse a more client-centered position through their admonition that "a lawyer shall abide by a client's decisions concerning the objectives of representation . . . and shall consult with the client as to the means by which they are to be pursued."[3] The rules themselves thus are ambiguous on this point (Strauss 1987; Haskell 1998), leaving lawyers free to make their own choices in relation to these competing expectations.

Defenders of the agent or hired gun role for lawyers believe it to be essential in the adversary legal system. Since that system assumes there will be a third party to adjudicate conflicts between parties, each side must have an advocate who will zealously and nonjudgmentally argue its position. Key to the lawyer-client relationship, in this view, is the lawyer's neutral position toward her own client. Regardless of how morally repugnant or unrealistic the client's objectives may be, once the lawyer has agreed to represent the client, her role as advocate is to defend or pursue those objectives (Freedman 1966). Such advocacy actions do not compromise the lawyer because she is simply enacting the prescribed professional role and thus is not accountable for the client's decisions.[4]

A different set of arguments promotes a professional role that enhances clients' self-determination and aims to empower them. For example, "a client-centered practice takes the principle of client decision making seriously" and encourages lawyers to practice in ways that will strengthen the client's role (Ellmann 1987: 720; and see Binder and Price 1977). That is, lawyers should not make decisions that rightfully belong to their clients and should provide helpful guidance and sensitive interviewing to elicit the relevant information that enables clients to make their own decisions. A participatory role for clients that encourages their active involvement in the formulation of legal strategy, the evaluation of alternatives, and the final decision on disposition may reduce conflicts of interest between lawyer and client, increase client satisfaction, and also produce a better case outcome (Rosenthal 1974). Not only will the client benefit but also arguably so will the law. "Law arises out of experience. Clients are the source of that experience" (Cunningham 1989: 2493). Hence, lawyers must attend carefully to clients' words, values, and understandings in order to work effectively with the language of law.

These advocates of a greater role for clients in decision making disagree on the reasons for—and the exact nature of—the ideal professional role for lawyers, but they share a skepticism about lawyers' independence. By contrast, others argue that a lawyer's single-minded pursuit of client interests ultimately does the client—and the law—a disservice. In this view, lawyers must exert their independent judgment in legal decision making whether balancing the client's wishes or even overriding them on occasion. As Gordon (1988) argues, a professionalism based on lawyer independence is better not only for clients but, more important, for society. By remaining independent of their clients, lawyers can better fulfill the ideal of law as a *public* profession. Therefore, "the independence of lawyers has a social and political value going well beyond the value of effective client service" (Gordon 1988: 10; see also Parsons 1962 and Kronman 1993).

Although the weight of commentary on legal professionalism now leans toward the independent advisor role, most current observers do not believe lawyers act that way. "In recent decades the hired gun model has become predominant," writes Haskell (1998: 86), citing Glendon (1994) and Linowitz (1994), among others. Empirical research on lawyers, however, suggests a more complex picture, with variation in the lawyer's role according to size of law firm, type of clientele, and area of practice (Harrington 1994; Abel 1995). Lawyers in large firms representing corporate clients show a close identification between lawyer and client and limited attorney independence (Heinz and Laumann 1982; Nelson 1985). But lawyers representing individual clients in areas of criminal defense, legal services, family law, and personal injury law more frequently appear to dominate their clients in decision making.[5] As a result, there is a "basic paradox that lawyers at the bottom of the professional hierarchy are most autonomous" (Abel 1995: 15). The competing pressures of client autonomy and professional authority create serious dilemmas for lawyers, and they resolve them in their own ways reflecting, for example, the nature of the work, the norms of their communities of practice, and individual values and particularized relationships to clients.[6]

These competing pressures were especially evident among the divorce lawyers we studied. Many of them had thought about these issues and had evolved strategies to try to manage clients in ways that appeared to minimize the conflicts. The dominant approach was to shape client expectations so that they were aligned with those of the lawyer. This was not always easy because of client resistance, however. Divorce involves a wide range of issues in which client expectations often collide with what lawyers understand the law to require or what they believe will be best for the client in the long run. Consider the following examples. A wife expects that her husband should have no contact with their children because "he has been a rotten father," but the wife's lawyer knows that the court will insist on the father's visitation and that the law presumes joint legal custody. Or a husband argues that his retirement pension is entirely his own, but his lawyer knows that the law considers pensions to be marital property and thus an asset to be divided between husband and wife. Or a wife says she wants a large amount of alimony, but her lawyer knows that that is completely unrealistic because of the couple's limited resources. In each of these scenarios and countless others like them, lawyers must respond to their clients' unrealistic expectations, either by articulating and representing their positions or by persuading clients to abandon them. Throughout the divorce process, as we shall see, lawyers have considerable leverage in their relationships with clients that enables them to bring pressure to bear in aligning their clients' perspectives with their own.

Moving from Emotion to Pragmatism: Challenges of a Divorce Clientele

The initial challenge for divorce attorneys frequently involves redefining the divorce in largely pragmatic terms when clients first come to them focused on its emotional aspects. Indeed, the lawyers we interviwed generally perceived marital clients to be different than clients in other legal cases due to the intensity and extent of the emotions involved.[7] "Divorce is *all* emotion," said one lawyer, while another explained that marital clients are different "because I am asked to legally solve an emotional problem." Attorneys noted that such emotions were understandable because divorce affected every aspect of a client's life—emotional, financial, social, sexual, physical living situation—whereas other kinds of cases tended to be more limited in their impact.

> I see people who are dealing with so many issues that the actual legal issues many times are the easiest thing. . . . They have the feeling that if they are hiring an expert, that expert can give them advice in all areas—in their love life, in how to parent their children, should they sell their home for such and such a price?

Thus, lawyers perceived divorce clients to act in ways that are less reasonable, less patient, more desperate, and more volatile than many other clients. In divorce, one lawyer said, "you're seeing people at their absolute worst. I mean, I represent people who've killed other people . . . and they're emotionally much easier to deal with than . . . many divorcing people!"

Out of this experience of working with what they see as a distinctive clientele, communities of divorce lawyers constructed varying notions of professionalism that generally elevated their own authority and encouraged them to exercise greater control over clients and responsibility in decision making. Many lawyers therefore responded to their emotional divorce clients by asserting their professional expertise for their clients' own good. Even advocates of a client-centered lawyering acknowledge that the emotional disabilities of clients may prevent them from participating effectively in their own decision making and thus may justify greater influence by lawyers (Ellmann 1987: 768–770).

In talking about client control, some lawyers emphasized the importance of gender differences among clients in terms of the issues that they presented.[8] According to the stereotypical views of these attorneys, wives typically expressed greater need for emotional rebuilding and support, whereas husbands were more concerned about finances. As one lawyer said, "Husbands tend to be a little bit more closed-mouth or not quite as open with the attorney as women will be. However, husbands . . . will take more of an objective approach than the wives will. Sometimes the wives get very emotional and let their emotions control that." Another attorney put it more bluntly: "Women will be more emotional . . . and men like their toys."

As intermediaries between their clients' perceived interests and the law, lawyers draw on their understandings of legal entitlements and outcomes, as well as on their clients' interests, as they define their legal roles in practice.[9] The result, according to Sarat and Felstiner (1995: 50–51), is a lack of communication between lawyer and client and consequent client dissatisfaction, as clients insist on "the language of guilt, fault, and responsibility," while their attorneys try to limit discussions more narrowly to the legal terms of divorce, which typically take little account of these concerns. In doing so, "the lawyer's construction of meaning works to justify his authority and invites client dependence" (1995: 51; and see Merry 1990). Lawyers' interpretation of the legal framework for divorce, as well as the emotional state of divorce clients, dictate a professional role that favors lawyer independence and professional authority more than client autonomy. When conflict between lawyer and client arises over decisions about strategy or case settlement, the independent lawyer urges what she thinks is "fair" or "best" for the client. The problem of client control thus refers most often to lawyers' efforts to redirect the investment of anger, emotion, and blame in divorce and to moderate the positions of clients that may get in the way of reasonable settlements.[10]

Where conflict emerged between lawyer and client over the direction of the case or settlement in divorce, we found support in our interviews for both pictures of divorce lawyers. When attorneys saw clients as vengeful, seeking to wreak as much havoc as possible on the lives of their spouses, lawyers typically reported attempting to moderate or soften the clients' positions. Yet the reverse also occurred, namely, when the client who—as a result of guilt, intimidation, or exhaustion—simply wanted to finish the divorce as soon as possible without seeking rights or assets to which she was entitled. In such cases, lawyers often described themselves as trying to bolster the client's self-confidence and encouraging her to claim legal entitlements.[11]

The emotion and anger that so frequently accompany divorce thus present several choices for lawyers. Certainly, as chapter 4 makes clear, many but not all attorneys believe that their expertise does not extend to emotional counseling. Equally important, because clients see the divorce through an emotional lens, they are thought to be less able to make the crucial decisions about the terms of a divorce. Furthermore, emotion may lead clients to have unrealistically high or low expectations about divorce outcomes. For these reasons, divorce lawyers believed they must invest considerable effort in shifting the perspectives and expectations of clients. Lawyers' efforts to influence client perspectives began with their first meeting and the lawyer's decision to accept a client.

Screening Clients

Lawyers first confront the question of how much control to exercise over a client in their initial interviews, when a decision must be made about whether or not to accept that client. Lawyers reported that during such interviews they typically listened carefully to clients as well as explaining their style of practice to them. These interviews were crucial to the screening that the overwhelming majority of lawyers said they did.[12] If they sensed that the client was "unrealistic" and also unlikely to be amenable to education, then most reported that they would not represent him. Several divorce attorneys described this initial screening:

> What I like to do is I try to talk to them a bit, and I tell them there's no charge for [the initial] conference. . . . They decide if they can work with me, and I decide if I can work with them. The door does work both ways, and I want to find out what their expectations are.

> [I rarely part ways with a client] because of the process that I go through up front and the fact that I'd say to the client—because I feel that clients are interviewing me as much as I'm interviewing them, and I tell them that—"If you're not comfortable, don't for gosh sakes hire me because you're just doing yourself a disservice."

Thus, according to our interviewees, negotiations between attorney and client began even before the lawyer-client relationship was formally established. Rather than waiting for conflicts to surface later, lawyers tried to anticipate them and head them off—either by redirection and education at the outset, or if that did not succeed, by refusing representation. Some lawyers relied on their secretaries for help in screening clients, getting cues about those who were rude, obnoxious, or especially demanding.

When we asked lawyers to describe the cases or clients that they might reject, the stock response (volunteered by about half of the lawyers) was a client who was "difficult." "Difficult" clients were variously defined as vengeful, unrealistic, stubborn, or demanding, such as those "that are totally out for blood." Since most divorce lawyers prided themselves on being "reasonable," they were wary of potential clients who were not. One attorney explained, "I don't like to take people coming in to me and saying, 'I want to nail the other side, and that's what I really want.' Particularly when there are children involved, I won't take that case."

Not only did the initial interview help attorneys identify those clients whom they did not want, but it also provided an occasion for teaching about the lawyer's style and approach to divorce law. One lawyer said, "I sort of lay it on the line in the initial interview what my philosophy is." Or as two other attorneys explained:

> I won't take a client who comes in and presents himself or herself as wanting everything and that I get a sense that is going to be totally unreasonable. . . . I don't think I can tell a client in good faith that I can get them everything. . . . And if somebody feels that way, then I do suggest that they retain another attorney.

> People come in with unrealistic expectations, and I often feel like the client and I are at odds initially because I'm trying to give them a

realistic sense of what they can expect to get out of this process. And I'm up front with people when they walk in, and I tell them that I'm not a heavy hitter.

Most divorce attorneys claimed that to head off such problems, in the initial interview they would begin the process of client education, of promoting "realistic" expectations, and of identifying themselves as reasonable lawyers. From the start, they reported asserting a degree of authority over their clients. But while lawyers sought to convey "realistic" information, they were simultaneously assessing their clients' ability to hear and appreciate their advice. As one lawyer put it, "sometimes you just have a general feeling that this is somebody that you aren't going to be able to get along with . . . that they aren't going to listen to you," and if that were the case, many lawyers said they would not represent that person.

A few lawyers pointed to another type of difficult client whom they would be reluctant to represent, namely, the client who would demand too much of the lawyer's personal attention.[13] As discussed in chapter 4, most lawyers said they tried hard to avoid becoming embroiled in their clients' emotional problems. In cases where lawyers anticipated that clients could not maintain a clear focus on the legal issues, they often would decide against representation.

> People . . . who look like they are going to think that they are my only clients. . . . Someone who is going to want to be able to pick up the phone and call you four, five, six times a week and want you there to hold their hand and to talk with them about everything. . . . You can get a perception from someone at an initial meeting whether these are folks that you want to establish a long-term, sort of personal, relationship.

Other lawyers invoked the terms "long-term personal relationship" and "marriage" to depict their relationships with their divorce clients. And some said they avoided "clients I don't like" or "clients I'm not comfortable with." Attorneys tended to believe that a successful lawyer-client relationship required clients who respected their lawyer's expertise, who listened to their advice, who were honest and straightforward, and who understood the limits of the lawyer's role.

One indicator of a potential problem client (mentioned by about one-quarter of the attorneys) was a "a recycled client," who had previously been represented by another attorney. The fact that the client was unhappy with one lawyer suggested that she might also be dissatisfied with the next one. Many lawyers interpreted this dissatisfaction as resulting from a client not listening to "reasonable" legal advice and demanding to call all the shots in the case. Thus, a client who had switched from another lawyer "always raises the red flag." One attorney described the problem this way: "If you've got somebody coming in from another office, then you instinctively smell trouble. . . . If they have been a pain in the rump to another lawyer, then they are going to be a pain in the rump to you." These comments especially point to the importance of the professional community of practitioners and the cues they take from one another in practice.

Nonetheless, many such clients do find new attorneys. Our docket data reveal that in cases where both parties are represented, about 10 percent of the parties have more than one attorney listed as lawyer of record. Switching lawyers is half as likely in cases where only one party has representation. Examination of the docketed cases for the lawyers we interviewed shows them to have the same pattern of second-lawyer representation as in our aggregate sample.

The processes of lawyers' screening of clients and of clients' switching from lawyer to lawyer suggest a sorting mechanism at work. One way that "difficult" clients ultimately find representation is by seeking out lawyers who specialize in a more aggressive or litigious practice. Indeed, examination of docketed cases for the lawyers we interviewed shows that those most likely to be the second lawyers (with 15 percent or more of their clients in the rebound category) scored significantly higher on seeing litigation as an important skill in divorce practice.[14] Lawyers most specialized in divorce practice (75 percent or more of their cases) also were much more likely to be second lawyers than those with less specialization or a more general practice.[15]

Lawyers who wanted to avoid or reject those whom they saw to be problem clients often used their fee to do so. That is, they purposely set high initial retainers to ward off all but the most serious clients and to ensure that, if the client did end up being difficult, the lawyer would at least get paid properly. In the words of one attorney, "I don't mind a pain if they are going to pay me—but if they are not going to pay me, then I don't need their garbage." Other lawyers described how they set their fees partly according to the degree of difficulty they anticipated with the client: "I make my retainer even bigger," said one attorney. "If I can't turn down the case, I say, how much do you want to pay for this?" Another explained that she didn't tell clients that "I don't want to represent them. What I do is I structure my fee in such a way as to know that they can't afford it. And then, every once in a while, I get hurt by that if they can afford it."

The comments of these lawyers underscore four important themes in a divorce lawyer's work. First, while clients have power in the relationship through the fact that they pay the bill, lawyers have corresponding power to determine the amount of the bill. Second, while fees have an iconic, ostensibly neutral, appearance to the client—something predetermined like the couch in the office or the picture on the wall—in fact, they can be easily manipulated by the attorney. Through their fees, lawyers can try to accomplish indirectly (rejecting clients) what they are reluctant to do directly (telling the client how unrealistic or demanding they are). Third, as much as divorce lawyers would like to screen out all the undesirable clients, they acknowledge that the demands of making a living regularly intrude on such decisions. And fourth, it is the divorce law specialists and the most litigation-oriented lawyers who are most likely to inherit clients who have left (or been left by) their previous lawyer.

How Lawyers Influence Client Decision Making

Because of the perceived need to shift a client's perspective from the emotional divorce to the pragmatic issues of the terms of the legal divorce, and then either to bolster a client's demands or to moderate them, lawyers often faced difficult negotiations with their clients—perhaps even more difficult than those with opposing counsel. As one lawyer put it, "The hardest part of divorce practice is . . . not the other side, not the courts. It's dealing with your own client." How do divorce lawyers manage to assert their pragmatic and professional views of the case while also allowing clients to participate in decision making? Lawyers reported drawing on an array of resources and tactics to influence clients throughout the divorce process.[16]

Setting Clients' Expectations

Once the basic decision has been made to accept a client, the next important stage of lawyer influence lies in educating that client by setting expectations and helping to shape goals. Many attorneys we interviewed believed they could avoid conflicts over case settlement later in the process simply by setting clients' expectations properly at the outset. Experienced divorce lawyers said they had a clear sense of the likely outcome of most divorces, at least in Maine and New Hampshire. No-fault standards predominated. Court decisions had clarified that marital property would be divided in a roughly 50–50 split, and child support was largely determined by formulaic statutory guidelines.[17]

The lawyer's task is to convey such legal realities to clients at the beginning of the case in order to reorient their expectations and set goals consistent with the attorney's understanding of the law. Since judges ultimately resolve so few divorces, however, it is the lawyers' own views of legal outcomes that may actually create the law. Thus, lawyers become significant actors in constructing legal entitlements since, in divorce at least, "the shadow of the law is being cast by the lawyers, who declare their expectations of judicial behavior" (Erlanger, Chambliss, and Melli 1987: 599).[18] Client education thus involves teaching realistic expectations about likely case outcomes.

> In some cases obviously it's just impossible to get what your client wants. They come in asking for custody and that just may not be realistic at all. They come in asking for some large amount of alimony that may not be realistic. I mean, people do have unrealistic expectations sometimes. I try and reduce their expectations right away if that's in fact what it looks like to me.

Part of my thing is teaching and setting the goals. . . . I take the view that it is my job to lay out the parameters to the client. What I think based upon my experience and the law, what I can achieve on their basis, what I think it may be.

Lawyers generally proceeded on the assumption that if they succeeded with client education and set appropriate expectations at the beginning of the case, they could avert serious conflict with clients over final case settlement (see Kritzer 1998a). Several attorneys pointed to this strategy to explain why problems with unreasonable clients did not occur frequently in their practices.

That does not happen a lot with my clients. I would like to think part of the reason that doesn't happen is because, through the course of interviewing and through the course of working with a client, I hope that I educate the client as to what the law deems appropriate.

One of the things I do with my initial interview is, we outline the goals for the client. "What do you want out of this divorce?" And we cover everything from the uncontested versus the fault-divorce right to who pays for the uninsured medical and dental bills and everything in between: the real estate, the bills, the pension plans, the insurance. We cover that all, so that if the client is unrealistic, I know right away, and I tell them, "You may want that, but I'm telling you what's likely to happen based on my experience." And so, you can give them a range of what's a fair goal or settlement. So that alleviates a lot of the problems you're talking about. So we're not into the case five months down the road with these kinds of problems. We've got the same direction and goals right from the start. That's very important.

The setting of client expectations occurred not only in the initial interview but also in the later meetings leading to the outline of an opening offer to the other side. When lawyers said they preferred to open with a settlement offer they thought was fair—rather than highly inflated—they explained this approach not in terms of what it conveyed to the other party, but in relation to its impact on their own clients. That is, a realistic proposal to an opponent served to reinforce realistic expectations, whereas an extreme demand could create false expectations.

I think one of the biggest problems [in negotiation] is the client expectations involved. If the lawyer takes an unreasonable position, and unless the lawyer made it clear to the client that this is an unreasonable position—"I am pursuing this for my own personal negotiating technique"—the client begins to have some expectations that that is reality. And then it is impossible to settle the case.

If you say, "I'm going to ask for this," then they [clients] think that is great, and then they think, like, they are going to get all of that! I think you have to keep your clients being somewhat realistic with the way things are going to be.

Learning to set client goals is a critical part of the work of a divorce lawyer, but it is not a strategy that is always apparent to those just starting out. Rather, it is a skill attorneys learn over time, often after some unhappy experiences with clients. One lawyer, for example, explained how she learned to shape client expectations from the start of the case:

> It used to be quite frequently I'd have to talk my people into things, which is, when I look back on it, I'm sort of dismayed, because the whole trick there is to get their expectations on the right road initially. And if they are giving indications early on, on some issue that this is what they want to have happen, you need to recognize that that's, if it is true, that that's not possible, and you have to straighten them out.

Both lawyer roles—the independent advisor and the agent of clients—give room for lawyers to teach clients realism and to reshape their expectations. For those lawyers who saw themselves as independent advisors, it was natural to assert their own views and expectations and employ varied techniques to gain their acceptance by clients. For those lawyers who saw themselves as client-centered, similar efforts at client education were justifiable as ways of providing clients with the information that permitted them to exert their own autonomy in making final case decisions—decisions that were then within the parameters set by the lawyer.

Verbal Persuasion

Not all clients could be "straightened out" by their lawyers at the beginning of the case, and some would continue to express unrealistic expectations. Lawyers then drew on their professional knowledge and power over clients to persuade them to accept their interpretations and recommendations. Verbal persuasion included a range of talk, explanation, philosophical musing, questioning, cajoling, preaching, yelling, name-calling, storytelling, and role-playing. Lawyers used these techniques to get clients to see what is fair and reasonable, and they required the most basic and common lawyering skills. With unreasonable clients who expected too much from the legal process, one lawyer explained, "I would probably try to talk to them logically, try to talk to them with common sense in mind and hope that they're listening." Another said, "I spend a lot of time trying to defuse what I call the nonsense or the bullshit, and I will be very firm with my client that this is not a matter of spite, and I have a whole pitch I give to them."

With clients who were willing to sign an agreement that would sell them short, lawyers would respond by asking clients, " 'Are you sure?' You ask her ten times, 'Are you sure this is what you want to do?' " Or, as another attorney reported, "I ask them lawyer questions—of the kind that are particularly maddening to clients, like 'What happens if a year from now . . . ?' " Listening to these lawyers speak, we heard them trying to persuade clients by being variously firm, loud, stern, constructive, logical, or common sensical.

Other lawyers embellished these persuasive strategies, introducing more elaborate (and more coercive) means to convince their clients. One divorce attorney, for example, employed a mixture of talk, humor, sarcasm, ridicule, money, and the specter of the judge, in describing his role-playing with unreasonable clients.

> I'll try to talk to them and get them to see it. Make them laugh at it, make them understand that they're just trying to kill the other party. I tell them they're paying me two dollars a minute. "You go and have a fight, nobody can win. This is ridiculous." You know, I'm pretty direct about it, and I'll basically slap them around verbally and laugh at them if they think they're going to go in and have a judge listen. . . . I tell them to put the black robes on. Literally! I'll even get up out of my chair and say, "You put the black robes on. You're the judge. Do you think you're going to listen to that?" And I'll say, "Now look at me. This is what the judge is doing inside!" And I'll just shake my head.

Another lawyer referred to role-playing in explaining how to encourage parties to take a stronger stand in divorce. By invoking the familiar image of Santa Claus, she tried to persuade clients not to give everything away as presents to their spouses.

> I usually tell folks, "You don't dress like Santa Claus, you don't look like Santa Claus, don't act like Santa Claus. You've got children. You've got responsibilities. I am as concerned as you are about trying to get this divorce over with as quickly as we can, but on the other hand you are going to have to live with this. I go home at the end of the day, and I don't have to live with it. And you make sure that there is enough money available so you will be able properly to take care of your children."

Lawyers also shared their own philosophies of life with clients in an effort to convey advice about case settlement. Most often these philosophies counseled fairness, the importance of long-term goals, the value of good parenting, and effective communication with the other party. By occasionally providing narratives drawn from their earlier divorce cases, lawyers would also communicate lessons about the fate of stubborn and vindictive people or about those who gave up without claiming their rights. Such lessons also worked to reinforce the client's sense of lawyers' experience and expertise in divorce, thus buttressing their professional authority.

Referring to the Judge or the Court

The law itself provided lawyers a significant resource to use in negotiating with unreasonable clients. [19] But the legal rules and entitlements were typically invoked in terms of what the judge would do, or what the court would accept. At first glance, this language of law might appear to communicate "the message to the client . . . that it is the judge, not the rules that really counts" (Sarat and Felstiner 1995: 97). In our interviews, however, the judge or the court were simply the vehicles for articulating the law, which lawyers emphasized was generally predictable rather than "idiosyncratic and personalistic" (Sarat and Felstiner 1995: 101). For example, one lawyer explained:

> There are a lot of times when you have to say, "It isn't going to happen. The judge is not going to do that," when they start telling you, "I want this and I want that." The judge is not going to do that. Period. "You can argue about it. We can go to court, and you can say this is what I want, and I can tell you it's not going to happen. Nothing's 100 percent, but I can tell you 99 percent that it's not going to happen."

Reference to the outside authority of the court allowed attorneys to avoid direct confrontations with clients and could also create a sense of identification with them, as in "I can understand your position, but the judge simply won't allow it" or "Perhaps you're right, but that argument will not be accepted by the court." New child support guidelines considerably reduced judicial discretion and made part of the lawyers' job of persuasion much easier. One lawyer explained, "You can say to your client, 'The judge won't accept [it] . . . unless exceptional circumstances exist.' Do they exist here?" Judges and "the court" were thus portrayed as the instruments of a reasonably consistent "law" and therefore set clear boundaries on case outcomes that clients could expect.[20]

Lawyers also reported that they would tell their clients that unreasonable or overly aggressive behavior was not appropriate conduct and might be sanctioned by judges. For example, "If you want to go and fight this, fine, but my recommendation is not to, and I think all we are going to do is aggravate the court." Or, as two different lawyers put it,

> I will tell them that it is inappropriate to use the system as a method of retribution and that they are probably absolutely justified in being upset, and their spouse is probably very bad. . . . And then I try to get them to draw back from that. I point out to them that that is actually going to have a possible negative effect on the way they are perceived by the court. It could in a strange way hurt them in terms of the result they finally get.

> If this is what you want to fight about, I'll tell you what the judge will say. He's going to say exactly what I am saying: "You're being a jerk." And you're going to end up losing more because when you get into that courtroom and you're making the judge go through a hearing because you're fighting about these stupid little things, he's not going to like you any more, and judges are like other people, they will take it out on you.

Thus, not only did lawyers employ references to the law and likely legal outcomes in order to constrain client expectations, but they also referred to the character of legal proceedings and their claimed intolerance of "unreasonable" claims and positions to dampen client demands.

Communicating with Other Lawyers

Because most divorce lawyers reported sharing within their communities of practice a general sense of realistic case outcomes, they were also able to draw implicitly on each other in negotiating with their clients. If a client insisted on a settlement demand that the lawyer considered to be extreme, the lawyer might convey it to opposing counsel, while emphasizing that it was the *client's* demand, not the lawyer's. "You make clear [to the other lawyer], you say, 'This is what my client wants,' " said one attorney. Another explained that where clients were unreasonable in their expectations and continued to resist the attorney's persuasion, then she would simply say to the other lawyer, "It is my client's settlement proposal. It's not mine." In this way, the lawyer could maintain her cooperative reputation among peers by distancing herself from an unreasonable proposal.

> I wouldn't [send an offer I] consider outrageous or unfair, except in rare circumstances where I am trying to stall it or . . . expressing something with the client who wants [something] expressed that I ultimately know isn't going to happen, but I haven't quite gotten around to telling them that.

> I believe it's the client's case and so I say, if they're going to reject what I think is a reasonable offer, the final line is up to them, and if the client wants me to transmit—I mean, I'll tell them, "I think this is ridiculous. I think that you are making it very difficult to negotiate in the future," . . . but I'll certainly transmit an offer my client wants me to transmit.

By transmitting "unreasonable" demands in this fashion, attorneys could reinforce their relationship with clients and show respect for them as decision-makers, but without jeopardizing the lawyer's reputation with professional colleagues or undermining negotiations. Such a strategy also undermined effective client power over outcomes by discounting their claims to the other side.

Delay

Delay provided another source of leverage for lawyers to persuade clients to accept their advice. Lawyers could rely on the built-in delays of the court process or consciously stall case progress themselves.[21] Delay presumably permitted emotional parties to work through their feelings about the divorce, and several attorneys used the cliché "time heals all wounds" to describe changes in clients through the divorce process. The injured parties would calm down, get over some of their anger, and be able to think more clearly about the details of case settlement; the guilty parties would move beyond their own feelings to think about the future; and the submissive parties would gain some confidence and self-esteem. That, at least, was how the lawyers constructed it. Several attorneys described the positive effect of delay or, as one put it, "benign neglect," on the angry client who makes unrealistic demands. "I have to say that court delays are a help.... Time heals. I hate temporary hearings held three weeks after the libel [divorce] gets filed. These people are angry and hurt. They can't think straight." Or, as another lawyer said,

> A lot of that [unreasonable demands] I find is easy to deal with by just delaying things, by letting things calm down. I'm a great believer in delay in the system in situations like that. It really works to defuse the divorce. After awhile, people get tired of fighting, and they just say, "O.K., fine. Whatever she wants. I just want this over with."

Thus, the angry, vengeful party would either be worn down through sheer frustration at the lengthy legal process or would become more calm and rational and hence more susceptible to entreaties about a reasonable settlement.

Attorneys also described the positive virtues of delay for the party who demanded too little, just wanting to end the marriage quickly. As one attorney noted, "The thing to do is wait a while. Just hold on because fair is fair and you are still going to have to live, Mr. Guilty Husband." Others described similar efforts on their parts:

> I try to make them [despondent clients who want to walk away] realize that they will go through a series of emotions as the case ages and that what they're telling me at this moment is not what they'll be feeling two months down the road. And in those cases I'll stop an attempt to make a quick settlement if I feel that what they're settling for is insufficient.

> I quite often intentionally delay a case until the party is ready to make a reasonable decision and until you know how the two parties are going to function in their separate lives. People will come in and say all they need is $50 a week. They have no idea what the real costs are until you go over the financial affidavit.

For divorce lawyers, then, forcing case delays could be a deliberate tactic to bring clients around to the attorney's view of a fair and reasonable divorce outcome.

Fees and Expense

If the tactics of educating a client about the law and courts or delaying the resolution of the case did not succeed, lawyers could always remind clients of fees and expenses to influence their decisions about case outcomes.[22] Unlike all of the other techniques discussed thus far, this one applied only to clients who wanted too much, not the ones who wanted too little. Unreasonable and litigious actions demand time and energy from the attorney and translate into additional costs for the client. Thus, another way lawyers could express their disapproval of unreasonable client demands was to remind them of how costly they would be.

You can scare them off with a higher price or you can say, "I don't do those things." . . . I would tell them it is going to cost. . . . It's like if you want to use your energy and resources to give me a vacation in the islands which I haven't taken as yet, that is what it comes down to.

If children are involved, I'll use the metaphor of "If you do not . . . soften, and we have a contested hearing, the approximate cost of the contested hearing—with your contribution and your husband's— . . . will approximate eight years of child support. . . . If you soften, isn't it better for it to go to the kids?"

While these reminders about additional fees often worked to dissuade paying divorce clients from their unreasonable positions, there was no such leverage for attorneys with pro bono clients. Not only did lawyers find it difficult to limit these clients' demands for personal counseling, but they also found that the altered lawyer-client relationship made it harder to influence client decisions about the case itself. When clients were paying no fee, various lawyers complained, "You lose part of your leverage"; "They feel as if you ought to be their hired gun forever"; and "It's very easy for the client to want to litigate everything at your expense and there's no deterrent because of the fee about going to trial." Another lawyer commented, "I have never had an uncontested pro bono case and I consider myself very reasonable," and then went on to explain, "It doesn't cost them anything so why not take full advantage of it. So, yeah, let's go fight over the raincoat." Another lawyer told a story of finally discharging a pro bono divorce client who wanted a two-day hearing and wouldn't even try to negotiate with the other side.

If it was a private client, I would have done exactly the same thing. Although with a private client, I would have told them that I wasn't going to take another step forward until they came across with a significant additional retainer because if their position was they had to litigate, then they're going to have to pay for it in advance.

Legal fees thus generally provided a powerful tool for influencing clients who were paying the bills. But lawyers in pro bono cases lacked resort to the leverage of cost and thus sometimes found it much more difficult to persuade clients of the value of their advice.

Threatening to Part Ways

A final tactic for influencing client decisions mentioned by lawyers in our interviews was the threat to withdraw from the case. This approach called attention very directly to the power of each party in the lawyer-client relationship.[23] The client may make the ultimate decision on whether to accept a final settlement, but the lawyer makes the choice of whether or not to represent that client. Attorneys spoke at great length with us about which client demands they would be likely to accept and which ones they would not. Lawyers themselves differed on how quickly they would part ways with a client and for what reasons.

Some lawyers explained the usefulness of threatening to part ways with a client who was being unreasonable. One attorney responded that when a client wanted to sell himself or herself short, "If it's a real bad situation, I might even go so far as to withdraw from the case and get them another lawyer, if I think that's what it would take to wake them up." Others commented:

> I can think of cases where I said, "No, I'm just not going to be involved in that, and nothing's scheduled here, and I really think we're on a different wavelength, and you really ought to find somebody else." That usually scares them into changing their mind.

> It is not unusual in a particular case for me to mention maybe at some point or another, if the client's being particularly unreasonable or has expressed expectations that no one is going to be able to meet, that I might make a statement to the effect, "If those are your expectations or if that's what you want me to do, I just cannot represent you. Because either I will not do that or I'm not going to achieve those results, nobody can achieve those results" . . . I threaten more often than I do anything.

The threat of losing one's lawyer (even a lawyer with whom one has been arguing at some length) may provide a strong incentive for clients to accept their attorney's advice.

Firing Clients

At the end of unsuccessful negotiations between lawyer and client, the lawyer may face some difficult choices. Should the lawyer go along with a client who wants to sign an agreement that sells him or her short? Should the lawyer take the client's excessive demands to court, through motions and adversarial hearings, even when they are not realistic? Here the competing demands of professional advice and client self-determination collide. Some lawyers spoke quite openly about their anguish in resolving such dilemmas.[24] Interestingly, the actual resolution of conflict between lawyer and client depended somewhat on the particulars of the situation. Where clients wanted to sell themselves short, attorneys typically said they would probably continue with representation; but where clients made unreasonable demands in order to strike back at their spouses, lawyers were more than twice as likely to say they would withdraw from the case. We examine each of these scenarios in turn.

When faced with a client who was willing to settle for far less than she was entitled to, lawyers reported first trying their various persuasive techniques of education, advice, delay, reference to the courts, and so forth. But if the client was adamant about her decision, then lawyers typically said they would let the client go ahead with the agreement—unless it was outrageous: "They're the client and I'm the lawyer"; "It's their decision, not mine"; "They're adults. They can make their own decisions"; "As long as they understand what they're doing, I have no problems with it"; or "Bottom line is they're free to do it." Lawyers in this situation leaned toward client self-determination. However, they also would attempt to protect themselves through some written documentation about their objections to the agreement their client was signing.

Many lawyers (almost 60 percent) indicated that they would write a "CYA" letter, explaining that the client was accepting the agreement against the lawyer's advice.

> I tell my client that they're the client, and I am the lawyer. I give them my advice, they're free to ignore it. I don't get angry. I might get a little exasperated, but I tell them if they want to do that, they get the "CYA" letter, the "cover your ass" letter.

> All I can do is tell them what I think they should and shouldn't do and give them legal advice. If they then decided that they just want the damn thing over with and they didn't care what happened, they just wanted to get out, it was their decision to make. And then I'd make them sign a little memo saying I explained all this stuff to you so that they don't call me up two months later and say, "Why did you let me do this?" I'm a firm believer that in the end it's my client's decision to make.

Sometimes this letter would be addressed to the client, and at other times it was simply a memo placed in the client's file. Through this device, lawyers could both assert their own professional autonomy and acknowledge the final decision-making role of their clients.

> Sometimes I've gone as far as writing a letter. Make them sit down, read it, sign it, and have a witness that they went over this. I've gone through that experience before. First of all, to make an impression. No, first of all to cover myself. Second of all, to make an impression on them that they will think this is something they really ought to think about.

> If the client insists on going through with it, then what I would generally do is write a long letter that I will require them to sign before I'll continue representation. That serves a couple of purposes. When they see it in writing and show it to some friends, by and large, they will change their mind and decide not to go through with it. But in the event they do go through with it, I won't be sued for malpractice.

As these comments suggest, the "cover your ass" letter serves both as a last-ditch effort to dissuade clients from making foolish decisions and as a necessary protective measure against legal malpractice or bar grievance complaints. Comparison between lawyers' references to CYA letters and their specialization in family law revealed a statistically significant relationship between them.[25] For example, lawyers whose practices consisted of 75 to 100 percent divorce cases were twice as likely as those with under 25 percent divorce cases to volunteer that they wrote CYA letters in situations where the client wanted less than the lawyer recommended. Given the frequency of malpractice complaints filed against lawyers in the divorce area, lawyers who specialized in family law were especially sensitive to the need for such self-protection.

Client self-determination was given less deference, however, if it appeared to conflict with lawyers' public reputation among their peers and in court. More lawyers said they would withdraw from a case in which the client was making unreasonable and excessive demands than in the reverse situation described above. The difference between the situations seemed to center on the reaction the lawyer would receive from peers in the legal community.[26] The repercussions from legal colleagues, and especially from judges, were perceived to be more severe for attorneys who argued unreasonable positions in court. As one attorney said, "I'm not going to make a fool of myself in that court!" Another commented, "It's ridiculous, you're going to get laughed out of court. I can't even make this argument with a straight face." A third explained:

> I'm not a heavy hitter. I don't try to bluff my way through this process by intimidating the other side. The bar [here] is small enough that for the most part you're dealing with the same lawyers over and over again and you want to play pretty fair.

Reputation matters to lawyers in continuing interaction with one another and while the labels of "patsy" or "unreasonable hired gun" were both undesirable, the latter image was perceived by lawyers as more harmful, especially when presented publicly to the court.

Besides a concern for their reputations within the community of divorce practice, some attorneys articulated personal values to justify their resistance to unreasonable clients who were excessive in their demands. In particular, they explained their belief in the importance of avoiding excessive family conflict in order to protect the children's interests. Thus, some lawyers distinguished between divorce fights involving children and those involving property and said that they didn't mind engaging in legal combat over financial matters but would refuse to do so over child custody.

> But the reality is I tell clients that that [child custody] is not a fight I'm going to fight. They're not going to use the kids that way. . . . Having said that, I then divide off the money issues. What I then tell clients is, if they want to get even with him, let's get even by stripping him down to his underwear. I'm perfectly willing to take the other guy to the cleaners financially.

> Those people are tough. If they are only going to hurt each other, I might go along with it if they want to go around mudslinging and do whatever they have to do. But if there are children involved, I don't go through with it. I say, "I can't represent you if you're going to take that position."

Ellmann (1987) describes concern for the interests of third parties as a justification for lawyers to deviate from a client-centered practice and to exercise greater control over clients. As a result of particular concern about the effects of protracted legal combat on children, some lawyers redefined their professional roles to include their personal views about children. And these lawyers reported exercising greater client control when they perceived that an unreasonable parent could hurt the children.

Client Resistance and Legal Professionalism

Clients may use some of these same techniques to resist their lawyers' advice (Sarat and Felstiner 1995), and it is useful to consider these tactics from the client's point of view. Clients have their own expectations of what they should receive in divorce, and they can sometimes stubbornly insist on a version of reality quite different from the lawyer's. Verbal persuasion is not only a lawyer's skill but also may be exercised by clients—by talking and by silence. Just as lawyers can delay the divorce process, so can clients stall in producing documents, fail to show up for appointments, or put off signing papers.

Clients can also use financial leverage and this is undoubtedly the most powerful resource that some clients have. Those with sufficient resources can simply insist that the lawyer follow their wishes, since they have the money to pay the increased fees that the lawyer may demand. If the lawyer balks, the client can threaten to part ways, just as the lawyer can. As the consumer of a service, the client can simply take her business elsewhere, and her search for a willing agent is limited only by the depth of her pocketbook. The capacity of well-to-do clients to seek a second lawyer might help explain the more aggressive and litigious strategies found within the community of divorce specialists. As one marital master said, "even with one of the best attorneys, when you get a litigant who wants to fight and has got the money to do it, even that lawyer might take the case to trial."

Examination of these tactics of client resistance, however, underscores the imbalance of power between most divorce clients and their attorneys. While lawyer and client may jointly construct meaning in law office talk, decisions about and the attainment of final outcomes may reflect the lawyer's greater influence. As one attorney said, "I tell every client within these four walls, they can say anything they want but when they walk out of here, I'm in charge of the decisions that have to be made." In determining the power of lawyers over clients, who does what and who gets what in divorce ultimately matters more than who says what (cf. Sarat and Felstiner 1995: 144).

Other persuasive techniques also suggest how lawyers can dominate decision making with most clients. Although both lawyer and client can use delay, lawyers control the timing of filing of motions and can influence the scheduling of hearings. Their knowledge of the court process and familiarity with court personnel also enable lawyers to use delay as a tactic in ways that are invisible to the client. Furthermore, clients have few resources to resist the lawyer's greater knowledge of what the law requires and what a judge will do, or how the lawyer will present the client's proposal to other lawyers (whether with a wink and a nod, or as a serious proposal in negotiation). The costs of legal action generally impact on paying clients more than on lawyers, and the actual amount charged is within the control of the lawyer. Not many divorce clients have unlimited resources for legal combat.

The picture of the divorce lawyer's professional role toward clients that emerges thus far is therefore somewhat mixed, but more closely approximates the lawyer as an independent advisor than as a hired gun. Two lawyers captured this point well:

> I have had a number of people [clients] say, "Wait a minute, who are you representing?" And usually I can straighten that out by explaining that part of what I perceive to be my role is to help a person come to the right expectations as far as what's going to happen.

> There's a great gradation between how much beating over the head you have to do as far as getting them to comprehend that what they want is unreasonable. It's not that you're telling them what to do but telling them that the positions that they are taking are unreasonable and unsupportable.

Professionalism in practice entails framing situations for clients so that their choices are within the bounds of what the lawyer sees as reasonable, fair, and likely to be achieved. For clients whose choices lie outside those bounds or who are not amenable to reeducation, lawyers have the additional option of withdrawing from the case. While clients too have this choice, the cost of exit in divorce is generally higher for clients than for lawyers.

Conclusion

The attorney-client relationship in divorce presents a problem for professional practice with no clear or certain solution. Neither the codes of professional responsibility nor the academic or legal literatures provide definitive guidelines about how much responsibility for decision making lawyers should exercise on behalf of their clients. In the context of this ambiguity, lawyers' day-to-day decisions about professional authority and client control are not isolated ones, affected only by the lawyer's personal disposition and the particular client. Instead, these decisions occur within communities of practice, and lawyers come to share certain understandings about levels of appropriate and inappropriate client control as a result of experience with divorce clients and their cases, knowledge of likely divorce outcomes in court, and the constraints of ongoing relations with professional colleagues.

The relationship between divorce lawyers and their clients is enacted through a long and complex series of discussions and negotiations between the two parties and is also realized through decisions and action. It is a relationship fraught with tensions and ambiguities. It is not, however, a relationship between equals. Lawyers can invoke a variety of means not available to clients to resolve those tensions in favor of their understanding of the situation. Judging by their own accounts, divorce attorneys employ these tactics frequently and with considerable success.[27]

The lawyer's authority is asserted initially through the decision to accept or reject a potential client. Once the lawyer-client relationship is established, attorneys employ an array of tactics to redirect client expectations and shape decisions: client education, advice, appeal to the law, use of other lawyers, delay, increased fees, and threats to withdraw from the case. If the lawyer is still facing a particularly stubborn, unrealistic client toward the end of the case, the lawyer can recommend that the client seek representation elsewhere. Invariably such tactics are invoked "for the client's good," since the attorney knows from experience that an unreasonable client can harm himself, his former spouse, and his children. And the attorney also believes that divorce clients must be moved from their emotional concerns to focus on more pragmatic ones. As divorce lawyers engage in such redirection, they are sensitized to the malleability of client interests and the difficulty of acting as pure agents for their clients (Gordon 1988; Simon 1984). The indeterminacy of client goals, and the gap between a client's focus on blame and the law's focus on no-fault, remind attorneys that they cannot avoid responsibility for the independent influence they provide in constructing the legal divorce.[28]

Furthermore, the lawyer knows that by representing unreasonable clients one can gain a reputation for being an unreasonable lawyer. Few divorce attorneys aspire to join the ranks of the "pitbulls" and the "Rambos." As important, clients with unrealistic expectations are almost certain to be dissatisfied customers, who may be reluctant to pay bills and who not only do not make the attorney feel successful but also refuse to recommend him to their friends.[29] By asserting an appropriate measure of control over clients' expectations and decisions, therefore, divorce lawyers believe they help their clients. Such control also serves to maintain the lawyers' own sense of satisfaction, a flow of new clients, a steady income stream, and credibility with colleagues and judges—all of which are crucial to their professional survival.

6

THE MEANING OF ADVOCACY

Q: When you are negotiating a divorce case, would you say your primary goal is best described as reaching a settlement fair to both parties or getting as much as possible for your client?

A: The right answer from the bar association stand is probably to get as much as I can for my client, but it is the other one, that's what I do: a reasonable settlement, I guess, fair to both parties.

—a New Hampshire divorce lawyer

Partisan advocacy, in which lawyers pursue legal strategies in an effort to maximize their clients' interests, is a central tenet of legal professionalism. In this "Dominant View" (Simon 1998b: 7) or "Standard Conception" (Luban 1988: 393) of the attorney's professional role, lawyers owe complete loyalty to their clients and should pursue the clients' goals through any and all legal actions. This ideology of adversary advocacy rests on the principle of neutrality, which "prescribes that the lawyer remain detached from his client's ends" and of partisanship, which "prescribes that the lawyer work aggressively to advance his client's ends" (Simon 1978: 36). As Simon writes, the phrases "partisan advocacy" and "adversary advocacy" are used interchangeably to refer to the combined principles of neutrality and partisanship in legal conduct (1978: 37).

Legal scholars such as Simon and Luban have attacked the principle of partisan advocacy, and vigorous debate over it has continued in both the legal academy and the bar. But is this view of advocacy actually dominant in day-to-day legal practice? Much of the commentary on the legal ethics of advocacy focuses on criminal defense lawyers or stems from incidents such as Watergate or, more recently, the behavior of attorneys at the law firm Kaye Scholer representing Lincoln Savings & Loan (see Simon 1998a). What advocacy principles guide lawyers in a more routine civil law practice?

Divorce lawyers, as we reported in chapter 3, generally rejected single-minded devotion to partisan or adversary advocacy. Professionalism in divorce practice meant behaving as a "reasonable lawyer"—a lawyer who balances fairness to both parties with protection of the interests of one's own client, who cooperates and shares information with opposing counsel, and who avoids unrealistic, inflated demands in negotiation. Unlike the highly contested divorces reported in the mass media, the average divorcing couple lacks the resources to support—or the property to justify—extended legal combat. Furthermore, even among affluent couples, the long-term interest in family harmony for the sake of children discourages the escalation of conflict. Divorce law in the two states— with a no-fault framework, presumed equitable distribution of property, shared legal custody, and child support guidelines—provided a fairly predictable legal framework for attorneys in most divorce cases. Divorce lawyers in the small cities and towns of Maine and New Hampshire thus typically defined their professional role according to widely shared informal norms of the reasonable lawyer, not by reference to the formal norm of the zealous advocate.

In this chapter we describe the informal norms of advocacy in divorce and show how those beliefs developed in the legal and social context of divorce practice. We also consider differences in advocacy across communities of divorce lawyers—those distinguished by income of clients and by gender and specialization—as well as the relation of advocacy to reputational concerns among divorce practitioners. Some of these communities of lawyers defined advocacy in ways that more closely resembled the partisan ideal. Such differences in legal professionalism in practice reflect Nelson and Trubek's observation of "multiple and often conflicting ideas about what lawyers should and should not do" (1992a: 187).

The Debate about Zealous Advocacy

Canon 7 of the 1969 Model Code of Professional Responsibility states that "A Lawyer Should Represent a Client Zealously Within the Bounds of the Law" (American Bar Association 1979). Widespread criticism of the legal profession in the 1970s and internal debate within the bar led legal scholars to reexamine that ideal of zealous advocacy. Frankel wrote that "we should begin, as a concerted professional task, to question the premise that adversariness is ultimately and invariably good" (1975: 1052). Simon (1978) developed "the case against adversary advocacy" further, and others (e.g., Schwartz 1978; Rhode 1985) joined his critique. These attacks, along with widespread public dissatisfaction with the legal profession, persuaded bar leaders to modify rules for conduct. In 1983, the American Bar Association (ABA) adopted a new code for lawyers, the Model Rules of Professional Conduct that has since been adopted by about three-quarters of the states (Haskell 1998: 22). New Hampshire was one of the first states to adopt the Model Rules, but Maine resisted wholesale adoption.

The Model Rules omit Canon 7 and situate the admonition on advocacy in the preamble, rather than as a separate rule. The Model Rules also qualify the norm of zealous advocacy by explicitly acknowledging that advocacy is only one of the many different functions that lawyers perform in representing clients:

> As advisor, a lawyer provides a client with an informed understanding of the client's legal rights and obligations and explains their practical implications. *As advocate, a lawyer zealously asserts the clients' position under the rules of the adversary system.* As negotiator, a lawyer seeks a result advantageous to the client but consistent with requirements of honest dealing with others. As intermediary between clients, a lawyer seeks to reconcile their divergent interests as an advisor and, to a limited extent, as a spokesman for each client. [emphasis added]

This formulation preserves the principle of zealous advocacy, but *only* for lawyers when they are operating in an adversarial mode. The newer rules thus respond to Schwartz's (1978) argument that different principles should apply to lawyers in adversarial and nonadversarial settings. Professionalism in the adversary system, writes Schwartz, requires lawyers zealously to advocate their clients' interests before a third-party decision-maker, but different professional principles should apply when lawyers act as negotiators or counselors (1978: 671). The impartial arbiter in the adversary system provides a key difference between the two modes. In an adversarial mode, "putting one's best foot forward by stepping on the feet of the other side makes sense because of the presence of an impartial arbiter. That presence legitimates the zealous advocate model of the lawyer" (Schwartz 1978: 677). In nonadversarial situations, however, lawyers lack the constraint of a third-party arbiter and hence should be more accountable for their actions.[1] Negotiations that require judicial approval, according to Schwartz (1978), obligate lawyers to play two different roles. Prior to reaching agreement, lawyers should negotiate wholeheartedly and honestly for the client, but once an agreement is reached, the lawyer's role changes to that of an advocate for the agreement.

For lawyers in daily practice, unfortunately, no neat line separates preagreement and postagreement modes in negotiation. In contrast to the formal distinction in the Model Rules preamble, the empirical realities of legal work require continual movement back and forth between adversarial and nonadversarial approaches to case settlement. At the same time that lawyers are counseling clients and negotiating, they also need to be alert to the possibility of trial. And as they prepare for trial, they have to remain open to opportunities to reach a consensual agreement. A key dimension of divorce law practice involves addressing such choices that are imposed by the interweaving of negotiation and trial preparation—what Galanter (1984: 268) calls the "litigotiation process." The divorce lawyers we studied most often constructed their professional role as advocates in relation to a working environment characterized by a small community of professional colleagues with generally shared norms of cooperation, avoidance of extreme conflict, and concern for fairness.[2]

Such construction of professionalism in practice raises serious questions for attorneys. Even in the newer Model Rules, the comment on Rule 1.3 continues to admonish lawyers to be "diligent" in representing clients and authorizes "whatever lawful and ethical measures are required to vindicate a client's cause or endeavor. A lawyer should act . . . with zeal in advocacy upon the client's behalf" (American Bar Association 1995). The gap between these formal rules and the realities of divorce practice creates a tension that Kressel (1985: 59) calls a "professional dilemma": official legal codes mandate zealous advocacy, whereas informal norms and the realities of professional life require cooperation among lawyers (see also Gilson and Mnookin 1994). Divorce lawyers responded to this conflict by developing their own guidelines for decision making. These guidelines were created, understood, and maintained within the different communities of divorce practice.

Advocacy in Divorce

The American Academy of Matrimonial Lawyers (AAML) addressed the professional dilemma over representation in 1991 by adopting standards of conduct for divorce lawyers entitled *Bounds of Advocacy* (American Academy of Matrimonial Lawyers 1991). In this report, the Academy criticized existing bar codes for not providing adequate guidance to divorce lawyers and for ignoring the uniqueness of family law. The AAML standards rejected overzealous representation of partisan advocacy and articulated instead "the much greater level of professionalism" to which matrimonial lawyers should aspire (American Academy of Matrimonial Lawyers 1991: 4). The norms for professional conduct set out in the *Bounds of Advocacy* are indeed the informal norms of the "reasonable" divorce lawyer that we encountered in our interviews with divorce attorneys: prescriptions to encourage settlement; to avoid hardball legal tactics; to treat opposing counsel with candor, courtesy, and cooperation;

and to refuse to engage in vindictive conduct toward a spouse, even if requested by a client.

As discussed in chapter 3, the common norm of the reasonable divorce lawyer defined both typical and expected behavior for handling most divorce cases. Through this norm, attorneys found guidance from their peers in how to make the difficult judgments that are central to the professional role. Reasonable lawyers advocated for their clients by knowing the law of divorce and making independent judgments about how to apply that law rather than by identifying too strongly with clients. They sought negotiated settlements where appropriate and avoided unnecessary litigation. In short, the norm of reasonableness in divorce appeared to respond to and incorporate some of the critiques of adversary advocacy. Reasonable lawyers were said to reduce costs (financial and emotional) for clients, more accurately apply substantive law (rather than being caught up in strategic maneuvers), and produce qualitatively better and more equitable case outcomes.

Divorce lawyers are not ordinarily portrayed as behaving in this way. The press and popular culture depict the "Rambo" lawyer, who files every conceivable motion, seeks everything and more from the opposing side, refuses to cooperate in settlement, and argues vigorously and bitterly in a long, drawn-out trial. Nevertheless, our research on the divorce process confirms that few divorces actually go to trial, and that most attorneys in divorce seek settlement. Similarly, Sarat and Felstiner observe that although "clients think of the legal process as an arena for a full adversarial contest, most divorce disputes are not resolved in this manner" (1995: 108). Griffiths (1986), Erlanger, Chambliss, and Melli (1987), Ingleby (1992), and Gilson and Mnookin (1994) also have found that divorce lawyers dampen legal conflict far more than they exacerbate it and generally try to avoid adversarial actions. In our interviews, lawyers frequently identified a few Rambo lawyers whose visibility highlighted by contrast the more common norm of reasonableness.

Most divorce lawyers we interviewed rejected overzealous advocacy. Instead, they drew on their experience with divorce cases and family law to define advocacy in ways that incorporated fairness to both parties. When asked whether their primary goal in divorce was best described as reaching a settlement fair to both parties or as getting as much as possible for their client, the lawyers varied in their responses: 35 percent of the lawyers chose "fair settlement," only 23 percent chose "most for client," and 42 percent refused to accept the forced choice and instead combined the possibilities, as in, for example, "reaching a settlement fair to my client."[3]

Lawyers who said they sought the most for their clients defined advocacy in a partisan way. In their explanations, they underscored the lawyer's obligation to serve the client's interests—and *only* the client's— and argued that ensuring "fairness" was the responsibility of the court, the mediator, or "the system," but certainly not the job of the lawyer. Some of these attorneys explained their position in the classic terms of defenders of the ideal of partisan advocacy. "Your goal is always to advocate the strongest position for your client and to get the best result possible. You aren't concerned with the other side, except to the extent that this agreement is going to pass judicial scrutiny." Another lawyer described her goal as "getting as much as possible for my client. Because I believe in the system. The other lawyers are usually doing the same thing. And if you stand back and you look at the whole thing, you can see that each side got something." A third lawyer said of his negotiating goal:

> I can't be fair. There's a part of me that wants to be fair. I'm Catholic. I think that most attorneys are basically decent people—they want to be fair, but that's not their role. That's the judge's role, to be fair. My role is to represent what the client wants.

Strikingly, however, less than one-quarter of the divorce lawyers we interviewed embraced the goal of partisan advocacy. Over three-quarters of our respondents defined their role as advocates in relation to notions of justice and fairness. Some of the lawyers who chose "fair settlement" as their negotiating goal expressed concern that this was not the "correct answer" in terms of professional values. That is, they recognized at some level that they were not complying with the admonition to be zealous advocates. Other attorneys spoke openly of the tension they felt over this professional dilemma. For example, one replied, "It is a difficult question to answer, and I have had an argument with one of my partners over this very question."

Why did the majority of divorce lawyers respond that they sought fairness instead of, or in addition to, getting the most for their client? Their answers variously emphasized the legal framework of no-fault divorce, the equitable property distribution that the court would most likely impose, a concern for clients' long-term future, and the self-interested concern of lawyers to avoid future involvement in post-divorce litigation. One lawyer, for example, said, "You won't get it settled unless both parties at least perceive it as fair. And if you overreach, even if you get an agreement from the other side, in some cases, you might go to court and the judge might say, 'I'm not going to endorse this, you've overreached.' " Another attorney put it this way:

> I think the goal is the fair settlement to both clients for the client's benefit. If it's fair, there will be less post-divorce legal proceedings. If you go in to get it all, all you're setting it up for is a good pat on the back from the client, and future legal fees, because there will be critical faults in this post-divorce foundation, and they'll break wide open.

Experience with divorce cases can be a great teacher about the value of fairness in the negotiating process. One divorce lawyer explained her preference for fairness by describing a case that went on for years with much legal wrangling. She concluded by reflecting on the costs of overly zealous advocacy: "I think it is in my client's interest that the other person not leave the marriage feeling soaked. If you create a situation where there is long-term resentment, you'll pay. There is no doubt in my mind about that . . . whether it is emotionally or financially, you'll pay." Indeed, many divorce lawyers claimed to have learned over time that highly partisan advocacy was counterproductive to the continuing, long-term relationship required of divorced parties, especially those with children. Lawyers referred to their case experiences—shared by their peers in divorce practice—to explain why they had adopted a perspective that incorporated fairness into client representation.

The lawyers who attempted to combine the alternatives of "most for client" and "fair settlement" described similar lessons. One said, "I think you want to get the most for your client. But I think you realistically know that you have to be somewhere in the parameters of what's considered fair." Another attorney explained:

> Well, obviously I'm interested in getting the best possible deal for my client. But that has to be considered in the context of fairness because I know that if the case goes to court and the judge makes a decision, that's still going to be the criterion. . . . It's going to be easier for them to deal with the former spouse, particularly in matters involving children, than if the other spouse tends to feel that he's been taken advantage of, it's not going to be good for anybody.

Unabashed advocacy for one's client may be the lawyer's role as learned in law school and reinforced by codes of professional responsibility, but our evidence suggests that most divorce lawyers rejected it as an exclusive goal for representing divorce clients. Scholars of legal ethics have challenged concepts of legal professionalism on just this point, arguing that "surely the professional standards must ultimately impose upon him [the lawyer] a duty not to accept an unconscionable deal . . . an arrangement that is completely unfair to the other side" (Rubin 1975: 591). The divorce lawyers we studied seem to have constructed this view out of their common experience, as most agreed that pursuit of a divorce client's interests should occur with concern for a fair outcome for both parties.

Just as lawyers' negotiating goals developed out of their practices, so too did their negotiating tactics. Unlike the "hard bargaining" of personal injury negotiations (Genn 1987), the typical divorce negotiations reported by the lawyers we studied were consensual, occurring within a generally predictable and shared normative framework of outcomes.[4] In other words, negotiations were generally *not* what Kritzer (1991) describes as concessions-oriented, maximal-result bargaining, in which lawyers start with extreme positions with the expectation of repeated rounds of concessions and behave strategically in what they view as a zero-sum game. The elaborate posturing and extreme position-taking common to personal injury settlements did not make sense, according to the divorce attorneys we interviewed:

If you deal with a lawyer that knows the law, there's no point in playing those games because it's not that hard to figure out who gets what. It's not like in a personal injury case where who knows if a lost leg is worth a million dollars or a half of a million dollars. Who knows? That's not what you're dealing with here. You're dealing with the presumption that it's going to be 50–50.

The law merely sets down the rules that you're playing along . . . you're working within . . . a rather narrow framework. You have limitations that you're not going to go far below or high above. You can predict that pretty well as opposed to a personal injury claim. . . . The [personal injury] case could be worth $200,000, or it could be worth $60,000, and there's just so much play in between.

Since the parameters for divorce were relatively narrow, and experienced divorce attorneys knew generally what to expect, most lawyers chose not to represent their clients through competitive bargaining.[5]

Another aspect of advocacy in divorce was revealed through lawyers' descriptions of the appropriate methods for negotiating cases. When we asked attorneys how they preferred to open divorce negotiations, only 3 percent said they started with an extreme position in anticipation of later compromise, whereas 70 percent of the lawyers said they preferred to begin with an offer close to or only slightly higher than what they thought would be a fair outcome (and 27 percent said "it depends.").[6] Most of the lawyers reported that they rejected extreme posturing designed to extract as much as possible for the client and instead saw fairness as the guide for calibrating an opening offer. To a certain extent, Maine and New Hampshire attorneys characterized divorce law in ways similar to some of the plea bargaining studies that found norms of shared agreement on likely case outcomes.[7] Divorce attorneys reported that they engaged in some give and take with one another, exchanging offers and counteroffers, but that their negotiations were generally cooperative. Their opening bids had "some room to move," "some fat to throw away," or "some padding." But they were not the highly inflated offers characteristic of other areas of law such as personal injury.

What aspects of the divorce law workplace led lawyers to reject or qualify partisan advocacy? One key factor was the legal framework of no-fault divorce, which presumed equity in property distribution, and of generally nonnegotiable child support guidelines. Second, lawyers considered the costs of zealous advocacy and said they defined their representation in part according to the stakes of the cases and how much their clients could afford. Finally, the small size of the divorce law community and lawyers' concern for preserving their reputations reinforced a role of reasonableness. Taken together, these factors shaped the nature of advocacy within communities of divorce law practitioners. Furthermore, where differences arose—in the legal framework, in the stakes of cases, or in the relation of lawyers to their peers—lawyers defined their professional roles in ways that diverged from the norm. These differences in role definition regarding the principles of advocacy thus reflected not only general concerns about individual reputation but also patterned differences across communities of practice based on the economic resources of clients and on the intersections of specialization and gender.

The Legal Framework

The law provides the basic structure for defining advocacy. As the comment on Model Rule 3.1 states, "The law, both procedural and substantive, establishes the limits within which an advocate may proceed" (American Bar Association 1995). The grounds for divorce in both Maine and New Hampshire allowed both traditional fault criteria and no-fault, with equitable distribution of property and presumptions of shared legal custody of children. Lawyers perceived this substantive legal framework for divorce and the pattern of judicial decision making in divorce to explicitly discourage outcomes weighted heavily to either side. For example, in no-fault divorce cases, lawyers negotiated settlements against the expectation that the court would order a 50–50 division of all marital property. One lawyer explained how the legal change to equitable distribution influenced her preference for a fair outcome rather than the most she could get for her client: "Ten years ago, I would have said otherwise. . . . I think the law has changed. . . . It's much clearer what the guidelines [are] the court must use in dividing up property."[8]

Knowledge of the law and experience with judicial decision making in divorce have led lawyers to construct informal norms about how to advocate for their clients. The communities of divorce lawyers have developed standards and shared reference points that define professionalism in practice. Not only does divorce bargaining occur "within the shadow of the law" (Mnookin and Kornhauser 1979), but so too have attorneys' ideas about the meaning of advocacy developed and changed within that legal shadow. Arguing zealously that a divorce client is blameless and deserves the bulk of the marital assets simply makes no sense to lawyers operating within a legal framework that ignores fault and presumes a 50–50 division of property. As one lawyer explained his role:

> When you talk about negotiating, the framework for negotiations has been set up by the statute, and that is an equitable distribution of marital assets, with the exception of nonmarital property. So, you start out with a goal—the legislature has given you the goal, so all you're doing is fashioning. . . . "Well, would you rather have the money come out of the bank account or would you rather have the money come out of the equity?" I mean, to me, that's the negotiating.

In other words, for most divorce cases, lawyers saw themselves engaged in something more closely resembling problem solving than adversarial negotiation (Menkel-Meadow 1984).

In addition to the shift to no-fault, the introduction of child support guidelines significantly changed the law of divorce. Congress passed a law in 1984 to encourage child support enforcement,[9] and states seeking federal funds were required to institute numerical formulas to guide judges in setting child support awards. The federal Family Support Act of 1988 further strengthened the 1984 law by making mandatory these mathematical formulas to set support amounts and strictly limiting deviations from them (Melli 2000). Both Maine and New Hampshire rewrote their child support laws to comply with these federal mandates. The first New Hampshire law passed in 1988 and calculated support amounts based on a percentage of gross income—25 percent for one child, 33 1/3 percent for two, 40 percent for three, and 45 percent for four or more children. Similar guidelines[10] for Maine went into effect in 1989.

Given these mathematical formulas to determine support, divorce lawyers redefined certain aspects of their roles. Nearly 70 percent of the lawyers we interviewed said that the new child support guidelines made their divorce practices easier[11]—largely because the new rules removed much of the uncertainty from the process and reduced the number of contestable issues. A marital master described the guidelines as "the greatest thing since sliced bread." And a lawyer explained how the guidelines made life "so much easier. You can just tell your male clients . . . 'This is what you can expect to pay. And that's that. There is nothing that you can do about it.' " Another attorney said, "I used to joke that I referred to myself as Monty Hall. You get on the phone and make a deal. 'How does 40 bucks a week sound? How about $47.50? $45?' Now you sit down and calculate everything according to the child support guidelines and that is it." In sum, lawyers praised the guidelines because they substantially raised the amounts of support awarded to custodial parents; parents accepted the amounts more readily on learning that they had been legally mandated; the guidelines made divorce settlements easier to arrange ("It's a no-brainer"); and the rules on child support reduced adversarial conflict between the parties ("[There is]less room for being wild and crazy").

The decrease in adversarial advocacy caused by the guidelines paralleled the shift to no-fault and equitable division of property. Divorce lawyers said they altered their settlement goals from seeking maximal amounts to the easier—and far less contentious—one of equitable division of property. As one New Hampshire attorney said, "I mean, anyone can negotiate a 50–50 split of property in a divorce. A moron can do that."

Both New Hampshire and Maine retained the option of a fault-based divorce, even after the adoption of no-fault in the early 1970s, but attorneys only infrequently made allegations of fault. New Hampshire law allowed marital fault to be a factor in property distribution, whereas Maine law excluded it, regardless of the grounds for the divorce. Not surprisingly, New Hampshire attorneys reported more frequent use of fault grounds than did attorneys in Maine. Lawyers in both states described courts as reluctant to find fault in divorce, and consequently most preferred to file on no-fault grounds instead.

> The attorneys as a rule . . . very quickly fell into line with this no-fault business and very, very rarely do I ever see a divorce brought on fault grounds, even if there is grounds to do this because . . . courts aren't particularly interested in hearing any fault grounds.

For example, New Hampshire lawyers said they rarely alleged adultery in their case filings because they believed that a finding of adultery would not greatly influence the court's division of assets. As one explained, "Adultery isn't worth all that much, maybe 5 or 10 percent." And another lawyer said that judges simply "aren't interested in who's sleeping with whom or who's done what." One told the story of a colleague in Maine who "had a case . . . where the guy actually came home and found his wife in bed with another man, went bananas, and he did bring adultery grounds in Maine. And the judge simply told him, 'I don't want to hear any of this.'" Thus, most divorce lawyers adapted their representation to reflect the practical reality of the rules and generally avoided the fault basis for divorce.

Not only did the reluctance of judges to hear allegations of fault shape lawyers' decisions, but so also did their concern for limiting conflict and promoting settlement. A few New Hampshire lawyers said they believed that professional rules compelled them to file on fault grounds when the facts suggested such a claim, because of the possibility that marital fault could affect the property division. For example, one said, "I think the way the law is written, if we don't file on a fault ground, at least on the alternative, then we're liable. . . . I think we're guilty of malpractice." But most lawyers emphasized instead the harm that fault allegations could do to the divorce settlement process. Simply by stating fault grounds in the formal legal complaint, lawyers knew that they would fan the emotional flames of the divorce and create more conflict in case negotiations. One lawyer acknowledged, "I think twice [about alleging fault] because with fault grounds, if you have got a divorce that is close, that you think may not become too contested, fault grounds will enrage the other party." Another attorney explained that she tried not to file on fault grounds "because I think that just tends to keep the legal process going and makes negotiation that much more difficult, and it keeps emotions higher, and it keeps the conflict [going] between the parties." The small likelihood of gain for a client from a finding of fault, along with the high risk of creating new obstacles to settlement from the increased emotional conflict discouraged allegations of fault.

Another legal rule that decreased adversarial conflict was the presumption of "shared parental responsibility" (Maine) or "joint legal custody" (New Hampshire) of children. This legal language discouraged fights over custody and facilitated negotiations—in part, because it was hard to succeed in overturning the legal presumption of shared or joint custody.[12] Lawyers acknowledged that the reality of joint legal custody

did not mean very much, but it did strengthen lawyers' hands in negotiating with their clients:

> I think "joint legal custody" is a nice word that has no real meaning.
> It placates fathers very nicely. You can tell the father that it gives him
> all sorts of important legal rights, whatever they may be, and allows
> you to tell the mother . . . that it means absolutely nothing.

> I just let my clients know that there is a presumption that it's in the
> best interests of the children to have joint legal custody, so unless they
> can come up with some real good reason why the other parent should
> not have joint legal custody, then let's move on to something else. . . .
> I think psychologically it helps the other parent to feel better about the
> situation because, "Hey, you know, I've still got this major input into
> my child's life." But I don't know that practically it really makes any
> difference.

In contrast to the predictability and clarity of the rule on legal custody,
the rule for physical custody—"best interests of the child"—was subject
to wide interpretation. "The court still has a lot of discretion in custody
and visitation matters," as one attorney said. Yet even in this situation,
lawyers generally preferred to avoid extended legal battles. Divorce lawyers had seen the adverse impact of prolonged litigation on children, so
they typically tried first to resolve custody conflicts through mediation or
with the help of a guardian *ad litem*. But they said they also took custody
cases to trial if warranted.

Another area of legal uncertainty that led lawyers to advocate more
aggressively than usual included alimony ("Alimony is a big wild card"),
as rules governing alimony awards had shifted over the years.[13] Also, in
New Hampshire, legal guidelines on what constituted "marital property"
were not clear, so that parties might contest questions such as "Does her
inheritance count? Does his land that he had before marriage count?" in
determining marital property to be divided.[14] Experienced divorce lawyers
believed that these gray areas of law and the uncertainty of judicial decisions called for more adversarial advocacy. Yet they also saw few divorce cases that clearly warranted such a role. Economic forces aug-
mented these legal influences on professionalism in practice.

The Costs of Zealous Advocacy

"Winning" in divorce was not only unlikely as a matter of law, but it
was also a costly goal to seek. That is, the costs of pursuing every possible
avenue for a client within the bounds of the law often outweighed benefits to be gained. Divorce lawyers thus tried to convince clients to settle
divorces by touting the comparative advantage of settlement over trials,
rather than talking about fairness in settlement (Sarat and Felstiner
1995: 120–121). A custody fight imposes costs on the "winning" party
in terms of damaged long-term relationships that lawyers believed usually
outweigh any gain.[15] Family law attorneys did not see divorce conflicts

as zero-sum games. As one lawyer said, "I don't think in terms . . . of win-lose in family law cases. I think that it's not a win-lose thing." Legal advocacy in divorces with modest stakes was generally tailored to reaching fair and amicable settlements in part to minimize the costs—both financial and emotional—to clients.

The transaction costs of fighting for a greater share of property or more generous visitation were high, lawyers felt, and those costs rarely made economic sense for their clients. Thus, lawyers were attentive to the costs of alternative strategies in negotiation.[16] For example, one explained why she avoided inflated offers: "I just think an incredible amount of money can be wasted on that. And I see it, and it is really too bad, you just go all the way around the mulberry bush." Another lawyer responded firmly, "I will never take a negotiating position that I think is completely unfounded. . . . I think it just prolongs the process, it makes the first few forays into the negotiation process senseless and wastes your client's time and money." A full-court legal press takes time, and therefore money, and usually with only a small chance of gain, especially for clients with limited resources.

Some lawyers emphasized how tempered advocacy saved their *own* time, as well as their clients' resources. For instance, one attorney said he preferred to start negotiations "pretty much with what you want," because "I just don't have enough hours in the day to mess around with ridiculous offers." Another lawyer said, "I don't think I ever come in with a very extreme position. . . . I would more often say this is what I think is fair and this is my offer. I don't want to waste my time going back and forth and playing games."

Professional practice requires understanding what a job entails so that it can be done efficiently. Seeking a fair settlement rather than the most for a client, and opening divorce negotiations with a reasonable offer rather than an extreme one, provided lawyers with an efficient solution to the problem of negotiating an agreement. As one attorney explained, "It's a much more expedient approach. Everything takes so damn much time. You know, that muscling and chest beating and all of those ape-type maneuvers." When attorneys knew their clients simply could not pay for more than 10 or so hours of their time in a divorce case, cost considerations were overwhelming.

For some cases, however, the payoff structure led lawyers to adopt a different approach. When sufficient financial assets were involved, lawyers were more likely to perceive the benefits from adversarial posturing to outweigh the transaction costs. Just as in criminal law, where lawyers engaged in explicit, protracted plea negotiations to settle serious crimes,[17] lawyers representing clients in high-asset divorce cases more often pursued greater legal contest, through extensive settlement negotiations, pretrial motions, and trial. High stakes in a divorce not only presented lawyers with greater opportunities to earn fees, but also provided more complex issues for lawyers to negotiate:

Usually where you have two people, both working, both with their own IRA accounts, both with their own economic lives, then you get some tailoring and shaping. But if you have the fellow working at the Navy Yard, the wife is at home taking care of a couple of kids, the only asset is the home and car, then there's not much negotiating. Because most attorneys . . . know what the legislature is requiring as well as I do, and so they're not going to be trying to get creative because there's nothing to be creative with. Your child support is controlled by this, the custody is usually agreed upon by the parties, so there's not a fight over the kids. So the only thing you have left is how do you pay for the VISA and the Sears card? You know, how do you divide the house? And that's about it.

Advocacy for clients in working-class divorce cases meant fairly straight-forward problem solving, whereas lawyers believed that advocacy for higher-income clients required more "tailoring and shaping" of settle-ments. Moreover, the wealthier clients could better afford to pay lawyers to pursue time-consuming legal strategies and detailed negotiations. Given the different payoff structure for high-end divorces, a wealthy di-vorce litigant might be able to buy off an otherwise cooperative attorney and cause him to "defect" from reasonableness (Gilson and Mnookin 1994: 543). A few divorce lawyers thus made their living by being un-reasonable gladiators or pit bulls—by cultivating a reputation as advo-cates who would fight tooth and nail, regardless of the inefficiencies of time and money.

Resources of clients could also influence the approach lawyers took in divorce negotiations—for example, whether they preferred to make the first settlement offer or wait for the other side.[18] Financial concerns led some lawyers—especially those with working-class clients—to prefer to wait to receive an offer. "Who's got the money? Who's going to take the time and prepare that document? Is there any money in this case?" For lawyers in this situation, cost was the overriding factor. As one admitted, echoing Henry Genrus, "I prefer not to write the agreement. It's quite expensive because the agreements themselves can be eight, ten pages long and they can take three or four hours and that's a lot of money for a client to have to shell out for a proposed agreement." Another lawyer with a predominantly working-class clientele said, "If the other attorney says, 'We'll put something together,' that's great because it saves my client having to pay me to do the stipulations." Thus, the shared context of limited resources to invest in negotiations shaped the norms about advocacy for the community of lawyers serving working-class clients.

That lawyers would expend more time and energy fighting in high stakes cases is supported by docket data on various measures of the court process. Table 6.1 shows that among the lawyers we interviewed, those who represented upper-middle-class clients raised significantly more ad-versarial motions per case than those with middle-class and working-class clients. Similarly, Table 6.2 shows how the average length of the

Table 6.1 Average Number of "Adversarial" Motions Per Case
Initiated by Lawyers by Social Class of Their Clienteles

Clientele	Mean Number of Adversarial Motions
Working Class	0.53 (n = 64)
Middle Class	0.64 (n = 55)
Upper-Middle Class	1.26 (n = 32)
All	0.73 (n = 151)

F = 11.16 with 2 and 148 d.f. (n = 151); p = .000

case—the period from date of filing to date of final disposition—increased significantly for lawyers depending on the class of their clientele.

These data reveal significant differences in the duration and nature of the divorce process especially between the high-end clients and those in the middle and working classes. Couples with substantial assets obviously presented greater challenges to attorneys than did those with few assets. Lawyers had to establish values for businesses, second homes, or trusts, explore pension and retirement funds, and be certain that all assets had been located (or protected, depending on the client). All this took time and could require legal motions and court hearings. But at the same time, lawyers for wealthy clients were more likely to assume the role of partisan advocate and to initiate various legal actions, since the benefits for clients (and lawyers) of doing so could exceed the costs. The informal norms guiding professional conduct in high-end divorces placed greater value on meticulous legal representation and vigorous assertion of a client's interests, the kind of advocacy that leaves no stone unturned.

Facing similar workplace demands from wealthier clients and having experience with the complexity of divorces involving substantial assets, the small community of attorneys serving the upper and upper-middle class tended to share a view of advocacy that comes closer to the dominant view in the bar, that of partisan advocacy. A less charitable interpretation of their behavior would point to its self-serving quality. Adversarial advocacy in high-end divorce cases generated high legal fees for the lawyer. The same type of advocacy practiced routinely in cases in-

Table 6.2 Mean Length of Cases of Lawyers by
Social Class of Their Clienteles (in Days)

Clientele	Mean Number of Days
Working Class	251 (n = 64)
Middle Class	264 (n = 55)
Upper-Middle Class	341 (n = 32)
All	275 (n = 151)

F = 5.93 with 2 and 148 d.f. (n = 151); p = .003

volving fewer assets would bankrupt a divorce lawyer. Economic incentives thus contributed to the nature of professionalism in practice. According to Rhode (1985), an obvious problem with professional legal standards mandated by the bar

> involves the financial underpinnings of advocacy, a point on which most defenders of the adversary ethos are diplomatically silent. Almost without exception, *Model Rules* commentators who invoked fundamental values simply ignored the vast array of civil matters in which the stakes do not justify or the claimant cannot secure a "champion against a hostile world." (608–609).

The relative infrequency of high-stakes divorces—at least in Maine and New Hampshire—helped to explain why the reasonable lawyer ideal was so widely shared among the divorce lawyers we interviewed. The stakes of most divorces simply did not justify adversarial advocacy.

Advocacy from Women Specialists

The emergence of a specialized family law bar that especially concentrated its representation on affluent clients in divorce coincided with the sharp increase in women in the legal profession. Women lawyers were always overrepresented within family law (Epstein 1993), but their increase during the 1970s and 1980s had a particular impact on changing advocacy in divorce in Maine and New Hampshire. Not only were women lawyers more likely to practice divorce law, but they were also more likely to specialize in divorce. As discussed above, it was the specialists with divorce cases involving upper-middle-class clients who saw greater value from adversarial advocacy because the high stakes in their cases and the pocketbooks of their clients would justify and support the costs of it. Thus, the economics of a legal practice with high-end clients encouraged both male and female lawyers to file more motions, ask for more court hearings, and engage in more aggressive advocacy. But, at the same time, gender played a role in accentuating the differences between advocacy in divorce by general practice and specialist lawyers.

An important characteristic of the legal community was its nearly all-male profile until the 1970s. As women entered the legal profession in large numbers over the next two decades, they frequently struggled to gain acceptance within each local professional community. Bar surveys in both states revealed perceptions of an old boy network among lawyers and the exclusionary, discriminatory atmosphere such a network created (Crowley et al. 1996; Shanelaris and Luneau 1998).[19] Some women attorneys we interviewed said that while informal communication and reasonableness may have worked well for those in the old boy network, it was disastrous if one was not a member of "the clique." In part, because the male professional community excluded them, some of these women rejected the informal norms of moderation and reasonableness and sought instead to put into practice the vigorous advocacy skills they had learned in law school. Other women lawyers brought to divorce the techniques of civil litigation and chose to rely more on formal motions, discovery, and interrogatories than on informal conversations with their peers.

For example, in each of the two states we studied, several women lawyers—all of whom specialized in divorce—claimed that they were personally responsible for introducing interrogatories into divorce practice as part of their commitment to taking divorce seriously. One woman lawyer defended the change by asking sarcastically why, since few lawyers would dissolve a client's business based on verbal assurances about financial assets, they were so willing to dissolve a marriage that way. Another woman lawyer explained:

> When I came into the family law bar, I brought with me a lot of the litigation techniques I had used in all kinds of other cases. . . . I have an obligation to the client not to accept the fact that just because someone tells me they have a pension worth $20,000 [that they do]. If that means interrogatories or subpoenas, then that's what it means. . . . I see a lot of bad lawyering that's based on "Oh, let's be buddies." I'm not a member of the clique.

Andrea Wright (in chapter 2) similarly described how she began using these formal discovery techniques in divorce work in the early 1980s and faced strong opposition from her legal brethren for doing so.

One result of introducing greater formality and more adversary advocacy to divorce practice was that these women lawyers created a reputation for themselves as "difficult," "hardball," and "aggressive." Thus, some divorce lawyers we interviewed said that women were disproportionately represented among "unreasonable" divorce lawyers. "The women would make a greater percentage," one male attorney explained, of "the so-called hard-nosed lawyers that we are talking about." Another lawyer noted:

> Maybe that's a broad statement [that women are the unreasonable lawyers] but some of the more aggressive ones that I have dealt with I would say have been women. I think that they have manifested less willingness to try and resolve this thing and to try to work out the differences and reach a settlement.

Thus, efforts intended to approach divorce by employing the same legal tools used in civil litigation were viewed by other lawyers as violating the informal understandings so crucial to much general practice work with clients of modest means.

The gender differences in divorce advocacy identified by some of the attorneys we interviewed showed women disproportionately as the more zealous advocates and men as the more reasonable, cooperative ones. What might explain a finding that is so contrary to feminist predictions? Since a higher percentage of the women lawyers than men specialized in divorce and also reported representing primarily upper-middle-class clients, these women—like almost all attorneys engaged in high-end specialist practice—were more likely to use adversarial legal tactics. Also, women attorneys were far more likely than men to represent wives in divorce, and this may have led them to a more partisan identification with their clients and their clients' goals. Furthermore, male comments about Rambo-like qualities of female advocacy may simply have reflected an unwillingness to accept women in the role of advocate. Finally, exclusion from informal relationships in the professional community and discrimination from their male peers may have led some women lawyers—especially in the 1970s when their numbers were small—to rely more on the formal advocacy of civil litigation and the Model Code and less on the informal advocacy characteristic of much of divorce practice.[20] As more women entered divorce practice, they became more integrated into communities of practice, but those communities were redefined by their new approaches to divorce representation.

Lawyer's Reputation

Reputation within the professional legal community matters enormously. Lawyers frequently remarked that they constructed their own styles of advocacy with an eye on their reputations. Almost all divorce attorneys said, for example, that they avoided extreme opening offers and preferred reasonable ones instead, because of how they would be viewed by their professional peers. The divorce bar in both states was small, and attorneys had considerable first-hand experience handling cases against one another. As a result, divorce lawyers typically did not want to be perceived as uncooperative or unreasonable. In this way, the reputational market for lawyers served to reinforce cooperative behavior and diminish overly zealous advocacy (Landon 1990; Gilson and Mnookin 1994).

"Credibility" was the word lawyers typically used to explain position taking in negotiations. In order to be taken seriously by colleagues, lawyers said they must operate according to the known parameters of divorce law and to the informal norms of divorce advocacy—norms that strongly discouraged exaggerated offers and counteroffers. These informal norms functioned, as Gordon (1988: 33–34) argues, to promote independent legal judgment in representation. Norms of reasonableness helped lawyers resist client pressures (as discussed in chapter 5) and the reputational market for lawyers reinforced cooperation. "I never start with an extreme position," one lawyer explained, "[because] if you make an extreme offer, all you're doing is ruining your credibility." Another attorney who avoided inflated offers said, "My feeling is that if you're ridiculous with your demands, or your suggestions of settlement, the other side will never take you seriously, and you have no credibility." The verbal content of negotiations matters to lawyers (Eisenberg 1976), and consequently, an offer that is inconsistent with what "everyone knows" about divorce can damage the lawyer's reputation. Such behavior also "takes away the credibility of other arguments you may make in the case," as one lawyer put it.

Lawyers explicitly referred to their reputations, saying that they didn't want to be "labeled" as one who makes outrageous offers, takes unreasonable positions, or is going to "bullshit" the other lawyers. Reputation is a precious commodity for professionals. As repeat players, divorce lawyers in small communities encounter one another over and over, and thus the costs of being unreasonable are great. A lawyer who said she would never put forward an extreme position explained, "People know you're blowing smoke. I mean, you don't have to practice law more than six months to be able to spot somebody who's pulling that nonsense." A lawyer with the same response put it this way: "You like to preserve some aura of reasonableness among our fellow professionals so that they will respect you and want to deal with you. I mean, nobody wants to be known as somebody who takes ridiculous stands and paints everybody else in a corner."

When lawyers tender offers in negotiation, they communicate important information about their own judgment and operating style, information that is easily and quickly shared within a small legal community. At the same time, lawyers' offers communicate something to the other lawyer about how she is viewed—as another professional to be treated with respect and courtesy or as an adversary to be fought. Several lawyers used the same phrase to evaluate opening offers in divorce negotiations: the "straight face test," which determines whether the offer lies within acceptable bounds. Other attorneys explained that they would never make an extreme offer because it would show "contempt" for the other attorney or would "insult" her.

Gilson and Mnookin suggest that the incentives individual lawyers have, as repeat players, to maintain a reputation for cooperation may be undermined in two ways: through client pressures that cause "a previously cooperative agent to defect" and through "collusion" between lawyers "to exacerbate conflict when that behavior serves their own interests" (1994: 513). The first situation comes into play especially in high-stakes cases. The second situation is not one lawyers acknowledged, but they did identify a third situation, whereby the adversarial conduct of one lawyer induced reciprocal behavior from a normally cooperative and reasonable attorney.

We asked divorce lawyers if their negotiation style varied with the identity of the opposing lawyer, and 85 percent said that it did.[21] Although most claimed to mirror cooperation, attorneys also felt they had to adopt a more aggressive approach if such conduct was introduced by their opponent. One said bluntly, "If somebody wants to be reasonable, I'll be reasonable. But if somebody wants to be an asshole, then nobody can be a bigger jerk than I can." Another described his negotiating style as "a mirror of how the other party is behaving. If I am negotiating with an attorney who is clearly friendly and collegial, then I will be. If I'm negotiating with somebody who is just a rat-assed bastard, then I will be a rat-assed bastard back." What is striking about these responses is that nearly all denied *initiating* adversarial moves but then readily acknowledged adapting to them and responding in kind. The "collusion" between lawyers to abandon cooperation, as suggested by Gilson and Mnookin (1994), develops not from an explicit and joint decision or a self-interested one, but rather from a tacit understanding that both lawyers should be operating in the same mode or "playing the same game." The "game," however, is most often defined by the most adversarial lawyer's moves and not the reverse. In this sense, the community of divorce practice lacks the capacity to enforce its norm of the reasonable lawyer.

Sarat and Felstiner (1995) found the metaphor of ball games and playing fields to be invoked frequently by divorce lawyers, and attorneys we interviewed also used it often to characterize the different approaches one might take in the divorce process:

> If this is the way somebody wants to do it, I'm willing to do it that way. If somebody wants to have a battle of dueling word processors, then I'll do that. I don't like to do it. . . . If somebody wants to have a shouting match, we can do that too. I like to think that I can play a variety of games.

> If you're dealing with somebody who is, say, a litigator, who is more hard-nosed or just unreasonable or whatever, then I tend to turn it up a notch on my end. You've got to let them know that it's the same playing field and that you might be an easygoing fellow, but that this is an important case and you're going to do this and that.

Other attorneys referred to the "game" of negotiation only in reference to an especially adversarial mode of interaction, reinforcing the notion that reasonable, cooperative negotiations were the norm. For example, if a difficult attorney is on the other side, one lawyer said, "then you have to play all kinds of games, pretend you want something when you don't, and ask for things even when you don't care about them. And it's wasteful. Unfortunately, it's sometimes necessary." Another responded:

> If it's an attorney who I know who's very aggressive and is going to play the game, then I'll play the game. I won't like it, but I'll do it. If it's an attorney who does stuff more like me, then I will call them and say, "Listen, this is what this is about. You and I know what in the end is going to happen. Why don't we sit down and talk about this and settle what few problems there are and get it over with?"

This comment underscores the central questions we have been exploring: Why did most divorce lawyers think it "necessary" to adapt in this way? Why did they perceive greater rewards from joining the style of a colleague—even a style they disparaged—than from remaining loyal to their own beliefs about professional conduct? One answer, clearly, lies in their belief that the client could be hurt in the particular case if an attorney did not respond in kind to unreasonable behavior. That is, the zealous advocate could take advantage of the more restrained party on the other side.

At a broader level, however, the willingness of lawyers to adapt to the style of their colleagues may reflect something about the cohesion and identity of the wider legal profession. "A critical but often ignored method of sustaining the solidarity of the profession lies in norms governing relations among its members and between its members and lay people" (Freidson 1994: 203). Differences between nonlawyers and the general lawyer community, discussed in chapter 3, may help to explain why divorce lawyers generally adjust their own behavior when opposing their more aggressive peers. Lawyers have all been schooled in the zealous advocacy ideal of the profession. Even where divorce lawyers reject the appropriateness of that ideal for family law practice, they may not want to appear weak or lacking in the ability to play the more traditional advocacy role. A perception of weakness in advocacy could also hurt a lawyer in later negotiations by damaging her reputation, suggesting she is a "pushover" when faced with hardball negotiating tactics. This pattern exemplifies the inconsistency between overlapping communities of practice as the older ideal of zealous advocacy from the entire legal community tends to trump the tempered advocacy of the narrower divorce law community.

A smaller group of lawyers (15 percent of our respondents) denied adapting their style of advocacy according to the attorney on the other side and said they would assert their own reasonable style, even when facing an unreasonable opponent. Some said they would try to change the other attorney by writing letters that would be seen by the opposing client[22] or by attempting to coax the lawyer into cooperative behavior.

> I usually try to shame them out of it, if they're being too extreme. I just get a little more gray-haired, old lady-like, and say, "Come now. This seems like an awful waste of time and these good people's money to me. Why don't we talk about something that's reasonable?"

Through such cajoling, a few lawyers tried to educate their peers and thus reaffirm what they believed to be the professional norms of the divorce law community. These efforts were the exception, however, and they underscored the weakness of collegial enforcement mechanisms.

With this small group of lawyers we return, in a sense, to the theme developed at the beginning of this section on the importance of professional reputation. Not only is a reputation for being cooperative a positive asset in the market for clients (Gilson and Mnookin 1994), but it also serves lawyers' professional interests in getting their work done—easily, smoothly, and in ways that keep client costs down and reward the attorney's knowledge and expertise. A cooperative reputation must not be perceived as weakness, however, and consequently, most lawyers said they became more aggressive when confronted with a different kind of lawyer, one who chose to play hardball in case settlement.

Conclusion

Lawyers working in routine family law practices have developed norms of advocacy that loosely resemble those articulated by critics of "zealous advocacy." We found that divorce lawyers constructed and shared an ideal of advocacy within their professional communities that preferred cooperative problem solving to adversarial posturing.[23] The norms of these lawyers were constructed in relation to the nature of divorce, the legal framework of divorce law, and the economic incentives and legal complexities of the cases lawyers undertake. These norms of cooperation shaped the ways that lawyers approached negotiation and the uses of formal legal strategies.

Legal rules, concepts, and procedures in family law all influenced the nature of advocacy in divorce. The substantive legal rules of no-fault divorce rejected one-sided case outcomes and presumed instead an equal division of property and some sharing of legal responsibility for children. Strict child support guidelines further removed issues from legal dispute. The resulting legal framework thus provided few incentives for divorce lawyers in most cases to try to "win big" for their clients.

Within the community of divorce practitioners, however, we found certain differences in their professional norms that stemmed in part from the economics of practice and the values of practitioners. We saw in chapter 4 that the importance lawyers placed on skills of negotiation and litigation varied according to the class of their clienteles. That difference reappeared in this chapter through the type of advocacy lawyers deemed appropriate. Hence, for most divorces, the costs of adversarial conflict— both financial and emotional—did not justify the small chance of additional gain for clients. But as the stakes of divorce cases increased, the payoff structure for lawyers—and their clients—could change and influence lawyers to adopt a different advocacy role. Not surprisingly, then, we found a strong and significant relationship between the resources of their clients and the number of adversarial actions taken by lawyers in their cases.

Because women lawyers tended to predominate among specialists with upper-middle-class clients, women divorce attorneys often saw themselves and were perceived by their general practice peers as tough, aggressive advocates. This approach to advocacy in divorce reflected in part the values and understandings of the world that these women brought with them to their work. As women, they took especially seriously the rights of wives and recognized the huge economic consequences of divorce. These individual perceptions led them to redefine reasonable practice and to develop expectations for advocacy that became broadly accepted among specialists. But it also may have been exaggerated by sexist attitudes within the bar. Some of the older women lawyers described their feelings of exclusion or discrimination by their male colleagues. Perhaps in response to their lack of acceptance within the informal community, some women lawyers placed greater emphasis on formal advocacy skills.

Of course, the ability of specialist, women attorneys to redefine practice depended on the presence of upper-middle-class clienteles. Similar to the intraprofessional competition discussed in chapter 4, these divorce lawyers appealed to a particular client base and sought to establish their own niche in the market for legal services. But at the same time, through these efforts to advocate more vigorously for their clients, specialists and female lawyers aimed to increase the prestige and status of the divorce bar.

The legal, economic, and gender-based influences on divorce lawyers were reinforced by the various social bonds of the professional community. Reputation defined one's professional identity, and lawyers generally sought to establish and maintain reputations for cooperation and trustworthiness. Lawyers with reputations for reasonableness shared an understanding of appropriate and expected case outcomes and could work together smoothly to negotiate within that framework. Professional control over colleagues through the reputational market had its limits, however. Thus, even reasonable lawyers would typically adapt their advocacy approach to match the behavior of their unreasonable colleagues.

The meaning of advocacy for lawyers thus grew out of their day-to-day experiences with clients of varying resources, with legal rules and institutions, and with one another. These shaped overlapping but not entirely consistent communities of practice in which reputation mattered but had limited capacity to control conduct. These communities rested on knowledge of legal norms and procedures, on the economics of law practice, and on the social networks of professionals who knew and trusted—or distrusted—one another. The overlapping communities of practice revealed varying approaches to advocacy and different conditions under which one or another approach would be followed. Many of these approaches were far from the ideal of zealous advocacy, as they were constructed in everyday practice to reflect the particular field of divorce law.

7

SERVING CLIENTS WHILE PROTECTING THE BOTTOM LINE

I've become really tough, and it's hard for me because I'm not a good business person, I guess. And I have called one guy who's a businessman, and I said, "Look, I can't keep carrying you. You have to pay your bill or else I'm going to have to withdraw." I felt horrible about doing it. I'm not good at it.

—a New Hampshire sole practitioner

The ideology of legal professionalism includes a commitment to altruism. The realities of practice, however, place limits on selflessness. Scholars of the professions see as a core problem of professional practice "the tension between the provision of affordable and conscientious service to others, and the economic interest of those who provide it" (Freidson 1994: 199). The American Bar Association's Commission on Professionalism placed the tension between service and self-interest at the center of its inquiry, questioning whether the profession has lived up to its public service commitment (American Bar Association 1986: 10). The formal rules of professional responsibility highlight this conflict without resolving it, although they give increasing room for lawyers to choose their economic interests. The informal norms of practice and the exigencies of law firm organization create pressures for redefinition of the meaning of service by members of the bar. Even so, many divorce lawyers still find that their practices demand they provide considerable unpaid legal assistance to clients in need. The varying judgments of these lawyers about how to balance a commitment to public service and their own economic interests are a central dimension of professionalism in practice.

The importance of service is articulated and reinforced by formal codes of professional responsibility. At the same time, these codes increasingly permit self-protective actions by lawyers to ensure that they are paid for their work. The early codes made hortatory appeals to a spirit of altruism while underlining in various ways an attorney's obligation to serve clients.[1] For example, the Model Code asserted that "the rendition of free legal services to those unable to pay reasonable fees continues to be an obligation of each lawyer."[2] The newer Model Rules turn these rhetorical appeals into a black letter Rule 6.1, now titled "Voluntary *Pro bono Publico* Service," that asserts: "A lawyer should aspire to render at least (50) hours of *pro bono publico* legal services per year."[3] The last Comment [11] that follows Rule 6.1 notes, however: "The responsibility set forth in this Rule is not intended to be enforced through disciplinary process."[4] The emphasis on aspiration and voluntariness makes clear that what initially appears to be a sharpening of expectations for service is little more than a renewal of the hortatory language of the past.

A more subtle reading of this change suggests that the calls for voluntary service have been narrowed rather than expanded. The two prior codes implicitly saw pro bono work as integral to day-to-day practice. By defining such service as official charity, the new approach places it outside of regular practice and at the same time sharply limits it. These shifts in bar rules reflect changes in the organization and economic conditions of law practice that effectively marginalize the altruism of those lawyers whose work demands that they donate their time informally simply as part of what they do every day. For many lawyers with lower-income clients, the conditions of work and practice themselves foster altruistic behavior. These lawyers often understand service differently than do colleagues with well-to-do clients, although the formal rules about service presumably apply to all attorneys.

Divorce lawyers experience these shifting norms of altruism not only through changing bar rules but also through what they see and hear from their professional peers. Greater attention to efficient law office management (including billing) has become a common theme for professional publications of the ABA's Law Practice Management Section, the *ABA Journal,* and state bar journals, as well as a theme for bar meetings and continuing legal education.[5] These issues also are a staple topic of conversation among lawyers, particularly within law firms. "Concern with the bottom line" challenges "the spirit of public service" as a central theme of professional discussion. Both expectations, however, provide the context for many day-to-day decisions by divorce lawyers, decisions through which lawyers both construct and enact the variable meanings of professionalism in practice.

Signs of Altruism: Formal and Informal Pro Bono Work

Altruism was very much apparent among the divorce lawyers we studied. Virtually all of them provided services to some needy clients who were unable to pay the full fees for legal assistance. Some of that service was formally organized through bar programs that refer no-fee or reduced-fee cases to volunteer lawyers, the *pro bono publico* work that the Model Rules now promote. Most of the service, however, was delivered without any formal referrals and was largely invisible to colleagues and to the public. In some instances, lawyers simply accepted as nonpaying clients sympathetic and economically hard-pressed people who appeared in their offices. Much more frequently, attorneys found themselves inadvertently providing service at reduced fees when they chose to discount bills for clients who could not afford all of the legal assistance required to complete their cases effectively.

Formal Pro Bono Service

As elsewhere in the United States, pro bono service has been formally organized in Maine and New Hampshire.[6] In both states, participating lawyers place themselves on referral lists and agree to accept a certain number of cases from a central intake and screening agency that examines the nature of potential clients' legal problems, as well as their resources and eligibility. Referrals generally are tailored to a lawyer's particular expertise.[7] The New Hampshire Pro Bono Program concentrates its efforts on family law cases, which constituted 84 percent of the case referrals in 1991.

Most members of the bar feel an obligation to do pro bono work, but lawyers implement that obligation differently depending on the nature of their practices. Overall, 76 percent of the lawyers we interviewed reported that they currently took formal pro bono referrals for divorce cases. Others, like Edgar Prosper, accepted referral of nondivorce cases. However, participation in pro bono family law work varied by the size of law firm and the social class composition of an attorney's client base. At first glance, it looks as if those lawyers in larger firms and with more prosperous clients did more than their share of work. While 72 percent of lawyers in firms with four or fewer attorneys indicated that they accepted formal pro bono referrals in divorce cases, 87 percent of those in firms of five or more did so.[8] Those lawyers with working-class clients were less willing to take referrals—68 percent, compared with 85 percent and

77 percent among lawyers with middle-class and upper-middle-class clienteles, respectively.[9]

Those figures are misleading, however. In reality, small firm lawyers and those with a heavy representation of lower-income clients appear to be more committed to providing free or discounted service as a regular part of their practices. Some, like Henry Genrus, felt that since they already were doing a service for low-income people, they did not need to participate in the formal pro bono program. As one practitioner in a two-person firm put it: "I do enough work just for people who walk in off the street who can't afford legal service." Another explained why he had recently suspended his participation in the formal program:

> Lately, I haven't because I've had one or two cases that have gone bad on us as far as the client's ability to pay, and it's work as it is. And what happens in a small law office, if you spend too much of your hours during the week on those kinds of cases, you can't meet the overhead. We have a staff of six here.

What may be most remarkable is not that some of these attorneys refused to take on pro bono referrals, but that so many did so in addition to representing clients whose limited ability to pay ensured that some services had to be discounted or done for nothing. The net result is that at second glance, as one lawyer observed, "It is the small firms that are doing the vast majority of work. Those that can least afford to do it are doing it." That fact becomes clearer when we examine more closely the patterns of informal pro bono service.

Informal Pro Bono Work: Altruism or Bad Office Management?

Most divorce lawyers find themselves doing some informal pro bono work by accepting needy clients or discounting bills. It is the sole practitioners and those with low-and moderate-income clients who bear a disproportionate share of this burden. Although attorneys generally understand this work as "service," they also know that it is not recognized as such by the organized bar. Even more important, it is difficult for lawyers to feel good about their generosity in a professional climate that increasingly values effective office management and sound business practices.

A few attorneys talked to us about their willingness—or even compulsion—to help people in particular need by taking them on as clients, despite knowing that they could pay none or only some of the anticipated bill. One said, "I occasionally have someone who is extremely sympathetic, and I know they can't afford any lawyer, and I might say I'll do something for a flat fee knowing that I am not going to be paid fairly." Another attorney noted:

> Even people that come in, that don't have any money, and you just kind of feel like, "Gee, you know, I should help this person." And that

happens a lot. I mean, I don't know, my secretary is always giving me a hard time about it, you know? I feel that I'm able to afford it because I have a successful plaintiff's practice.

Some of these lawyers described the good personal feeling that doing informal pro bono work gave them, while others emphasized their sense of obligation to do such work. George Elder, whom we met in chapter 2, represents the old-fashioned general practitioner with a heart of gold, whose motto is "We are here to help people." But for another lawyer, informal pro bono work reflected her feminist principles: "I have been known to say that 'I never met a lady with a black eye that I didn't love,' and I tend to take on some clients that I know will never be able to pay me and not really expect them to." At least one attorney with a lucrative practice in other fields saw divorce work as a unique opportunity to do important service work: "This is a socialist enterprise. Generally, in divorce there is no ability to pay. I mean generally there are other things that subsidize divorces, not divorces subsidizing something else." As we shall see later in the chapter, the few lawyers who openly embraced this altruistic approach recognized its financial implications and often faced pressures from partners or employees to restrain their generosity.

In response to such pressures, several attorneys had adopted a strategy for converting unofficial pro bono work into officially credited service. When they were contacted directly by a potential client with limited means, these lawyers would advise them to call the pro bono referral organization and ask to request them specifically as the lawyer. Thus, the client would receive representation at no cost, and the attorney would "get credit" for the pro bono work. These examples, though infrequent, suggest the pressures to transform pro bono work from an integral but invisible part of practice into a distinctive, charitable act.

The few openly altruistic lawyers who found it hard to resist helping people of limited means were joined by a much larger number who felt an obligation to continue representing clients whose resources proved insufficient to pay all the costs of representation. As a result, 77 percent of the attorneys we interviewed reported that they at least sometimes "determined their fees based on the client's ability to pay." In fact, the practice was so routine for many lawyers that they needed some prompting in our interviews to recognize that they did adapt fees to fit client resources. The typical method was to discount a bill at the end of the case. Another approach described by several lawyers was to systematically undercount the time that they put in on a case. A very few attorneys instead reduced fees by adjusting their hourly rate downward for lower income clients in what one lawyer called "a sliding empathy scale."

Lawyers were not all equally likely to adjust fees downward for impecunious clients, however. Attorneys in the largest firms showed the *least* willingness to do so—62 percent in firms of five or more compared with 82 percent in smaller firms. In addition to firm size, class of clientele was related to willingness to adjust fees.[10] Only 53 percent of those lawyers serving largely upper-middle-class clients indicated that they adjusted fees based on a client's ability to pay compared with 80 percent of those with a largely middle-class clientele, and 86 percent of those with mainly working-class clients.[11] These patterns of informal pro bono are the inverse of those of formal pro bono participation. They reflect both the capacities of clients to pay fees and the different approaches to billing in smaller and larger firms.

Lawyers understand the reasons for discounting bills in both altruistic and pragmatic terms. Getting to know clients as individuals at a difficult time in their lives and understanding quite precisely what resources clients have can promote feelings of sympathy. "My philosophy has been to try to get them to pay and if, in the end, after you have done the work and they can't pay or they don't pay, it is probably because they are worse off than I am, and I don't pursue," explained one lawyer. Another noted:

> I think they both enter into [my discounting bills]: my own feeling about how much time I spent, plus me knowing that I'm gonna have to send this bill out to that client that I've gotten to know pretty well and feeling bad knowing that it's going to take them forever to pay this off.

At the same time, reducing a bill to encourage some payment might be a realistic alternative to waiting in vain for a client to pay an impossibly high bill. According to one attorney: "We discount when we think it's necessary. Also, if we think the person basically isn't going to be able to pay it, you might as well discount it. I think that helps encourage them to pay the difference." Another commented:

> [At the end of the case,] that's where we really take a look at, and maybe it's because by that time we really know, more than anybody else exactly what their economic circumstances are. And that's when I think we can really be flexible and creative about how to get this bill paid, whether it's by discounting or payment schedule or barter.

For both these altruistic and more pragmatic reasons, then, lawyers—especially those with less financially secure clients—found themselves regularly adjusting fees downward.[12]

Yet, because of the very real financial challenges of running a law practice and the attention given by the legal community to improved office management, this informal pro bono work seems just as likely to induce guilt as pride in lawyers. A tone of apology for unmet obligations pervaded the comments of those attorneys who faced billing problems, blaming themselves for their own poor business sense or for weak business practices. The moral imperative of "should" recurred in lawyers' acknowledgments of their failures to protect their own economic interests. One attorney, for example, asserted that "I should [have a retainer] but I don't," while a second apologized that "I'm not very good at keeping track of my time. I'm sorry, but I'm not." A third lawyer reflected similarly on his own limits:

I have nothing against making money and good money, but I'm not a good businessman. I feel like if I make enough to support myself and keep this operation going, then I don't have to chase people too hard, though I really should. It's not my nature.

It is not clear in most of these comments to whom the apology is tendered or the obligation owed. But it is certain that these and other lawyers in similar circumstances found it as easy to regard themselves as "chumps," who could not protect their own interests, as to give themselves due credit for altruistic service.

Whether lawyers understand pro bono work as an example of fulfilling service or evidence of poor office management, they must establish limits on it if they are to stay in practice. Consequently, the attorneys we studied commonly adopted one or another of three kinds of adjustments in their divorce practices, each with implications not only for obligations of service but also for other professional responsibilities. First, lawyers with the clients least likely to be able to afford substantial legal bills limited substantially the amount of time they put into cases. Second, some lawyers frankly conditioned each step of the legal process on the client's payment of bills or retainer, while other lawyers either threatened to or actually did withdraw from representation when clients were reluctant to pay bills. Third, all lawyers faced choices about rationalizing their practices and increasing business efficiency—although the pressures to do so were strongest in law firms. We shall consider each of these patterns of adaptation in turn in the next three sections.

Adapting Divorce Law Practice to Limited Client Means

Client resources are a strong predictor of the likelihood that attorneys will be faced with uncollectible bills. Partly as a consequence, lawyers whose clients had limited resources tended to approach the practice of divorce law with different expectations about the amount and kind of work they would do, compared with lawyers with more affluent clients. These systematic differences in divorce practices reflect both the different sorts of legal problems that poorer and wealthier clients face and the heightened concern of lawyers with low-income clients to protect their client's modest resources—as well as their own exposure to unpaid bills— by limiting the work that they undertake for them. These adaptations to practice expose divorce lawyers with clients of modest means to a series of difficult problems of judgment that attorneys with affluent clients usually avoid.

The fundamental issue is simple. As one lawyer put it, "The amount of work that will be done on a case will be based on the client's ability to pay. . . . Clients who want a Cadillac of a divorce but only will be able to spend $1,000 to $1,500 aren't going to get it." Another attorney wistfully observed:

I wish, you know, that everybody paid, and we could bill less, and money was never a problem. And we could concentrate solely on the legal issues and not the financial impact of following one course or another. That's a factor that you have to consider: How much justice can this client reasonably afford?

As a consequence, lawyers with working-class clients reported spending far fewer hours on the average divorce case than did those with upper-middle-class clienteles.[13] Operating at the margins of their clients' capacity to pay for their work, these attorneys had to limit their hourly rates and the numbers of hours charged to clients. They might have conferred less often with poorer clients, worked harder to cut off emotional outbursts, and encouraged clients to negotiate with their spouses. Yet, in such instances attorneys found themselves torn between their own interest in limiting their clients' costs and their professional obligation to represent them effectively.

> There are going to be cases that the person cannot afford to pay for it, but are going to be extremely complicated, and as a result of that I have to make adjustments to the bill because they can't afford to have the interrogatories done, but I can't allow the fact that they can't pay me to have the interrogatories done stand in the way of my doing my job. Once I'm into it, the monetary aspect of it is secondary. It basically plays no part in what sort of representation they're going to get, at least in my mind. I mean, subtly it does, but not intentionally.

Although this attorney initially insisted that client resources had no relationship to how he undertook his representation, in the end he acknowledged the subtle pressures at work. Another was more explicit about these pressures to limit what he did in a case.

> It would be very unusual in this practice [to charge $2,000 for a divorce] which is not to say . . . most of them couldn't use it. They can't afford it. So there are things we don't do that we might otherwise do. [Q: Like what?] Oh, more interrogatories, more questions, more information about data and whatnot.

Henry Genrus, whom we met in chapter 2, provides an extreme case of problems common to lawyers providing legal services to people of limited means. Like Genrus, these attorneys face serious questions about the extent and character of their professional responsibilities in representation of clients, problems that divorce attorneys with wealthier clients need not consider.

Lawyers who share these common problems—such as those in general practice—find similar ways of dealing with them that help to define a community of practice with its norm of the reasonable lawyer. Such communities play an important role in defining professionalism and in legitimating judgments, especially when these are contested by lawyers from other communities of practice, such as specialists. We saw in chapter 3 how reluctant generalists were to use formal discovery and a motion practice and how on occasion that reluctance put them into conflict with specialists like Andrea Wright who believed that being serious about divorce law required using the full arsenal of legal tools. Her view of the professional role found support in her professional community of specialists but depended on having clients who could afford both her rates and the amount of time that she devoted to cases. For those with lower-income clients, these tactics were out of the question, unless lawyers were willing to underwrite many of the costs of divorces.

Such lawyers relied less heavily on litigation tools and more heavily on informal negotiation with other lawyers and also encouraged their clients to do as much as they could for themselves. As was discussed in chapter 4, most divorce lawyers reported that they permitted or encouraged clients to do some or all of the negotiating, but the likelihood of doing so related to the social class of clients. Attorneys with an upper-middle-class clientele were less than half as likely (30 percent) as lawyers with a middle-or working-class clientele (64 percent) to report that most of their clients took responsibility for at least part of the negotiation. These latter attorneys were particularly likely to emphasize cost-savings. As one put it, "If I have informed my clients of what their rights are and they can deal with it and save themselves money, I just simply say I have other work to do. I am not here to run up your fees." In the words of another:

> I say, "This is a basis for you to sit down with your spouse if you can talk and negotiate. If you can settle things, it's going to be a lot cheaper for both of you. If you want us [the lawyers] to settle, every time we talk it is going to cost you money. So if you're able to talk without being intimidated, then do it."

By contrast, those attorneys with upper-middle-class clients had less need to be attentive to a mounting bill and thus could understand their role as requiring a more central and time-consuming part in negotiations. Lawyers with clients of modest means, however, always had to be mindful of limited resources, recognizing the practical limits on their responsibilities as client advocates.

Lawyers serving lower-income clients also faced other constraints that arose indirectly from the limited numbers of hours they devoted to each divorce case. To fill out their practices, these lawyers had to take on more cases in order to bring in the same number of billable hours as attorneys who devoted substantially more time to each case. Almost all divorce lawyers, in fact, faced some economic pressures, as one put it, "to take on more work than you can possibly do . . . just to see that the cash flow stays at the office." Lawyers with higher-income clients, however, can be more confident that they will be paid for most of their work and therefore need fewer cases to sustain the cash flow. A busy high-end divorce practice might include a maximum of 70 or 80 cases. By contrast, attorneys specializing in low-income divorce work can find themselves with caseloads two to three times higher.

Caseload size has significant implications for the ways in which attorneys approach their practices, placing special burdens on those lawyers with the heaviest caseloads (Gibeaut 1997).[14] Each new case competes for a lawyer's attention with other existing cases. Efforts to keep control over the course of any single divorce can easily be overwhelmed by the demands of handling many cases. As one hard-pressed lawyer put it, "You've got to keep all balls in the air at one time without letting one fall." Another lamented: "There is simply more than I can do. It is not even time management. It is just the fact that there are times when there are crises in cases, and things happen, and it all happens at once, and there is only so much of you." The competition for attention among many cases creates significant headaches for both lawyers and their clients. Clients understandably see their divorce as of primary importance and may call their lawyers frequently to find out what is happening. In response, attorneys who are faced with the crush of many cases, as well as the unpredictable responses of opposing party and counsel and the slowness of court scheduling, may delay or avoid responding because the answer is "nothing." The result can be client anger, frustration, and, particularly often in divorce cases, complaints of neglect to the appropriate bar agency.

In sum, having clients with few financial assets prompts attorneys to limit sharply what they do in the average case, while having clients with deeper pockets encourages expansion of billable hours and increased use of the formal legal process. Attorneys thus vary widely in their understanding of what constitutes "good representation." The practitioners who adopt the more expansive view, however, set the standard for the field. Their model is the one that Henry Genrus referred to when he said he sometimes does not feel like a "real lawyer." The legal profession itself provides changing signposts for attorneys struggling with these issues of service and fair payment for their work, supporting an apparent shift from informal pro bono work integrated into practice to formal pro bono as charity. As a result, lawyers for clients of modest means, who deliver affordable and competent, but limited, representation, may find themselves unrecognized and unappreciated for their approach to representation.

Holding Clients Hostage: Leveraging Payment

Maine and New Hampshire divorce lawyers commonly—although not universally—saw special problems in collecting fees in divorce cases. As a result, many attorneys thought hard about how to organize their practices to encourage payment and in doing so had to make difficult judgments about their professional responsibilities. Forty-three percent of the lawyers we interviewed reported payment to be a problem at least half the time in divorce cases, and another 39 percent reported occasional collection problems.[15] The experience of problems seemed to be tied more closely to client screening and billing techniques within firms than to the economic resources of clients, although lawyers with mostly upper-middle-class clients were three times more likely than those with working-class clients to see billing as "almost never" a problem.[16]

For a handful of lawyers, collection problems were substantial. The most extreme examples were a small firm lawyer who claimed accounts receivable of "$125,000, and the bulk of that is from divorce work," and a sole practitioner who agonized over $70,000 in unpaid bills. According to another frustrated sole practitioner, "We even went computerized this year. We billed $9,000 to $10,000 one month and got diddly back. The receivables right now are in the mid-to high $30,000s." These figures were atypical, but unpaid or partly paid bills constituted a problem for many lawyers.

Once a divorce has been completed, the attorney has little leverage with a former client. In essence, they have three viable options aside from forgetting the bill. By far the most common option among the lawyers we interviewed was to accept monthly payments, which might be as little as "five dollars a month forever" on a bill of several thousand dollars. Often these final bills would have already been discounted because of the client's limited capacity to pay. Yet, many lawyers felt it important to collect their fees, even at such glacial rates. One small firm attorney commented on the importance of being paid in full, even by people for whom it was difficult: "The fee is the fee. The *way* they pay me is based on their earning ability." Such an arrangement provided at least some return on the unpaid labor and also—importantly for some attorneys—provided an acknowledgment of reciprocity in the lawyer-client relationship. The moral return on the work done could be more significant than the financial return. Some attorneys also reported accepting payment in kind through items ranging from lobsters to artwork.

Whether an unpaid bill should be collected, reduced, or written off depends in part on how a lawyer perceives the client. The moral status of nonpaying clients varies, depending on their acknowledgment of an obligation to the lawyer. Attorneys in our study commonly distinguished between clients who "stiffed" them and those who simply could not afford to pay. It is only the latter who might have had their bills discounted. As one attorney put it: "On the poor people, I've never gone after somebody for collection. I just can't bear the thought of doing that. Somebody with money, I would do that. With poor clients, I'm not going to bother." Aggressive efforts to collect unpaid fees from such clients were widely regarded as not only "unprofessional" but also ineffective and mean-spirited.

An inability to pay differs from a refusal to do so, however. The more difficult cases are those where the attorney feels cheated—where a client who could pay at least a portion of the bill simply refuses to do so. In these circumstances, lawyers can either forget the bill or use a collection agency or small claims action to press for payment. In making judgments in such instances, attorneys reported considering the lawyer-client relationship, as well as the bottom line.

> If they are sending you money every month, you know, that's their effort. But people who just ignore you, then I have a policy of sending out for collection. At that point, obviously, your relationship with the client is so screwed up anyway that there is no harm.

Anger at violation of the norm of reciprocity could also press lawyers to take the more difficult step of suing a former client. Such an approach remained controversial among divorce attorneys, however, with only a few expressing unreserved commitment to its use.[17] Lawyers reported "not liking to" take clients to court, but doing so reluctantly when no other options existed.

> I can't go "repo" their divorce. If I could, I would have by now. Quite often we get embroiled by those kinds of problems. The matter is closed and then it takes an additional twenty hours of my time because I have to sue my own client. It gets very ugly and vituperative in court when you are doing that.

Unlike a collection agency that takes over the efforts to exact payment from the attorneys, lawsuits pit lawyers against their former clients, a practice that is neither satisfying nor good for the public image of the lawyer. In fact, the early Canons of Professional Ethics (American Bar Association 1969) warned in Canon 14 against such undignified and "ugly" proceedings:

> Controversies with clients concerning compensation are to be avoided by the lawyer so far as shall be compatible with his self-respect and with his right to receive reasonable recompense for his services; and lawsuits with clients should be resorted to only to prevent injustice, imposition or fraud.

The more recent Model Rules encourage the attorney to participate in procedures such as mediation or arbitration to resolve fee disputes—generally at the initiative of an unhappy client, not an unpaid lawyer—but say nothing to discourage suing clients about fees.[18] In the context of the greater permissiveness of professional rules, lawyers in Maine and New Hampshire agonized individually and within law firms about internal policies on collection. For example, a lawyer in a firm noted that "[Suing in court] is a tough issue, and we're discussing it now. We're even thinking about using a collection agency because we have a lot of accounts receivable." A sole practitioner reported wrestling with her own conscience about the appropriateness of taking a client to court: "I still have a real problem with suing a client. I feel somehow really strange about that, but I will get over that too." Indeed, many lawyers had learned through practice hard lessons about the need to protect their own economic interests and those of their partners and associates. Thus, the overhead costs of legal work, increasing reliance on firm rather than sole practice, and the subtle shifts in collective definitions of appropriate conduct seem haltingly but inexorably to be moving lawyers to make judgments that limit commitment to clients in favor of protecting the bottom line.

To prevent these sorts of difficult problems from arising in the first place, many of the lawyers we spoke with had evolved a wide variety of strategies, ranging from attempts to screen out potential deadbeat clients, to automated monthly billing systems, to requirements of payment before services were rendered. But when problems of payment arose, in spite of or in the absence of such precautions, lawyers had to make judgments about the appropriateness of various sorts of pressure to exact payment. One form of leverage mentioned was to hold up action on a case until money was paid. It was almost exclusively attorneys with low-income clients who described this technique, perhaps in part because their clients often did not own homes that would eventually be sold, generating the cash for payment of fees. Some attorneys admitted that on occasion they simply stopped work on a case or delayed a key event such as the final hearing in order to pressure a client to pay.[19] Said one attorney, "If I have the plaintiff, then I will probably tell my client that I will schedule a final hearing when my fees are paid. I will hold the papers to the extent I can." Another admitted, "I am sitting on one where the father sent me $500 from Virginia, and now it is contested, and he is supposed to send me another $500, and it has been two or three months. So I am just not working the case." The practice of demanding payment of fees in advance or of taking action contingent on payment resembles classic descriptions of criminal defense work (Blumberg 1967).

Both practical problems and issues of professional responsibility arise in making judgments about such a course of action. Lawyers do not always have control over the scheduling of trials or hearings and thus may have to proceed in advance of payment.

> You generally make it understood in the beginning that you can pay me a retainer now, but the rest of it has to be paid before we go in for that final hearing. The only time I end up getting stuck is if we end up with a real contested hearing, and I can't control that final hearing date.

Most lawyers did not talk about the use of such leverage, probably because they were reluctant to employ it. At least one noted the practice and explicitly rejected it: "Some attorneys I know require fees to be paid in full before they go into the final hearing, which I don't do. I ask people to try and do that, but I will go in and finish a divorce even if I'm owed a bunch of money." This lawyer did not fully articulate the reasons for rejecting leveraging tactics, but she seemed to weigh her obligation to serve clients more heavily than aggressive protection of her bottom line. She may also have recognized that by explicitly making their actions contingent on payment of bills, lawyers subtly alter a professional relationship built on some degree of tacit mutual trust. The attorney acts for the trusting client in dealing with important life issues, while trusting the client in return to pay for the services rendered. When a lawyer expresses doubt that money will be paid she is, in effect, voicing distrust of her client. In doing so, she may undermine a client's confidence that the attorney is acting in the client's interests rather than in her own. Thus, lawyers' judgments about the use of techniques to leverage payment implicate larger questions about their professional roles and relationships.

Attorneys who fear nonpayment have another form of leverage available—the threat to withdraw as counsel, using the client's emotional and financial investment in the relationship to extract money owed. Roughly 10 percent of the lawyers we interviewed—evenly distributed among all kinds of practices—reported that real or threatened withdrawal was a tactic they regularly employed to compel payment by reluctant clients or to escape those unlikely to pay in the future.[20] In some cases such conditions were written explicitly into fee agreements. Threats could provide the needed leverage to get checks written and need not have been carried out to be effective. Actual withdrawal would require more difficult decisions. Thus, attorneys distinguished carefully between threat and action, and more reported threatening to terminate relationships with clients than acknowledged actually doing so. One lawyer who described employing such threats explained: "I actually call people up now and say if you don't bring your retainer up now I'm going to have to withdraw. I haven't gotten to the point yet where I've withdrawn. But at least I'm saying something now. I didn't used to." Such reluctant threats led in some instances to actual withdrawals:

> I don't mind [monthly payments] as long as they take it seriously. Part of it is a personal reaction. I finally said to people—I remember saying it to one lady—"Well, if it is not important enough for you to pay my bill, your case simply can't be that important to me." And I got rid of that lady.

All the lawyers who mentioned withdrawal from cases over unpaid fees were from New Hampshire. Not coincidentally, New Hampshire's Rules of Conduct parallel the Model Rules in their permissiveness about withdrawal, in contrast to Maine where the Rule remains more restrictive. The new Model Rules broaden the lawyer's ability to take financial considerations into account when withdrawing from representation of a client. For example, the older Code cautioned that "a decision by a lawyer to withdraw should be made only on the basis of compelling circumstances" but permitted withdrawal if a client "deliberately disregards" an agreement about payment of fees.[21] The newer Rules substantially widen the conditions for withdrawal. They drop reference to "compelling circumstances" and "deliberately disregards" fee arrangements, thus making withdrawal for nonpayment, whatever the cause, professionally acceptable.[22] Maine's Bar Rules, however, by retaining the older language of "deliberate disregard"[23] may act to constrain Maine lawyers from withdrawing in cases where clients simply run out of money.

Concern about both the rules and about the welfare of clients were evident in the comments of lawyers who reported resisting the temptation to threaten or to undertake withdrawal when clients found it hard to pay their legal bills. These attorneys, including one from New Hampshire, explicitly framed their objections to withdrawal for nonpayment in terms of the rules: "I think the bar rules are fairly clear that you are supposed to continue to do the service. You are not allowed to stick the client because he is sticking you. So I continue to do the best I can and hope the money will begin to flow." This reading of the rules reminds us once again of their frequent lack of precision. Many rules are open to multiple interpretations that reflect the preferences of the reader, as much as the commonly accepted norms of the profession.

For other lawyers, leveraging payment by threatened withdrawal was distasteful because it violated their own personal commitment to helping clients:

> I'm not the kind of lawyer that will dump somebody because they can't pay me. Particularly a gal who is stuck at home with no job and a bunch of kids and her husband takes off. That's part of my pro bono. I will stay with that case 'til the end if it takes me two years and I never get any more money out of it. And I've got a pile of them.

Another attorney with a working-class clientele noted, "I guess I look at it as my pro bono when I see somebody in trouble and they can't go the distance, and I continue on."

In examining the difficult questions about what to do when a client in need fails to pay bills during the course of representation, divorce attorneys weigh fundamental questions about their professional identities and relationships to clients. Although there may be equally sound rationales for alternative approaches, the rules of professional responsibility have changed to give more room for economic self-protection. The judgments that lawyers make are likely to have significant effects on their relationships to clients that are premised on mutual trust. Although claims for payment can be based on reciprocity—"I am helping you, and it is only fair that you pay your bills in return"—they still may threaten to undermine a client's often fragile faith that the lawyer is dedicated to helping her. Equally important, these decisions reflect varying meanings that lawyers attach to client service and financial success in the context of different sorts of clients and practices.

Making Law More Businesslike: Controlling Formal and Informal Pro Bono Work

Without independent wealth, no attorney can maintain a practice over the long run without limiting in some way the amount of formal and informal pro bono work undertaken. Establishing such limits occurs through screening clients, making decisions about retainers and rates of pay, setting payment policies, and collecting unpaid bills. Each of these implicitly involves the lawyer in a calculation of the meaning attached to serving clients.

Managing formal pro bono work is relatively straightforward because of the formal and impersonal nature of most referrals. The lawyer can more easily say "no" to a referral agency than to an actual potential client. Many lawyers described an informal policy of accepting only one formal referral at a time, although some managed two or three or even more simultaneously. Informal pro bono work proves much more difficult to manage because it typically is unanticipated. Cases simply get "out of control"[24] or clients turn out to have fewer resources than anticipated.

The first stage of managing informal pro bono work occurs passively. Screening of clients for capacity to pay begins in the initial phone conversations and preliminary meetings between attorney and potential client. Through such communication and by reputation, attorneys with higher hourly rates and retainers discourage potential clients who have limited resources from seeking their services. The divorce attorneys with clients largely from the upper-middle class reported average hourly rates of $125, compared with $95 for the lawyers with largely working-and middle-class clients. The average retainer for attorneys with higher-income clients ($1,617) was triple that of attorneys with lower-income clients ($516). Indeed, several of those divorce lawyers with well-to-do clients acknowledged that their higher hourly rates and retainers shaped their clienteles. One admitted, "Quite frankly, I have reached a point where the people that come in, the people that are referred to me for the most part, either have that kind of money [for retainer and hourly] or have access to it." Another lawyer explained:

> I think that [my $1,200 retainer] tends to color obviously the kinds of people who come to me because if they cannot produce that initial retainer and give me assurances that they will at least pay me on some kind of regular monthly basis, I'm just not going to take that case, as much as idealistically I'd like to. I can't make ends meet, and I can't meet my own obligations if I do that.

"Prescreening" clients for ability to pay a particular lawyer's rates and to afford a higher or lower intensity of involvement in the case occurs to a large extent before clients ever reach an attorney's office. The result, of course, is that those lawyers with the fanciest offices and highest rates less often have to face potential clients with very limited resources who may require informal pro bono help. The burden of doing so lies largely with lawyers who charge less and demand lower retainers.

In addition to this passive screening process, all divorce lawyers have the capacity to turn down prospective clients at the first meeting if their resources appear insufficient. As one lawyer reported:

I screen out all clients who can't provide the retainer that I decide I want to have in the case. I screen out all clients who I don't think are going to either have the ability to pay what I think it is going to cost or who don't seem to have the desire to pay what I think it is going to cost.

Inflexible demands for retainers—whatever their size—served both to "ensure that most of the money is there up front" and to screen out those clients who lacked either the resources or the will to pay their bills.

Although all lawyers understood retainers as effective screening tools, they often employed them with some flexibility. Lawyers were about as likely to alter their retainers in order to help people as to enforce them rigidly to screen out deadbeats and undesirables. For example, a woman in sole practice with working-class clients reported: "What I'll do if people really come in and I feel really sorry for them—I won't make them pay the whole $500 retainer up front." A man in a two-person firm with a mixed clientele simply declined to establish a flat retainer for divorce cases.[25] He observed: "Some attorneys will ask for a $1,500 or $2,000 retainer right up front. Most people can't afford that. So, yes, I probably am not as good as some in collecting, but I'm adequately satisfied." Thus, the personal impulses of individual lawyers to assist those in need occasionally overwhelmed their business sense.

The use of the retainer—whether or not to require one, what it should be, whether it should be fixed or flexible, and what criteria to use in setting it in individual cases—was highly variable and in a constant state of flux. It was also a topic of much thought and discussion among attorneys. Lawyers' conversations about the retainer reflected larger issues of professional identity: How much do I commit my practice to assisting people in need regardless of ability to pay, and how much do I protect myself by ensuring payment of bills in advance? As we will see in the next section, these choices were substantially affected by the organization of law practice into law firms.

Lawyers' billing arrangements, like the retainer, varied widely and also mirrored different views of their professional role. Many lawyers saw value in regular and careful monitoring of client accounts and of monthly billing. Ideally, the costs of the case would be paid as they were incurred, and clients would not be surprised at the end of the case with one large bill. Problems of nonpayment could be identified and reacted to before the unpaid bills mounted up. As a result, in many practices, the client would "get an itemized statement every month that's computerized, and it tells them every breath we took regarding their case."

Although monthly billing was the predominant approach, it was not universal because of lack of time, staff resources, or systems for doing so. Some lawyers chose not to bill monthly because of their clients' limited means: "Frequently, I end up billing at the end of the case because they don't have the money when you're going through the case." Another said of monthly billing: "I know other attorneys do that, and it's something I've considered doing but again you need to consider [client] re- sources and all of that." Like the retainer decision, the decision to bill monthly and to hold clients accountable throughout the case for the money owed involves implicit or explicit judgments about how the in- terests of lawyers balance with those of clients.

A Shifting Balance between Altruism and Self Interest: Professional Socialization and the Pressures of Law Firms

Experience in divorce practice pressures attorneys to alter the delicate balance between public service and businesslike practice in favor of self- protection. Although a few of the lawyers we interviewed chose to deal with these issues on a case-by-case basis, many more struggled to fashion procedures, decision-rules, and strategies that reduced the conflict or dis- guised it. Almost 10 percent of the lawyers in our study indicated that they had grown tougher in demanding payment, often in advance, or in turning away clients who might later pose payment problems. No one reported changes in the reverse direction. As one lawyer described this shift, "I've become more hard-nosed about that [requesting retainers]. I can look them in the eye and say 'I need the money, or I'm not doing anything.' I didn't used to do that." Another remembered:

> And I was starting to practice, and, what the hell, I would take what comes in the door. And I did. And so I . . . was also infected with this idea of "Gee, I'm a lawyer. I owe it to the community to provide whom- ever comes to me with legal representation." And I did not take care of myself financially. And so for many years, I was not financially successful because . . . my sense of self was out of skew.

For these and other attorneys, the commitment to an ethic of service represented both the high ideals of the legal profession and their own personal values and aspirations. To make a law practice work, however, they found it necessary to limit that service. Having learned their lessons through hard experience, these lawyers began to make adjustments not only in their practices but also in their sense of what it means to be an attorney.

Lawyers who made this transition generally reported feeling uncom- fortable about it. Demanding money up front and refusing to represent needy clients creates awkward interpersonal situations, giving the ap- pearance of lack of sympathy and challenging assumptions about the obligations of lawyers to serve. Thus, attorneys' reports of their changed or changing behavior typically included explanations of the feelings that accompanied them.

> I have to be very strict with retainers. It took me four years to learn that—four years of getting stung just about every time. So somebody

could come in here and tell me their woes and really have some problems, and I say "Too bad." It's hard but, on the other hand, it's amazing how many times those people will come up with the money.

I'm going to have to start doing that [charging standard retainer] and I feel very badly about it. . . . My experience has been that less than half the people that agree to a payment plan carry it out. . . . I am really on the verge of a major revamping of my billing system, and I may just have to cut those people out, and that bothers me.

To place economic interest above service appears selfish to those who feel personally and professionally obligated to helping others.

The moral calculus of obligation to one's client or to one's own economic interest tends to shift as employees and law firm partners come into the picture.[26] The hiring of clerical or paralegal assistants in a sole practice can exert claims on a lawyer's "conscience" that compete with those of needy clients. The abstract need to "meet overhead" translates in practice into an obligation to earn enough to pay the salaries of employees, who depend on a lawyer's billing to support their families. And the needs of one's own family may compete with those of the clients that attorneys counsel and bill for services:

I try to resist [reducing bills]. I've got a staff of five people here. In the beginning you want to be the savior for all at no cost, but you learn quickly that there's a downside to that. So, yes, to some extent, [I do reduce bills], but I keep on looking at my photographs of my children on my desk and [thinking of] their college education.

Those staff members apparently do not refrain from voicing their concerns either. Lawyers in sole practice often described their office managers, secretaries, or bookkeepers as advocates for a more businesslike approach. For example, one sole practitioner sheepishly admitted that he was thinking again about raising his rates which at $85 were still "the cheapest around." He indicated that it had been his secretary who a few years earlier had told him "you better smarten up and raise your rate from $75." Another lawyer confessed that "I deal with them [problems of nonpayment] poorly, according to the office manager." As a consequence of such pointed reminders from staff, divorce attorneys in sole practice face substantial and repeated pressures to become more aware of the costs of serving clients without adequate payment.

Working in a partnership or firm further increases the pressures to be attentive to the bottom line and emphasizes the competing obligations of a lawyer to her clients on the one hand and to her firm on the other. When one partner gives services away, other partners lose money. This may result in the kind of situation reported by one small firm lawyer who found it hard to say no to clients: "Business-wise it's not [good]. My partners have screamed at me." Another firm member described a similar reaction from her partners to her generosity toward clients:

I was supposed to [demand a standard retainer] but I did it on a sliding scale. . . . I would ask her for whatever she had and then make some kind of payment plan. That did not sit well with my partners. Obviously, they have to pay the bills.

These pressures from law firm colleagues highlight the importance of the organizational context, as well as the economics of divorce law practice, in influencing the ways that attorneys define and understand professionalism in practice. The development of partnerships and firms alters substantially the moral basis of law practice by redefining the primary obligations of attorneys as being owed to their partners and their firms rather than to their clients.

Lawyers with partners or junior associates in firms reported having had their spines stiffened by colleagues and by the establishment of clear policies that they could—or had to—stand behind. "The firm" provided an impersonal scapegoat by which the attorney could explain financial demands on clients without undercutting her own commitment to the client's interests. Firm policies also diminished or eliminated the use of individual discretion in decisions about billing.

> Our firm has a policy; we get $1500 as a retainer. That can be waived provided you supply proper information as to why you're waiving it. Currently, under our present policy, we don't seem to be having a lot of problems [collecting fees]. There have been times in the past when we have had problems, before we started the policy.

The application of law firm policy was particularly clear and nonnegotiable for associates, who "don't have the final say in how things are billed." Such policies also put considerable pressure on partners. In addition, law firms permitted a division of labor for undertaking distasteful practices such as billing or suing clients to collect money in court. As one lawyer who could not bring herself to sue former clients for unpaid fees reported: "I don't end up in court but my partners do. I can't deal with it. They're really good about understanding that that's just a hang-up I have and they're willing to do that." Law firms thus set policies and provide resources that encourage and assist attorneys in making judgments that give priority to the firm's economic interests.

Law firms also frequently manage their accounting practices so as to make attorneys more attentive to problems of payment early in a case. The visibility of such problems, along with the sense of responsibility to one's partner(s), produced pressures to confront clients about nonpayment or to resist discounting bills.

> What I've been doing [lately], and I think that is the difference between being in a partnership or on your own, is that I have begun to track people fairly early on who do not do what they said they would do.

> We discourage our lawyers from mentally discounting on a daily basis, saying Sally can't pay so I won't write it down. We want to know exactly how much time we spend on these things.

As a consequence of such businesslike practices within law firms, decisions to provide services for free or at discounted rates became collective judgments that explicitly took account of the interests of "the firm" rather than the personal preferences of individual lawyers.

> We bill monthly, unless the divorce is uncontested. . . . and those monthly bills once they build up get some attention by me and by my partners in particular. It is easier to be pushed by somebody else than to push yourself because you have an emotional investment in the client and you want them not to be burdened by the bill.

> [Before deciding to reduce fees] I look at the client's income. I look at their asset level. I always discuss it with my partner. We decided the only way we could make rational decisions is to do it jointly.

The practice of making decisions collectively in law firms takes much of the pressure off individual attorneys to make difficult choices about accepting sympathetic clients or reducing fees.

Collective decision making does not always ensure that the firm adopts the tightest business practices, however. As we have seen throughout this chapter, lawyers in firms talked regularly with partners about their retainer, billing, and collection practices. In some cases, these discussions were resolved in favor of restraint in pressing nonpaying clients.

> We have a collection agency, and we send unpaid bills to them. They send [the clients] letters, and then they say to us, "Do you want to sue them?" And we don't. And you wonder why the trim on this house is so ugly? I would like to be harder about that, and my partners would like to be harder about that, but we are just not one of those firms.

Thus, as Kelly (1994) has made clear, the cultures of law firms vary. Firms constitute small communities of practice that play an important role in guiding significant judgments by lawyers about the balance between serving clients regardless of their resources and the economic well-being of the firm.

Lacking a division of labor and a sense of responsibility to the firm as opposed to the client or potential client, sole practitioners are left to their own devices with little institutional or moral support for tough business practices. We found that sole practitioners were less likely than firm lawyers to have rationalized their billing practices and could not easily delegate collection tasks to others.[27] Moreover, lawyers in sole practice had difficulty distinguishing themselves from "office policy." As one sole practitioner observed:

> It's always a fine line, though. It's hard to approach a client on that basis [to ask for new retainer] because I've had clients that were insulted by the request, and they say, "What, don't you trust me?" And you try to give them the usual stock line that, "I'm sorry, it's office policy because the largest part of the receivables are nonpaying domestic cases." . . . It's tough to say when you're the only person that's saying it.

When making demands on a client, the individual practitioner thus speaks, or appears to speak, only for herself. Under those conditions, such demands can jeopardize the lawyer-client relationship and undermine the appearance of loyalty to one's client. Most important, there is no powerful conflicting claim of loyalty by partners to override the personal and professional commitment to serving individuals in need.

In many ways, the organizational logic of law firm practice crystallizes the lessons that many individual practitioners learn through experience, however often they may ignore them. Attorneys who can afford office computer technology have available resources to support them in becoming more "businesslike" and attentive to the "bottom line" by setting retainers, billing clients regularly, and collecting unpaid bills. Moreover, the extensive professional publications and frequent bar journal articles and professional seminars about office management communicate collegial norms of business efficiency. However, the imperative to rationalize the practice of law reaches its height in law firms. "The firm" becomes an independent and powerful focus of attention, separate from the individual attorneys who comprise it. It also provides an organizational basis for creating and imposing policies about billing, retainers, and pro bono service. Furthermore, lawyers in law firms can look to partners for help in making hard decisions and assistance in undertaking distasteful tasks of fee collection. The law firm itself becomes a locus of loyalty and obligation that competes powerfully with devotion to the client.

Conclusion

The dual expectations of service to clients and sound management practices were the central theme in the Report of a 1991 ABA Conference. Conference participants—concerned largely with the practices of larger law firms with corporate clients—took as their problem "the deteriorating workplace," a state of affairs that they attributed to unsound management practices (American Bar Association 1991). In advocating the use of businesslike practices to improve the work lives of lawyers, they confidently asserted the essential compatibility of efficient management and client service:

> If we look at law as a profession and as a business, there are two core principles that should guide all management decisions in maximizing both these aspects: service to the client and creating an efficient, productive work force. . . . The core truth of the profession yesterday and tomorrow is that the client comes first. A law firm is run for the benefit of the clients who are served by it. Every issue should get resolved from this perspective. (American Bar Association 1991: 14)

These glib assertions of the ease with which client service and business principles could be reconciled led the conference participants to conclude optimistically that "the law is not a money machine, but it is a business that offers some financial rewards, great intellectual achievement, and a chance to do well for society" (American Bar Association 1991: 13). However true this vision of the profession may be when corporate clients have the resources to pay their bills, it has only limited application in the world of divorce law.

In the divorce practices that we have studied, efficient management practices often are at odds with a commitment to serving clients with limited resources. By emphasizing the economic welfare of firms and partnerships, those techniques effectively provide a counterweight to the commitment of lawyers to individual clients. As we have seen, they can lead to clear policies about client selection, retainers, billing, and debt collection. They may encourage lawyers to consider withdrawing from cases where clients appear unable to keep up with bills. Such management changes may indeed increase modestly the attention lawyers can give to cases where clients have the resources to pay. But they inexorably move the practice of divorce law literally to a fee-for-service activity, organized as much or more around payment as around the delivery of professional service.

This movement is most noticeable in those arenas of practice where payment and resources are most problematic. Where payment of bills can be taken for granted, service to clients remains the focus. Where client resources are limited, however, many lawyers face choices about how and how much to emphasize efficiency as opposed to service. The lawyers who most often resolve this dilemma in favor of service are seldom recognized for their professional contributions. With heavy caseloads and limited hours to give to each case, they have relatively low incomes, are vulnerable to client complaints, and are unlikely to have leadership roles in the profession or even in family law practice. Meanwhile, the recognized elite of the bar generally, and of family law practitioners in particular, tend to be somewhat insulated from many of these demands. Secure in the knowledge that clients can pay the costs of extended representation, they enjoy recognition for their visible but carefully limited pro bono work.

According to Freidson's vision of a profession, "The client's needs must take precedence over the professional's need to make a living" (1994: 201). As lawyers look to their colleagues for guidance about balancing client- and self-interest, however, they see increased support for self-interested choice. The literature of law office management contains important lessons about organization and responsible attention to billing and time management, but often carries implicit messages about success. On the one hand, lawyers cannot stay in business and remain satisfied with their work if they are not bringing in money. On the other hand, the message that these professional journals communicate is that lawyers who give away time in the course of their practices are bad managers, even "chumps." We heard the apologetic tone from those lawyers who felt it necessary to justify their commitment to helping clients. Thus, the legal profession itself pushes lawyers to give greater weight to making a living than to serving clients' needs. These messages set professional standards and help shape the meaning that lawyers attach to legal professionalism in practice.

The demands of practice are also reflected in changing bar rules that have increasingly permitted and thus tacitly encouraged greater emphasis on the business side of law practice. The Model Rules, for example, now make it easier to justify withdrawal for nonpayment of bills and have eliminated the taboo against suing former clients. At the same time, of course, these changes have highlighted the aspiration that lawyers will donate service. The formalizing of pro bono work in numbers of hours and organized programs gives precedence to the visible efforts of those lawyers most able to donate time outside their regular practices, while ignoring a bulwark of legal services—the donated time of lawyers working with lower-income individuals. Modifications in bar rules thus reinforce changes in the organization and the informal norms of practice that threaten to squeeze out informal pro bono work for people of modest means and transform the concept of public service into that of private charity.

8

CONSTRUCTING PROFESSIONAL MEANING AND IDENTITY IN THE PRACTICE OF DIVORCE LAW

> The sad part about divorce practice is, your clients aren't happy. There's really no way you can make them happy. This is such a horrible ordeal. Regardless of who gets the house, they are not going to leave beaming and blissfully happy. It just doesn't happen.
>
> —a Maine divorce lawyer

Divorce law practice does not offer up easily the idealized rewards of professional work. Indeed, some lawyers never find them at all. The ideology of professionalism promoted by the organized bar provides a framework and reference point for lawyers to imagine and interpret their own careers (Nelson and Trubek 1992b: 22). It sets out a series of tacit promises about the rewards of a career in law. These rewards include the intrinsic satisfaction to be derived from autonomy, from mastering and applying a complex body of knowledge, and from serving the public, as well as the extrinsic rewards of public esteem, comfortable income, and collegial respect.[1] These promises of professional rewards—implicitly supported by much of the scholarly writing on professions[2]—collide, however, with the stark realities of divorce practice. Even lawyers' income in family law ranks the lowest of all legal specialties.[3] Divorce lawyers thus find that a central challenge of their day-to-day work is to shape it—to the degree they can—to provide themselves with meaningful rewards in relation to their own personal standards and with reference to the communities of practice to which they belong.

Scholars and professional associations have identified the organizational context of lawyers' work as a primary barrier to achievement of the promise of professional rewards and a central cause of dissatisfaction among lawyers. In particular, the rise of the large law firm has been seen as a major source of lawyer unhappiness (Galanter and Palay 1991). The regimentation and constraints imposed by large firms presumably diminish the autonomy of lawyer's work and contribute to dissatisfaction and alienation.[4] The pressure in large firms to produce billable hours helps to create a "time famine"—the problem of working conditions most prominent in the bar's own examinations of lawyer dissatisfaction (American Bar Association 1991: 3).[5] This general approach to lawyer satisfaction and reward thus emphasizes the contrast between a bureaucratic model, where work is controlled by organizational rules and management-created incentives, and a professional model, where work is controlled by individual practitioners with reference to collegial standards.

The heavy emphasis on the impact of large organizations on professional practice stems in part from an implicit contrast to the idealized view of professionals as self-employed practitioners (Freidson 1994: 206).[6] Kronman, for example, argues that sole or small firm general practices—not those in large law firms—provide the best hope for restoring his ideal of the lawyer-statesman (1993: 379). Studies of general practice lawyers make clear, however, that they too face many problems of professional identity and conduct, although they may differ from those of large firm lawyers (Carlin 1962; 1966; Seron 1996: 31–47; Van Hoy 1997: 77–85). Thus, it is too simple to focus solely on firm size or organizational context in thinking about lawyer satisfaction and professional orientation. Instead, we need to think more broadly about both personal identity and "the mundane business of earning a living in the law" (Wilkins 1994: 465; Harrington 1994) as key variables for examining professional aspirations and achievements.

The mundane business of divorce law provides a varied array of opportunities for emphasis, allowing divorce lawyers to find different meanings and rewards in the "same" practices. Although divorce practices are filled with many routine elements, they also leave much to the discretion of practitioners, as we have seen throughout this book. Choices must be made about the breadth or narrowness of knowledge relevant to their work, the character of relationships with clients, interactions with other parties and lawyers, and the meaning of "service."

One reason that these choices challenge attorneys is because they leave open the meaning and markers of success. Lawyers wonder whether professional fulfillment is to be found in the respect of their peers (and if so, which peers), in the appreciation of clients, in meeting personal standards of performance, in contributions to the law firm, in financial success, or in some other form. At the same time, the indeterminacy of practice and professional standards provides opportunities for lawyers with varying personal values to find different meanings in their work. This means that attorneys can and do play an active part in shaping aspects of their practices and in constructing communities of practice that promote a sense of success and satisfaction.

Reference Points for Judging Professional Work in Divorce Practice

Attorneys generally discover that the most obvious measures of achievement in legal practice—winning a case or securing high dollar outcomes—simply do not apply in family law. The lawyers we interviewed usually disavowed "victory" as a goal and embraced instead "fair" or "reasonable" results as a sign of success in particular cases. For most, as we made clear in chapter 6, victory was simply irrelevant in their discussions of divorce law because of its paradoxical character.

> In a domestic relations practice you can gauge your success by the results, but in a different way. A criminal lawyer has so many convictions and so many acquittals. It's either guilty or not guilty, and it's a little easier to do that. But there's never any such thing in a divorce action.

> It's really hard to say who wins and who loses when you go into court because I don't think if you get a really one-sided lopsided decision for your client that you've won because they have to live with the ramifications of that for the rest of their life.

Divorcing parties, linked together indefinitely through on-going child support, visitation, or alimony payments, have ample opportunity to challenge or undermine one-sided legal outcomes. Winning, especially winning "big," may simply mean, as one lawyer put it, "a lifetime annuity for the attorneys" as parties continue to battle through post-divorce litigation.

As divorce lawyers attempted to evaluate their own work as professionals and draw meaning and satisfaction from it, they found two prominent but not always consistent signposts to guide their judgments—their own assessments of their work and the opinions of their clients.[7] The first approach reflects the idealized view of a profession, where lawyers define both their own goals and their success in achieving them. The second approach reflects the realities of practice, where client opinions are difficult to ignore or to discount. Dissatisfied clients can complicate a lawyer's representation of them by failing to pay bills and filing grievance complaints. Certainly, they do not help recruit new clients.[8] Most significantly, however, unhappy clients challenge the lawyer's view that she is helping people and developing good relationships with them.

Among the lawyers we interviewed, 46 percent either reported that they made their own judgments of "success" in divorce cases without taking into account client views (17 percent) or indicated that they balanced their own assessments with those of clients (29 percent).[9] Needless to say, lawyers' views of outcomes often diverged sharply from the clients' perceptions:

> I like to think it's by a client's satisfaction. But that is such a subjective factor, and truthfully, clients sometimes aren't satisfied, but I felt I've done a damned good job for them. There's no way that I can convince them that I have done a good job given the facts and circumstances that I had to deal with.

> If my client feels good, that always makes me feel better, but I also have my objective sense of, "Does this seem like a reasonable thing for myself?" Sometimes my client will not feel that it's wonderful, and I will know that it's a very good deal, and I still feel good, in that context.

Many divorce lawyers thus employed their own sense of "fair and reasonable" outcomes as an independent yardstick against which to measure settlements and court decisions. Indeed, several indicated special gratification when their case outcomes were close to what they had predicted, as if their competitive instincts had been translated into a guessing game with themselves.

Of course, lawyers do not create these internal yardsticks by themselves. Instead, they develop in relation to communities of practice through interaction, observation, and consultation with other lawyers. The standards of individual lawyers typically incorporate collegial norms. In our interviews, however, when asked about how they judged their own success in divorce cases, only six lawyers explicitly acknowledged looking to their peers—usually lawyers in the same or similar practices—to supplement their own judgments of reasonable outcomes.

> I have on a couple of occasions gone to see somebody, maybe Herb, maybe Marion, and said, "Hey, these are the facts, what do you think is fair?" And they tell me what's fair and if I get more than that, that's my judgment as well, or I'll say this is what I've been offered or this is what I want to do, and they will say, well if you get that you've really done a hell of a job. So I have a little bit of an external barometer, but I think I pretty much know what a good deal or a bad deal is.

Although lawyers may have only infrequently consulted one another in order to evaluate particular outcomes in specific divorce cases, their own standards for judging "good" and "bad" deals certainly developed through interaction with and observation of other lawyers' work. Divorce lawyers do not practice in isolation. They have many opportunities to see peers in action and to learn about outcomes of other cases. The internal standards of individual attorneys thus both reflect and help to constitute those of their communities of practice.

As important as such standards are to them, lawyers find it difficult to ignore clients' views about their own divorce cases. Just over half of the attorneys we interviewed explicitly included "satisfied clients" among the criteria they used for judging their success as lawyers generally or in divorce cases particularly. A significant number of these responses were brief—"client satisfaction"—and some were indirect—"referrals by past clients." Some attorneys explained in more detail, however, the importance of client satisfaction, as well as the difficulty of achieving it.

> I think initially what makes me feel good is whether the client feels good. That is my human nature that I think I look to other people sometimes to know my other feelings. I could get a very good result by "objective standards," and if the client is enormously displeased for completely oddball reasons, I would have a hard time thinking of myself as successful. I would need to really go over it a lot and reassure myself that I'd done all right.

A response such as this illustrates both the significance and fragility of client satisfaction as a measure of success in divorce cases, where emotions typically run high and expectations are often unrealistic. As another lawyer noted, "I almost never get a result that the client says 'It would have been impossible to do anything better than this.' " Very few lawyers reported receiving more than an occasional "thank you" card or gift as expressions of client appreciation of their work. Thus, it is not surprising that less than one-fifth of our respondents described client satisfaction as their *only* measure of success. To rely on it more heavily would be to put oneself at risk of substantial disappointment.

Nevertheless, client satisfaction is too important a part of most divorce attorneys' sense of success and reputation to be left to chance. As we discussed in chapter 5, divorce attorneys invested substantial effort in "client education" to align a client's expectations with their own. Because lawyers commonly perceived that clients came to them with unreasonable or unrealistic views about what could or should happen in their divorce, they typically began the task of negotiating the divorce by negotiating with their own clients. As two of our respondents said:

> I think that's probably how I evaluate whether the thing is a success or not. Are, at the end, a client's goals reasonably met? A lot of that has to do with were they reasonably set. That's something I can impact early on. What do we want? Let's be reasonable. I want more than half, but we're not going to get 90 percent.

> A good result may be obtained and a client may not be as satisfied as he or she would be with another result, but to hopefully take care of that, you'd have been able to explain what the ranges are and what's likely to happen, that type of thing. But again, you've got some wild

cards in there, for instance, you know, different judges do different things. Part of the whole thing is keyed into having reasonable expectations and explaining what the likely results are going to be.

In this process of client education, lawyers may sometimes overstate the uncertainty of legal outcomes, as a hedge against excessive expectations and disappointment. In the ideal case, the lawyer's professional standards, learned through socialization into the community of divorce practice, become the client's standards as well. Yet, as Sarat and Felstiner (1995) have clearly shown, lawyers often find that clients resist such efforts at education and the process may end in a standoff of mutually inconsistent views and expectations.

Without clear yardsticks, however, lawyers find themselves balancing their own practice-based judgments with those of their clients to gauge the quality of their work. The idealized vision of autonomous professional judgment meets the realities of practice, where clients make unreasonable demands, threaten nonpayment, and express anger. In this context of uncertainty and ambiguity in the goals of divorce work, lawyers with differing orientations toward their roles find their own ways to judge the success of their work. Varying communities of practice serve as reference points for these orientations.

Limits and Sources of Intrinsic Satisfaction in Divorce Law Practice

Professional work presumably offers intrinsic rewards to those who do it. As Freidson (1994: 200) argues, professionals labor not just for the money but for the pleasure and challenge of the work itself. Divorce lawyers not only gauge the effectiveness of their work as professionals in varying ways, but they also find differing rewards in the work itself. But what those rewards are depends heavily on how attorneys understand and approach their roles. The same features that attract some lawyers to divorce practice propel others away from it.

In the idealized world of legal professionalism, attorneys work autonomously and independently to provide legal advice to their clients. Without a bureaucratic employer to manage and supervise the work process, each lawyer presumably has the freedom to set his own schedule and pace and to ensure that work gets done that meets professional standards of performance. However, the lawyer's satisfaction in meeting those standards is threatened constantly with pressures to degrade practice (Freidson 1994: 205). The professional project that presumably secures autonomy and independence for the profession as a whole does not ensure complete autonomy for individual lawyers in their day-to-day work. A commitment to professionalism invariably harnesses a divorce lawyer to overwork. In describing the rewards of practice, only a handful of lawyers alluded in their interviews to their control over work pace and quality, while many more complained about the "pressures of circumstance" and the press of cases.

Personal freedom and reflective professional judgment cannot easily be exercised in the face of heavy caseloads and unending demands of clients, courts, and adversaries. Lawyer after lawyer from all sorts of practices described the trauma of piles of pink slips on the desk and constant phone calls that interrupted sustained work on cases.

> The telephone. It never stops. The other thing I have trouble with is sort of the obsessiveness of it. It's very hard to get away from it. If you're not at work, you're worried about your work, or worried about the fact that you're not there or something and it's very hard to . . . I work hard, but I worry that it's very hard to keep yourself mentally away.

These lawyers found that the promise of professional autonomy was challenged by the realities of practice that meant the next phone call or fax was as much in control of their work as they were (Seron 1996). The demands of the job spilled over into private life as well. It was difficult, especially for the sole practice lawyer, to take vacations and "to spend uncluttered time with my family." It could be difficult even to sleep at night.

> It eats me alive. My stomach went sideways the day I started practicing law, not during the dabbling period, but when I decided to go for it. My stomach went sideways and it's stayed there ever since. Even when you work 60, 70, 80 hour weeks sometimes you can't shut it. . . . I can't shut it off when I go home. None of us likes to wake up at 3:30 in the morning with a [snap of fingers] thought about a particular case.

For many lawyers what was hardest about their job was "the amount of time it takes to do it well." Lawyers complained that they never felt completely in control of their work, knowing that it could always be improved by more research, more thought, or more preparation. The lack of clear boundaries between work and nonwork thus becomes a central characteristic of professional practice, reflecting the expansiveness of the tasks that can never be fully under control—especially if one is devoted to doing them well (Kronman 1993: 373).

Although those lawyers with affluent clients and high hourly charges had the luxury of being able to screen clients more carefully and carry smaller caseloads, they were just as likely as other lawyers to report the pressures and constraints on personal autonomy. Yet they—particularly those who had chosen to specialize—had more control over the type of work they did than those general practice lawyers, who were economically dependent on divorce cases that they did not like doing.[10] These latter attorneys wanted to decrease the number of divorce cases they did, but found they could not. A sole practitioner responded to a question about whether he would like to reduce, maintain, or increase the number of divorce cases he was doing:

Well, I suppose, the most honest answer is I'll take any case that can pay me at this point. If I had more than enough work that I enjoyed doing more to occupy all the hours that I cared to work and being remunerated for it, I would probably turn away divorce work.

Such lawyers were constrained in the same way as their peers by the never-ending press of cases, deadlines, and phone calls. They also suffered the added burden of being unable to shape the kinds of work they did, which had the effect of limiting their intrinsic professional rewards.

In the idealized professional vision, lawyers presumably regulate their own work unconstrained by the rules of bureaucratic operation and free from market pressures to produce whatever consumers demand. The realities of practice prove different. Although most lawyers that we interviewed exerted some control over the kinds of cases they took, and certainly most tried to maintain some control over their clients and the direction of cases, almost all of them found themselves driven by the daily demands of the work. The lawyers' evident anxiety about this issue—the feeling so many expressed that they should always be doing more—reflects the open-ended character of much professional work. Indeed, that very sense of being overburdened appears to be an important part of professional identity, regardless of the communities of practice to which lawyers belong.

Lawyer Roles and Professional Meaning: Legal-Craft- and Client-Adjustment Orientation

The open-endedness of the divorce lawyer's professional role provides substantial room for choice in emphasis by individual practitioners. Consequently, attorneys engaged in divorce work vary significantly in their approaches to it. Some of this variation can be captured by distinguishing between lawyers' orientations toward two different aspects of their work.

This distinction is rooted in the fact that divorce work involves both the achievement of legal outcomes and effecting change in the lives of clients. The use of legal knowledge to secure legal outcomes that advance or protect clients' interests can be a complex task, even if the legal issues appear relatively simple. Its complexity derives largely from the difficult and uncertain relationship between achievable legal outcomes and the needs, interests, and emotions of individuals going through divorces. Attorneys must translate the human problems they encounter into the categories recognized by the legal system. This task places lawyers in the role of intermediaries between their clients and the law as clients' personal situations are transformed into plausible legal arguments and outcomes (Mather and Yngvesson 1980–1981). The legal outcomes then become part of the lives and experiences of clients. Divorce lawyers vary in the emphasis they place on one aspect or other of this intermediary role.

These variations are often subtle and certainly multidimensional, but we found that we could summarize them roughly by classifying attorneys as *legal-craft-oriented, client-adjustment-oriented*, or a combination of the two.[11] Legal-craft-oriented attorneys regarded their job primarily as the provision of legal advice and the deployment of legal knowledge on behalf of clients in negotiation or in court. Their goal was to produce the best legal results they can attain under the circumstances. They thus focused on the translation of individual problems into legal problems and in working the legal process to produce favorable outcomes. In contrast, lawyers with the client-adjustment orientation generally defined their tasks in relation to clients' problems of living. These lawyers tended to see legal outcomes not as ends in themselves but as means of improving the lives of their clients. They concentrated more on problem-solving, on seeking results—not all of which may be available through the legal process— that made a difference in the lives of clients. All attorneys mixed these role orientations to some degree, but it was clear to us in the interviews that individual emphases varied considerably. We capture that variation in our three categories, which classify 46 percent of the lawyers in our sample as legal-craft-oriented, 28 percent as client-adjustment-oriented, and 26 percent as having some elements of each.[12]

Those lawyers whom we identified as predominately legal-craft-oriented tended to think that their responsibility in divorce cases was mainly to serve as the client's legal advisor or advocate. These attorneys were especially likely to be put off by the emotional side of divorce and by the petty "nonlegal" details of such issues as personal property division and arranging visitation schedules. As one such attorney put it: "The worst aspect, there are children involved. You're personally involved, I think. Too emotionally draining. I don't enjoy them at all." Such concerns were the refrain repeated by the many general practice lawyers who predominated among the attorneys (one-third of the total), who wished to reduce their divorce caseloads or eliminate such cases altogether.

> It's just so frustrating—people fight over the foolishest things. Only the children suffer. It's like sitting in their kitchen and listening to them argue. You go to mediation sometimes, it's like sitting in the kitchen listening to the fight. They get in the office and they'll start—and it's tiresome, and frustrating, and bad—it's a bad thing. And I've seen people using children constantly to get back at the other party.

Some of these lawyers, including a few who had accumulated heavy divorce caseloads, found it difficult to replace those cases with other, less emotionally demanding, work. Instead, they found themselves diverted from what they saw as their "real work" by having to "waste my time listening to their problems which are not really legal problems." Another lawyer explained the burden of this kind of work:

> I'd say the aspect of it that I enjoy the least is the heavy emotional and psychological dependence that the divorce clients have upon their

lawyer. I realize that it's something that goes with the turf, but it's not what I'm trained to do. . . . [it] to me is not lawyering. It's part of what you have to do as a lawyer practicing in that area, but it's not lawyering with that meaning.

Seeing their primary role as providing legal advice and assistance, these attorneys tended to feel uncomfortable when they faced clients who demanded psychological support, financial counseling, parenting advice, and general guidance about life choices. What the lawyer should be doing instead, according to one respondent, is explaining to the client "what the law is with respect to whatever their facts are that I've culled from them, and then giv[ing] them some guidance about what to expect, and tak[ing] them through the process, whether it's through a settlement or through a contested trial or through an appeal." A recurrent point made by these respondents is that a lawyer must help the client be realistic about what can be achieved legally in divorce. Ultimately, however, the attorney aims "to try to get for them what they expect after I've talked to them." That means making "sure that [the client's] rights are protected, . . . [including] their support, property settlements, and everything else that goes along with it." For legal-craft-oriented attorneys, then, achieving legal outcomes that the lawyer viewed as reasonable was an important criterion for determining success and satisfaction.

By contrast, the lawyers in our sample that we classified as primarily oriented toward client-adjustment were likely to be attracted to divorce cases by precisely those emotional needs and problems of living that distracted or repelled legal-craft-oriented attorneys. Client-oriented lawyers saw their responsibility as, for example, "getting [the client] off to a new start—turning their lives around so that they are done emotionally and legally with one part of their life in order to get along with the rest." Some spoke specifically of the lawyer's responsibility for helping preserve "the things that . . . are important in terms of family life"; "a decent relationship with the ex-spouse"; or maintenance of a concept of the family group, "even if they are incorporating new and different people into it." To these attorneys, legal processes and outcomes were important largely because they could help or hinder their clients' long-term adjustment to divorce. Client-adjustment-oriented lawyers were especially likely to recognize that the divorce process "can be very emotionally traumatic, very wearing on clients," and they accepted their responsibility to be sympathetic guides for emotionally vulnerable clients.

In divorce work especially, it is real important to do not just the lawyering which is very important, but also just to try to assist people through the process emotionally. . . . By that I mean, invariably when a divorce starts there are a lot of angry feelings that sort of flare up, people say things, which for the most part, you are not going to carry out or really are not going to do. It is important to tell people ahead of time, if you can spot them, what is going to go on so that they don't allow [the process of the case] to bother them, so that they can make the transition to getting on with their life.

For client-adjustment-oriented lawyers, the opportunity to form a close bond with a client through such counseling was an attractive and perhaps unique aspect of divorce work. As one respondent put it, "I enjoy the interpersonal contact and intimacy from working on a divorce as opposed to the mechanical aspects of doing real estate transactions."

These client-adjustment-oriented lawyers frequently described finding reward in the intrinsic challenges posed by the complex human problems they faced and the opportunity to help those in great need with legal and nonlegal problems alike. One female specialist, for example, described the perfect match between her own personal values and divorce practice: "And it was just a very good fit because I love people, and I've always been very interested in human relations, and so it's just a natural." Two other specialists, one a woman and the other a man, explained further:

> That's why I like divorce law or family law—because it's people oriented. It's getting down to the nitty-gritty of life's issues. I think I'm a closet social therapist. And, I like to deal on that level, being able to see the changes people are going through and being able to help them go through it. And with my experience, and, I guess I'd say besides legal wisdom, [my] spiritual wisdom to help them and to empower them and to make them . . . and also try to demystify the legal system for them. Let them understand what they're going through. Make them feel that they're part of it.

> It's the only part of law I like and it's because it deals—it's not black and white—it deals with emotions. It allows me to personalize my involvement. If somebody comes to me with a contract case, it's either valid or it's not valid. [In divorce] there's no such thing as a black and white. You're dealing with people, and I think it's much more humanistic, much more options for me to express creativity and counsel people and help emotionally. So it's much more of a creative, fruitful and quite frankly I have much more success with family law than any other aspect of law.

To these lawyers, divorce practice provided the chance for personal and professional fulfillment in the open-ended and challenging arena of human relationships and emotions. In contrast, the legal aspects of divorce cases held little interest for them:

> I wouldn't say that I'm an intellectual lawyer. I don't ponder the law a lot because I'm frankly not very interested in it. I am very interested in people and their problems and helping them understand the way the law works so that they either don't have those problems or they can resolve the ones that they have currently.

The enormous variety and complexity of human problems offered to client-adjustment-oriented lawyers the intellectual challenge and fulfillment that few saw in the law of divorce itself.

These differing orientations toward legal roles served to predict attitudes toward the adversary system and both trials and settlements. Forty percent of the legal-craft-oriented lawyers, but very few of the client-adjustment-oriented practitioners, named the opportunity to try cases as what they liked best about law practice. As one of the first group of attorneys put it:

> Trials. I like being in court. And that was an easy question. To me that is what being a lawyer is all about, is being in court, trying cases. I really can't think of anything I like better than that. Being in court, thinking on your feet. The only thing better is when you win the case.

These lawyers found pleasure and excitement in the challenges and pressures of combat in the courtroom and appreciated the fact that their divorce practices permitted them to go to court on a regular basis.

By contrast, about 20 percent of the client-adjustment-oriented lawyers, but very few of those oriented toward legal-craft, indicated that what they liked *least* about law practice was the adversary system or the contentiousness of the legal profession and of divorce practice.[13] Several, in fact, admitted specifically to "disliking controversy" or "fighting on a day-to-day basis." "I'm not a fighter by instinct. I'm a peacemaker, a settler," acknowledged yet another attorney, although he added that "I can screw up my courage and go be a fighter—you have to be able to do that in order to be successful as a lawyer." Another noted, "I've always thought it was kind of ironic for me to be a lawyer because I'm not one who enjoys confrontation, and I do almost anything to avoid it." These attorneys not only found conflict personally difficult but also saw the limits of traditional litigation and the advantages of settlement in solving the human problems that they conceived to be at the heart of their work.

> I don't like going to court. I mean, the first thing that came to my head was "successfully resolving disputes without trial." That's why I got attracted to mediation. I like also going with clients to mediation and being successful there. I like finding creative solutions to difficult custody and visitation problems, that seem to make everybody feel a little bit better.

Those lawyers who disliked legal conflict often found solace in their ability to negotiate or mediate divorce cases, diminishing the adversarial character of the process and avoiding courts.

Divorce law practice thus offered those lawyers who enjoyed the thrill of the adversarial process substantial opportunity to argue motions or try contested cases. Others who preferred conciliation found that in a process in which most cases settle, they could try to solve their clients' problems through negotiation and mediation. Attorneys with different values and temperaments and with varying orientations toward their roles could each find rewards in some significant element of their work.

Our rough categorization of the role orientations of divorce lawyers permits us to examine how approaches to divorce law vary with the characteristics of both lawyers and their practices. Two striking relationships appear. First, as the percentages in Table 8.1 reveal, women were

Table 8.1 Lawyers' Role Orientations by Gender (in percentages)

Role Orientation	Females	Males
Client-Adjustment	30.2	27.3
Mixed	41.5	18.2
Legal-Craft	28.3	54.5
Total	100.0 (n = 53)	100.0 (n = 110)

χ^2 = 13.02 with 2 d.f.; p = .001 (n = 163)

much less likely than men to be legal-craft-oriented.[14] Conversely, women were more likely than men to express a primary or partial orientation toward client-adjustment.

Second, those lawyers most specialized in divorce were nearly twice as likely as nonspecialists to show an orientation toward client-adjustment, while specialists were only about half as likely as nonspecialists to emphasize a legal-craft orientation, as Table 8.2 shows.

Of course, we know that women lawyers in our study were more likely than men to be divorce specialists, but in multivariate analysis both gender and specialization (along with social class of clientele) showed independent, statistically significant relationships to our classification of role orientation.[15] Although women attorneys were younger, on average, than their male colleagues, lawyers' age did not explain this difference in role orientation. Gender and specialization were the key factors.

Table 8.3 illustrates these findings, showing that although less-specialized male and female lawyers differed from their more specialized counterparts, they also differed from one another. At each of the two levels of specialization, women were less likely than men to be legal-craft-oriented and more likely to be "mixed" in orientation. Men and women did not differ in the likelihood of having a client-adjustment orientation, however.

The relationship between gender and general role orientation might be interpreted in several ways. Perhaps women lawyers were disproportionately expressing the much-debated "ethic of care" that values harmony and maintenance of relationships, seeks compromise, and views

Table 8.2 Lawyers' Role Orientations by Specialization (in percentages)

Role Orientation	1–49% Divorce Practice	50–100% Divorce Practice
Client-Adjustment	23.8	36.2
Mixed	21.9	32.8
Legal-Craft	54.3	31.0
Total	100.0 (n = 105)	100.0 (n = 58)

χ^2 = 8.13 with 2 d.f.; p = .017 (n = 163)

Table 8.3 Lawyers' Role Orientations by Specialization and Gender (in percentages)

Role Orientations	1–49% Divorce Practice		50–100% Divorce Practice	
	Females	Males	Females	Males
Client-Adjustment	20.0	24.7	36.4	36.0
Mixed	45.0	16.5	39.4	24.0
Legal-Craft	35.0	58.8	24.2	40.0
Totals	100.0 (n = 20)	100.0 (n = 85)	100.0 (n = 33)	100.0 (n = 25)

$\chi^2 = 7.86$ with 2 d.f.; $p = .02$ (n = 163) $\chi^2 = 2.17$ with 2 d.f.; $p = .34$ (n = 163)

the social world as interdependent; men lawyers, by contrast, were articulating an "ethic of rights" that values formal rules, engages in abstract reasoning, and sees the world as composed of autonomous, separate individuals (Gilligan 1982; Menkel-Meadow 1985, 1995; Jack and Jack 1989; Cahn 1992).[16] An emphasis on client-adjustment in divorce work thus permits lawyers—often but not always women—to translate an ethic of care into practice; attention to legal-craft allows attorneys—often but not always men—to embody in their work an ethic of rights. In their study of family law attorneys, Hotel and Brockman (1994) similarly found that more women said that listening to clients was their personal strength, whereas men referred to their ability to "win" cases in discussing their personal strengths as lawyers.

Another interpretation of these data, however, recognizes that client-adjustment-oriented attorneys themselves vary. Some of the attorneys most committed to the client-adjustment approach in divorce were also strong advocates of the rights-based legal process as a means to that end.[17] In this view, women lawyers may be more likely than men, by virtue of their life experiences and gender identities, to see and understand the economic, social, and emotional costs of divorce, especially for women. This difference is further reinforced by the fact that women lawyers disproportionately represented wives in divorce, as we showed in chapter 4. Thus, the greater likelihood of client-adjustment orientation among female lawyers may reflect personal and political commitments as much or more than gender-based variation in "ways of knowing the world." Whatever the interpretation, however, these differences by gender underscore the potential for individual lawyers with varying views of the world to find differing meanings in their professional work and to define in markedly different ways their professional roles and responsibilities.

The decision to specialize in family law provided a particular opportunity for women and men with special interest in their clients' lives to organize their professional work in ways consistent with their views of the world. Those attorneys who chose to do a great deal of this work generally were not put off by heavy and repeated demands to attend to clients' emotions and to assist them with the infinitely variable personal problems of adjustment to change. Thus, the relationship between specialization and our classification of role orientation presumably reflects self-selection into specialized divorce practice. The distinctive orientations that specialists and nonspecialists often brought to their roles were reflected in the varying expectations of their communities of practice. As we saw in chapter 3, these varying expectations in turn provide collegial definition of and support for professional judgments. Thus, the individual values and perspectives of lawyers help to construct new professional communities whose norms in turn help to shape and reinforce the choices of some lawyers while challenging those of others.

The differing approaches of client-adjustment- and legal-craft-oriented lawyers to divorce work reflect the openness of professional roles to varying interpretation. Not only are these roles indeterminate but so also are the products of the work. Legal outcomes are uncertain, constrained as they are by law, court decisions, and the preferences and strategic behavior of other parties. The impact of legal processes and outcomes in clients' lives is even less predictable. Such uncertainty about what divorce lawyers produce through their efforts makes it especially difficult to arrive at ways to evaluate their own performance. As a result, it is not surprising that attorneys differed substantially in the criteria they employed to judge their own work.

Communities of Practice as Reference Points in Assessing Work

Long ago, Hughes noted that those who do "dirty work" come away soiled from their labor (1962). Clearly, many attorneys in the United States perceive divorce practice to be dirty work—a messy arena that lawyers enter at considerable risk to their reputations. As we have noted earlier, in their study *Chicago Lawyers*, Heinz and Laumann (1982) found that divorce law ranked second from the bottom in attorneys' prestige rankings of areas of practice. That ranking has not changed in the replication of the study (Heinz et al. 1998), despite efforts of specialists to bolster the image of family law. There is no reason to suppose that public perceptions of divorce lawyers are much better today than in the past. Financial reward generally does little to compensate for low prestige, since lawyers in general practice and in divorce law are among the least well paid of attorneys.[18] The extrinsic rewards of divorce practice in relation to the legal profession as a whole thus appear limited.

Communities of practice, however, help to insulate lawyers who practice divorce law from the negative assessments of their work by their professional peers. What mattered most for legal-craft-oriented lawyers was the regard of those with whom they had regular contact, their reputations among colleagues and judges. One attorney described his criteria for success as "the feedback I get from other lawyers and what they hear about me. And judges, how they react to me, appoint me guardian *ad litem*, and other things that would indicate that they have a high opinion of me." Another also defined success in terms of his reputation among colleagues:

> The way to measure it largely is how I'm perceived by other attorneys and for that matter judges. It's a small bar, and I want to be respected for my forthrightness. It is said here that if you don't live up to your word as an attorney, people will always remember it, and I don't want that said of me. One way to measure my reputation is that I get referrals from attorneys that I respect or requests to serve as co-counsel.

For several attorneys in larger firms, it was the evaluations of their immediate colleagues in the same firm that mattered most:

> I guess what I value most in terms of my own success is how I feel about the case, but at [this firm] there are some very good litigation attorneys, it was one of the reasons that I chose to come to this firm, people who I would consider to be good mentors, and they are also people who supervise and critique my work. If they say to me, "You did a good job in this case," I think that I did.

But for more client-oriented lawyers, success was measured in terms of client reactions at the end of the case or in referrals of new clients. Thus, even in practices that may be low in prestige and relatively modest in pay in comparison to the profession as a whole, lawyers can and do find extrinsic rewards both in making a decent living and in the respect of those with whom they work most closely.

For attorneys who specialized in divorce, communities of practice played an especially important role not only in providing professional identity and support to individual practitioners, but also by serving as a platform for improving their collective image and articulating their own ideologies of professionalism. Clearly, specialists have a vested interest in promoting their work. Groups of divorce specialists, such as family law sections of bar associations, have formed both nationally and locally to advance their professional standing.[19] The creation of the exclusive American Academy of Matrimonial Lawyers in 1962 provided another early organizational base for building the identity and prestige of the specialized divorce bar,[20] and it published *Bounds of Advocacy* (1991) to establish standards of conduct for divorce lawyers. On a local level, a handful of Maine lawyers—almost all divorce specialists with upper-middle-class clients—joined family therapists and psychologists in forming an organization called Resources for Divorced Families (RDF). Members of RDF exchanged information and developed programs aimed at helping divorced parents address their children's needs and lobbied for these programs before the Maine state legislature. These efforts of specialists to promote their field thus also helped to define anew and often with greater particularity the meaning of professionalism.

In some respects, the efforts of organizations such as Resources for Divorced Families, the family law sections of state and national bar organizations, and the American Academy of Matrimonial Lawyers constitute a "family law movement," resembling that of several medical specialties that "when threatened . . . hit upon a 'revitalization formula,' a means of incorporating new elements into the traditional mission of the segment" (Pawluch 1983: 460) in order to improve the professional image of the group and to defend it from encroachment by other occupations. By redefining their work as "family law practice," divorce lawyers "upgrade" the job in much the same way that Carlin found sole practitioners in Chicago "upgrading" divorce work by engaging in marriage counseling and thus identifying themselves with higher-status professionals (1962: 97).

As a prestige-building venture, this one is full of symbolism. Just as Carlin's lawyers tried to identify their work with making families whole through reconciliation attempts, today's family law bar has identified its work in terms of the positively valued symbol of "family" rather than the negatively viewed symbol of "divorce." In addition, the term family law conceives of the family both in its original and reconstituted form, not just of the dissolution of the marriage. It gives attention to the need to protect the interests of children as part of the family unit. With broadened attention to the family, this kind of practice can also encompass a wide variety of legal work other than divorce, including, for example, adoption and guardianship cases. Thus, the legal profession is experiencing through the efforts of some specialists a continuing redefinition of divorce law into family law and with it the potential rebuilding of the professional image of this specialty. At the same time, those lawyers who identify as specialists have found new identities as family lawyers, along with new ideologies of professionalism more suited to their evolving practices.

Conclusion

The general ideology of legal professionalism claims that lawyers are independent in their judgments and that they labor not only for money but also for the pleasure of the work itself. We have seen, however, that divorce lawyers struggle with such independence because the nature of the job itself pressures them to attend carefully to the opinions of their clients in their own assessments of their work. Many attorneys balanced these client evaluations with their own internal standards for success.

While most divorce attorneys did find intrinsic rewards in their practices, they differed significantly in what they understood those rewards to be. Some discovered rewards in—and fashioned their own professional identities around—solving legal problems and achieving reasonable outcomes for their clients. Others found satisfaction and established their identities largely through their relationships with clients and helping improve their clients' lives after divorce. Women and specialists appeared more often in the latter group, while men and general practitioners appeared more commonly in the first.

Clearly, individual differences in values and tastes affected the ways in which lawyers chose to define their professional roles and practice divorce law. It seems likely that divorce lawyers responded to the indeterminacy of their practices and professional roles by constructing identities and investing in work that suited their interests and needs. Often, of course, these choices were subject to resource and market constraints. Some lawyers took divorce cases, despite their distaste for them, and all members of the divorce bar sometimes found they had to do things they disliked—for example, trying cases or listening to the emotional outbursts of clients—as part of their work.

Although few acknowledged it, the choices that lawyers made in their roles and practices appeared to reflect those of the various communities of practice with which divorce attorneys identified. The individual efforts of divorce lawyers to find meaning and reward in their work took place collegially through these shared communities and thus together shaped professional norms and constituted professionalism in its various guises.

Lawyers' choices and understandings of their roles also have a significant impact on how law itself is constituted in practice. As the interpreters of law to clients, as the brokers who make the legal system work for individuals, and as the key representatives of the legal system to the public-at-large, lawyers play a crucial role in shaping the experience of law for many individuals and groups (Merry 1990; Sarat and Felstiner 1995). Whether an attorney approaches divorce law with a legal-craft- or a client-adjustment orientation is likely to have as great an impact on the client's experience of the divorce as is the actual legal outcome of the case. Attorneys who thrive on solving human problems may listen more carefully and extensively to the personal experiences of their clients and be more attentive to helping define and solve nonlegal problems. Attorneys who enjoy spirited negotiation and trials may be likely to translate most of their clients' experiences into issues amenable to legal argument and decision.

Thus, the vision of a unitary legal profession becomes even more fragmented than is suggested by the research literature demonstrating divided hemispheres of practice between personal services law and business or organizational law. The varying approaches of attorneys to divorce law suggest that even a single area of personal services law is itself fragmented into significantly different views of lawyers' professional roles and responsibilities.

9

FROM PROFESSIONALISM TO COLLEGIAL CONTROL

We began this book by asking how lawyers think about and make the decisions that constitute their daily practices. One vision of these decisions finds their roots in the organized profession—its educational processes, formal organizations, and rules of conduct. Another explanation sees these decisions as shaped by the economic forces acting on lawyers, with firm profits or client pockets controlling the choices that attorneys make in their work. Yet another perspective underlines the role of lawyers' individual values and identities in making day-to-day decisions. Each of these views addresses what we see to be the core issue in the debate about legal professionalism—namely, the question of who or what forces control or influence the discretionary work decisions at the heart of law practice. Our contribution to this debate has been to focus closely on that question through an empirical study of divorce lawyers at work. It has also been to emphasize the central importance of collegial control in answering that question and to identify multiple "communities of practice" as the key agents of collegial control. In this study, we have tried to identify the standards that develop in these varied communities, how they are created, how widely they are shared, how—if at all—they are connected to the formal codes and organization of the bar, and how effective they are as agents of collegial control.

Our microlevel examination of the ways in which divorce lawyers understand and make crucial work decisions thus provides a fresh perspective on the legal profession and on professionalism. As we have looked at lawyers at work, we have seen collegiality vested most importantly in the communities of practice with which attorneys have their closest contact and greatest sense of identity. Collegial norms and conceptions of roles are rooted in the informal understandings among those who contend daily with common substantive issues of divorce work and with clients of similar economic circumstances. We have observed lawyers who feel that their independence is under pressure in a competitive marketplace from the demands of clients to do what they want and from the expectations of partners in small law firms to contribute to the collective economic good. Nonetheless, we have also found practitioners who strongly identify themselves as divorce lawyers with principles, who care about doing a "good" job as they understand and can undertake it, and who think about the expectations of their colleagues when making crucial work decisions.

This bottom-up view of professionalism helps to reveal the implications of the multiple divisions within the legal profession. Divisions such as those produced by legal specialties and by the differences between serving individual or organizational clients (Heinz and Laumann 1982), as well as the even more particularized differences created by client resources, location of practice, and gender—all help to create communities of practice that reflect shared experiences and influence lawyers' conduct. These communities help to organize the ways that lawyers shape one another's behavior through informal norms and expectations.

At the same time, our perspective implicitly addresses macrolevel critiques that deny the possibility of professionalism in an occupation that turns out to be so highly differentiated. Because we identify the core idea of professionalism as being how collegial norms translate into personal expectations about appropriate conduct, we see the continuing relevance of particularized versions of professionalism in that differentiated world. Our research makes clear that such collegial standards are important, even if they are fluid and informal and only loosely connected to formal codes or to legal training.

If "lawyer professionalism" were to become an entirely relativistic concept—to refer to whatever any subset of lawyers defined as appropriate for their practices—it would lose its more general and unifying but contested normative meaning. Thus, our analysis of multiple communities of practice and "varieties of professionalism in practice" should be understood as our attempt, as social scientists, to observe and describe empirically the ways that norms are developed, communicated, and reinforced collegially in the work of divorce lawyers. It should not be viewed as an attempt to undermine the normative sense of the concept of professionalism(s) but rather to separate the empirical inquiry from the normative debate and to situate the latter in the social realities of divorce law practice. To underline that separation, we turn in the next section to focus on collegial control as the fundamental analytic concept for examining professional work. At the end of the chapter we will reflect on the implications of our data and the analysis of collegial control for the normative debates about professionalism.

Rethinking Professionalism: Toward Theory and Research about Collegial Control of Work

The contrast between bottom-up and top-down views of professionalism returns us to questions raised in chapter 1 about the meaning and utility of the concept. As Dingwall (1976) has reminded us, profession and professionalism are not "things" out in the world to be defined correctly or accurately. Rather, they are complex social constructions loaded with normative meaning. Efforts to define professionalism therefore must be understood in terms of the purposes served by the definitions. The campaign within the bar and among legal scholars both to define and promote professionalism may be intended to defend the bar from intrusive regulation, to protect and justify the monopoly over legal services, and to shape the self-definitions and normative expectations of practitioners.[1] In contrast, our interest lies in description and analysis of the nature of control over the work decisions of professionals. Although the ideological content of the concept of professionalism limits its analytical utility (Freidson 1994), it does point the way for social scientists to identify the core elements that may be most helpful in analyzing control over professional work.

Control over work proves to be the central issue for both the theory and the practice of professionalism. According to Johnson, "a profession is not, then, an occupation, but a means of controlling an occupation" (1972: 45). Building on Johnson's analysis in order to distinguish professional labor from other work, Freidson identifies the defining quality of professional labor as autonomy: *"the central principle that the members of a specialized occupation control their own work* (italics in original; 1994: 173). Discretionary work decisions are under the control of professionals themselves.

The notion that professionals control their own work stands in contrast to control over work by clients, by organizational superiors, or by the state.[2] Consumer-oriented decisions shape worker conduct in response to demands of the market. Bureaucracies control work through organizational structures that establish rules of behavior and provide supervision and distribute rewards and punishments to enforce them. The state provides a third alternative for control over work by establishing agencies that set rules for training and licensing and provide mechanisms for enforcing them. Each of these control mechanisms—clients, organizational superiors, and the state—is understood to limit or constrain work decisions by setting particular expectations for performance or conduct. These controls also provide incentives for decision making, by creating goals and rewards for practitioners.

In contrast with these alternative types of control, what has been identified as professional labor relies implicitly on collegial mechanisms to ensure that the work decisions of professionals are not arbitrary, self-interested, or idiosyncratic. That is, professionals work within an assumed context of collegially defined expertise and normative standards about appropriate conduct. What is missing from this picture of professional work, however, is an account of the forms and character of that collegial control. We suggest that it is in practice, and particularly in communities of practice, that the essence of collegial control can be found.

Collegial control of work has many dimensions. It includes shared languages, knowledge, and identities that together reinforce common understandings of the challenges of particular kinds of legal work. It involves internalized norms of conduct learned in life, in law school, and during socialization into practice. It includes pressures from peers to behave in particular ways in order to function effectively in a system of reciprocal relationships. It involves formal norms of conduct and the threat of sanction for violating these norms. Collective organization and identity strengthen collegial control over work. People who share strong occupational identities organize themselves to socialize new members, to formalize shared norms, and to sanction behavior that violates those norms. At the same time, of course, they may also promote the economic or political interests of members of the occupational segment they represent.

Throughout this book we have shown how these elements of collegial control operate in the varied communities of divorce practice. Paradoxically, these elements are often most apparent when they are threatened or absent. For example, we saw that professional identity as a lawyer emerged at its most basic level when lawyers faced *pro se* opponents—nonlawyers—in divorce cases. Through shared knowledge of procedure and legal discourse, lawyers recognized that they could assume some degree of predictability in divorces with a lawyer on the other side. But attorneys complained that such predictability was lacking in cases with unrepresented opponents.

Moreover, although divorce lawyers frequently invoked the concept of "reasonableness" to describe what they understood to be appropriate conduct, specialists and general practice lawyers understood its meaning somewhat differently. We also found that in the more particularized community of divorce specialists, lawyers shared a strong belief in the importance of knowing family law cases and rules and in defining their legal expertise to include a broad range of issues such as tax law, pensions, and family psychology. But such knowledge claims had less importance for general practice lawyers handling divorce. Identities based on geographic communities of practice also emerged in our research as attorneys adopted cities or counties as points of reference in describing expected ways of handling cases. Thus, shared identities and bodies of knowledge reflected and shaped how lawyers thought about and made their decisions in practice.

Formal and informal organizations reinforced these overlapping professional identities and norms. Groups such as state and county bar associations, family law sections within the bar, family law resource groups, and individual law firms provided occasions for discussion of work issues, helped to socialize new lawyers into practice, and developed informal norms and formal rules of conduct. Lawyers' day-to-day experiences of working with each other on similar kinds of cases, and representing clients of similar economic means, also created common understandings of the issues of practice. For instance, we found that specialists were more likely than nonspecialists to insist on a "cover your ass" letter in those instances where clients rejected their advice. Whether such a pattern of practice grew out of informal discussions among specialists sharing bad experiences, formal meetings of family law practitioners, or policy deliberations in specialist law firms, it constituted a collegial response to a difficult decision in practice.

Women attorneys share the obvious trait of their gender, and we found that for some women this was an important source of professional as well as personal identity. Women who had entered the legal profession when their numbers were few shared experiences of harassment, isolation, and frustration over not being taken seriously by their male colleagues. Their exclusion from existing communities of practice had prompted some to develop their own styles, norms, and, eventually, communities. Feminist ideals and the experience of representing wives in divorce may also have influenced women lawyers in their ideas about lawyering. We also found some gender differences in the relative importance attorneys placed on the value of listening to clients and in their role orientations toward clients. Although there were no formal women's bar organizations in either state at the time of our research, such organizations were formed shortly afterward.[3] Early programs of the first local women's bar association in New Hampshire, for example, focused on gender styles in negotiation, and the organization's leadership included prominent women in family law practice.

Besides the influences of formal and informal organizations, the actual work experiences of divorce lawyers provided them with incentives and behavioral cues. We saw that the economics of practice required lawyers with clients of modest means to figure out how they could responsibly do their jobs with limited resources, for example, by sharing the task of negotiation. Similarly, among lawyers with wealthier clienteles, understandings of responsible practice had evolved to include greater use of the formal legal process. Repeated interactions with other lawyers created patterns of practice and expectations about how to obtain information for discovery (whether through interrogatories or phone calls), about how to formulate initial offers of settlement, and about how to define advocacy. Such social practices were reinforced through informal etiquette and the interdependence of those who worked together over time. Informal sanctions in such settings included refusing to share information with attorneys who were considered untrustworthy, prolonging the negotiation process, and insisting on court hearings for matters that would ordinarily be settled without one.

Finally, we observed that formal rules and accompanying sanctions for misbehavior provided additional mechanisms for collegial control. The lawyers we studied learned through practice and through examples of sanctioned misbehavior what the often ambiguous rules of professional conduct really meant. They also learned which rules mattered, which did not, and why. As divorce lawyers, they learned to be especially attuned to potential formal sanctions, as they became aware of the frequency with which clients filed grievances against their attorneys.

Our study thus has prompted us to view collegial control as being vested in communities of practice and as being variable with regard to its normative content. Collegial norms may vary over time, from group to group, and may be mutually inconsistent. For social scientists, then, identifying the normative standards of collegial groups is an empirical question. We must also ask whether such collegial groups are formal or informal, whether their shared understandings of roles and conduct are consistent or inconsistent, how strong collegial identities are, and ultimately, how powerfully various communities act in shaping conduct.

The power of collegial control may depend on such things as the tightness of the organization of a practice community, the strength of members' identity with the group, the intensity of members' socialization into the group, congruence between members' self-interest and collegial expectations, the degree to which members of collegial groups share language and experience, and the availability of avenues for establishing and communicating prestige and status within the group. One of the crucial functions of law school education, bar examinations, and rules establishing clear distinctions between lawyers and nonlawyers is to reinforce collegial boundaries and controls. Our examination of divorce law practitioners suggests, however, that while these general professional identities mattered, they were less important to lawyers than their varied practice experiences. It was the more particularized communities of practice that played the critical role in shaping lawyers' identities and standards for conduct.

If one were to study lawyers in others arenas of practice, would the same conclusions emerge? Our data do not allow us to generalize to other practice settings that are organized differently from divorce. However, research on lawyers who represent individual clients suggests similar conceptions of local communities of practice, particularly in criminal law (Eisenstein, Flemming, and Nardulli 1988). And Kelly's (1994) study of law firms suggests ways in which they operate as local communities of practice. We believe that a focus on collegial control within still other areas of practice can open up a useful line of inquiry into the work of lawyers in varying settings, while also connecting studies of the professions to research on competing forms of control over work and on other types of occupations.[4]

This perspective on collegial control also leaves room for consideration of personal identity in research on professional work. As new participants enter an occupation or a particular kind of practice, they are taught to follow its norms. But at the same time new entrants can bring their own values, experiences, and interests to their work, potentially changing the norms and expectations in practice communities. If feminists' predictions that women would transform legal practice to make it more humane and less adversarial are unrealistic for the legal profession as a whole, perhaps such changes are possible within more local and differentiated communities of practice. Also, as women's bar associations develop and articulate issues of special concern to women, they may exert pressure on statewide associations to alter their policies and standards.

Collegial control thus is a microlevel concept, insofar as it identifies the influences on crucial work decisions in day-to-day practice. Our research shows how the nature of law practices, the values of lawyers, and notions of professional roles, norms, and responsibilities interact to help shape one another. But at the same time, these microlevel processes are embedded in much larger social and institutional developments that can profoundly affect the nature of collegial control of legal work. These forces extend far beyond those encompassed by the ideological model that envisions (or hopes for) a legal profession shaped by the decisions of professional organizations, the rules of professional conduct, and the substance of law school teaching. A theory of collegial control in law should take account of these macrolevel forces that influence the character of communities of practice, of legal work, and of legal institutions. In the next section we will examine a series of such changes in the world of divorce law and relate these to variation in communities of divorce practice.

Forces for Change in Collegial Control among
Divorce Lawyers

Much has happened in the past 40 years to transform divorce law practice in the United States. Such important developments as the rise of specialization, the increased entry of women into law, the decline in sole practice and corresponding growth of small firms, changing divorce laws, and changing institutions for handling divorce cases—all appear to have affected the nature of divorce work and both the conceptions and practice of collegial control.[5]

Changing Markets and the Rise of Divorce Specialization

Over the last century, the practice of law generally has become increasingly specialized (Abel 1989; Ariens 1994). Shifts in the organization of law practice, growth of new areas of law and legal knowledge, and a changing marketplace for services have all influenced the concentration of lawyers' practices in particular areas. Specialization in turn has reshaped the meaning and character of collegial control by redefining communities of practice and encouraging new individual and collective self-definitions of work.

Increased specialization in divorce law practice was facilitated particularly by changes in the rate and volume of divorces. Divorce rates in the United States increased steadily from the early 1960s until roughly 1980, when they stabilized at a level about twice the older rate (Goode 1993: 139). Even more important for legal specialization, however, the composition of the divorcing population changed as well. Through the 1950s divorce rates were inversely related to income (Udry 1967: 673), but during the 1960s divorce increased so significantly among high-income and highly educated couples that the relationship between income levels and divorce rate disappeared (Glick 1975). Growth in divorces among people of means, along with an increase in the overall volume and rate of divorce, substantially altered the legal marketplace and created new possibilities for lawyers to specialize.

With the expansion in volume, the number of divorce clients in particular geographic areas became sufficiently large to sustain law practices concentrated in that field.[6] The increased demand for lawyers' services by divorcing persons of middle and high income ensured sufficient resources to pay the larger fees that often accompany specialization. The resources of those clients—including professional practices, businesses, complex property holdings, and retirement annuities—encouraged the lawyers who represented them to expand their expertise to deal with these and related issues. Changes in the marketplace thus enabled the development of specialized divorce practices differentiated by the characteristics of clients, as well as by the substance of the knowledge required to do it well.

As we found in our study, these trends had facilitated the development of distinctive communities of specialized divorce practice in Maine and New Hampshire. Divorce specialists, representing mostly affluent clients, reported using and valuing different sets of skills and expertise than general practice lawyers. Not only did the specialists attach more importance to litigation skills and knowledge of the law but their view of the law itself was also broader and more varied than that of nonspecialists. Lawyers specializing in divorce were also more likely than those in general practice to employ the techniques of civil litigation in representing divorce clients. In response to both their clients' needs and resources and to their own individual interests and commitments, divorce specialists developed quite distinct conceptions of their professional roles and norms. Specialists competed with nonspecialists for clients in divorce, and they also sought to increase the prestige and status of this area of legal work.

Thus, specialization in divorce has emerged, as it has in other areas of law, in response to a changing marketplace for legal services. These changes themselves create pressures on professional organizations and legal scholars to rethink their views of professional identities and norms. Indeed, it was only recently that the organized bar formally acknowledged the de facto growth of specialization and permitted attorneys to list their legal specialties.[7] At the same time, these changes reshape and strengthen communities of practice that help to articulate collegial norms and define professional roles and obligations. By particularizing collegial controls, specialization both differentiates and stratifies the bar, thus providing the basis for multiple communities of practice that support differing views of appropriate conduct based on particular areas of work and conditions of practice.

Entry of Women into the Profession

As new cohorts of lawyers enter the profession, they can introduce different perspectives, expectations, and values into their practices, and perhaps redefine how legal work is done by reshaping communities of practice. As part of the overall growth of the bar in the last 30 years, there has been a dramatic rise of women in law practice from only 3 percent in 1971 to 20 percent in 1991 (Curran and Carson 1994). The substantial increase in numbers of women lawyers, and the social forces that have helped to propel that increase, have reinforced the growth of divorce specialization and appear to have influenced the content of collegial norms and roles in family law.

During the 1960s, women lawyers were more likely than their male colleagues to handle divorce cases (White 1967: 1062–1063), and this pattern has continued into the 1990s. Divorce specialists in Maine and New Hampshire, and probably in the United States as a whole, are disproportionately women. While some women lawyers may be assigned divorce work as a result of gender stereotyping by their employers, others prefer divorce law for the substantive issues it presents and the types of professional roles and identities that it permits them to assume. For some women, divorce law provides an arena for enacting feminist ideals; they choose it in order to advance the rights of women, thus linking the mundane, private work of divorce advocacy to more public issues of civil rights. The fact that women attorneys, as we found, frequently represent disproportionate numbers of female clients may reinforce this role. For the same or other women lawyers, divorce practice offers the chance to help people and to make a difference in their lives, an approach consistent with an ethic of care. In our study, for example, female lawyers reported giving greater weight than did male lawyers to the importance of listening to clients. Gender difference in the expressed values and goals of attorneys involved in divorce practice suggests the development of new role conceptions for this area of law.

Given the shifting nature of collegial norms, significant changes in the perspectives that practitioners bring to their work can redefine professional roles and normative conceptions of "best practice." There are hints that the increasing numbers of women in the field of divorce law—combined with changing societal perceptions of women, families, and divorce—have transformed divorce law practices for clients with means. These transformations have not been in a single direction, however. As we have seen in our study, women attorneys specializing in divorce law have also been strong supporters of the importation of civil litigation strategies into divorce practice to protect and advance their clients' legal interests. Women lawyers specializing in divorce thus appear to be striving to combine a commitment to aggressive legal advocacy with attention to clients' emotional needs. Much of this work has been accomplished by women who are divorce specialists, thus helping to give direction to the specialization movement during the last three decades and to shape new communities of practice.

Changing Organization of Legal Practice

The organization of lawyers at work has changed dramatically over the last half century as well, making law firms much more common sources of collegial control. The organization of private law practice has continued over many decades to move from the model of the independent practitioner to that of law firm partner or employee.[8] The long-term decline in sole practice and increase in size of law firms reflects, according to Abel, a "response to the growing complexity of the law and the need to specialize, as well as competition from legal clinics and non-lawyers" (1989: 235). At least as important, however, is the cost of setting up and maintaining a law practice and the clear efficiencies of scale that result from consolidation. The expense of running a law practice encourages the creation of small firms and diminishes the frequency of sole practice. The economic pressures of running a law office may also alter the nature of professional identities and obligations and influence the shape of collegial controls.

We have seen in our research how the development of partnerships and small law firms substantially alters the moral basis of law practice by redefining the primary obligations of attorneys. In firms of any size, lawyers can easily see themselves as owing at least as much to their partners and their firms as to their clients. Thus, we found significant differences between firm members and sole practitioners in their capacities to resist giving away their time and helping people with limited resources.[9] Law firm policies provide cover and the interests of partners furnish both excuses and moral claims that effectively harden the stance of firm attorneys to the needs of clients. In this sense, law firm organization itself—not the size of law firms—turns out to be a fundamentally important factor in influencing the nature of collegial control.

Both the organized bar and scholars studying lawyers have devoted considerable attention to the rise of large firms.[10] Unfortunately, this focus on large corporate firms has deflected attention from the implications for the nature of collegial control of the long-term shift from sole practice to firms. As Kelly (1994) suggests, the character of the firm—the ideologies of those who shape firm culture and their communities of practice—may also be a significant force influencing lawyer conduct. As lawyers continue to move into, or create, firms as a means of delivering legal services, it is important to examine the forms of collegial control that reside in firms as organized communities of practice.

Changing Divorce Law and the Nature of Advocacy

While collegial relationships and shared conceptions of professionalism influence expectations of lawyers, the law itself also helps to shape the structures and identities of communities of practice. The changing character of divorce law has altered the nature of the work that divorce lawyers do, and with it their relationships with clients and other attorneys and their conceptions of roles and responsibilities.

Beginning in the 1960s, sweeping shifts occurred in divorce laws. First came the no-fault revolution (Jacob 1988), followed by statutes and court decisions intended to equalize property division, provide greater balance in parents' rights and responsibilities with respect to child custody,[11] and protect children of divorce through standardized schedules of child support payments. Such transformations of divorce law have modified the character of legal advocacy and altered the bases of relationships with other lawyers and clients. They also have changed the criteria for legal judgments by removing discretion in some areas while creating new areas of uncertainty.

Fault-based divorce laws encouraged lawyers to employ highly partisan advocacy to obtain the most that they could for their clients. But in a no-fault system, in which the law presumes an even division of property and mandates set child support amounts, the meaning of advocacy changes for most cases. Thus, we found in our research that lawyers reported more consensual problem-solving in divorce settlements, as opposed to adversarial advocacy. Child support guidelines, in particular, removed a key area of unpredictability and contention from most divorce cases, thus redefining this aspect of the lawyers' advocacy role. Equally important, the guidelines provided points of leverage for attorneys to convince clients that their expectations were either too high or too low. Indeed, the greater clarity in the law may have reinforced a shift in the central role of divorce lawyers from advocacy to client education.

In the remaining areas of uncertainty in divorce law, however, we heard attorneys describe the greatest contention and the most strenuous legal advocacy. For example, lawyers saw child custody, with its gender-neutral "best interests of the child" standard, to be a highly discretionary and unpredictable area of law. There may in fact be more custody conflicts now than in the past because fathers as well as mothers can be considered appropriate caretakers for children. We found, however, that presumptions of joint legal custody or shared parenting buttressed lawyers' efforts to dissuade clients from bitter custody fights and aided them in client control. The move to divorce mediation, discussed below, is one response to conflict that has arisen in this area. Redefinitions of the legal framework surrounding child custody and greater use of psychological expertise to resolve conflicts over children also encourage attorneys specializing in divorce to broaden their knowledge claims to include understandings of family dynamics and child psychology.

In another example of legal uncertainty, despite greater clarification of the legal rules in property division, the question remains as to what counts as marital property to be divided. Feminist advocates in family law successfully campaigned for a more expansive definition of marital property that includes pension and retirement funds. Such changes have required lawyers in divorce to pay closer attention to detailed financial matters and tax consequences, and it has also increased the complexity of divorce settlements, particularly for higher-income clients. The law itself has become more rationalized in these areas, with more finely honed statutes and specific appellate cases to address different financial situations. The development of more detailed law in the area of property division also may have sharpened differences between those lawyers with more or less propertied clients and thus between specialists and nonspecialists in divorce.

Changing Institutional Framework for Divorce Practice

Finally, the institutions and processes available for those seeking a divorce have changed over the last several decades, with important consequences for lawyers' work and the normative content and strength of collegial control. Institutional change appears to have been driven largely by worries that children are harmed by adversarial custody proceedings, particularly when they are unrepresented, as well as by a perception that the courts do not do particularly well in resolving the issues of marital dissolution. Two significant institutional changes have resulted from these concerns—increased use of public and private divorce mediation (Rogers and McEwen 1994) and the expanded use of guardians *ad litem* to represent the interests of children in divorce (Muhlhauser 1990). These institutional changes have the potential to challenge and change definitions of professional roles and responsibilities and to alter the composition and the norms of communities of divorce practice.

In Maine, where lawyers participate actively in mediation, they may be encouraged to adopt a broader view of their roles as they hear parties express emotions and struggle with nonlegal issues, and as they themselves take part in mediated discussions about fair and appropriate resolutions of cases. Such continuing socialization may help to explain why most of the Maine lawyers we interviewed believed that mandatory mediation had reduced somewhat the adversarial character of the divorce process. Differences between Maine and New Hampshire in lawyers' self-described goals in divorce negotiations, and the reduction in adversarial motions in Maine following the introduction of mediation, gave modest support to this view of Maine lawyers. The involvement of mediators in the divorce process reshapes the norms and expectations of communities of practice by bringing mediators' goals and perspectives directly into the interactions among divorce lawyers. Thus, a crucial factor in mediation's impact, if any, on professional roles and identities of divorce lawyers is the extent and character of lawyer involvement in mediation.

Although far less well studied and observed than mediation, guardians *ad litem* appear to be increasingly appointed in contested custody cases and could conceivably alter lawyers' roles and senses of responsibility in divorce cases (McIntyre 1996: 1711). Some years ago, 10 states required by statute or court rule the appointment of a guardian in contested custody cases that met particular conditions (Federle 1994: 1552). During the course of our research, New Hampshire routinely appointed guardians in contested cases, but the mandate to do so was dropped in 1992 (Federle 1994). The roles played by these guardians, however, remain inconsistent and unclear; thus, their effects on divorce lawyers are uncertain and variable. We found some lawyers to be especially troubled by the challenge of representing clients in custody battles if they saw conflicts between their client's position and their own personal concerns about the welfare of the children. To the extent that the institution of guardianship in custody cases is expanded, it might influence lawyers' own perceptions of their responsibilities as advocates.

Increased participation of mediators, guardians, or others in the divorce process as a result of court-ordered or statutory change in the institutional framework of divorce not only introduces new participants but also may change the roles that lawyers believe they should play in divorce work.

Summary

Throughout this book we have presented a mostly static picture of collegial control in communities of practice at the point in time when we did our research. Yet we are well aware that collegial standards and controls change and that they are sensitive to the pressures that modify communities of practice. In this section, we have suggested ways in which social and legal changes and shifts in the organization of legal work may have had an impact on practice. Our brief and incomplete examination suggests the possibility that many such changes—in the nature of the market, in the organization of practice with regard to specialization and law firm organization, in the gender composition of legal communities of practice, and in substantive law and institutional structures—bear significantly on the work choices of lawyers, on the organization of collegial control of legal work, and on the content of the informal and formal norms of practice. In the context of these broader forces, our research shows how the characteristics of lawyers and clients and the rules and institutions of particular jurisdictions affect localized communities of practice. This view of collegial control—taking into account both the broader changes in society and law and the differentiated implications of those changes—provides a useful lens through which to consider the implications of our research for the future of legal professionalism in the United States.

The Implications of Collegial Control for the Bar's Debate about Professionalism

The concepts of collegial control and communities of practice can sharpen and guide the empirical study of lawyer decision making. They can also usefully inform and challenge the way bar leaders and law teachers think about professionalism. The discourse on legal professionalism is fundamentally about the power and normative content of collegial control in relation to other forces that shape discretionary work decisions in law practice. If a goal of the bar's persistent focus on professionalism is to encourage high standards and public accountability for lawyers, then we believe it is critical to understand both the nature of the norms and expectations that guide attorneys in practice and the mechanisms by which these are constructed and maintained.

Our research underscores the importance of normative guides in influencing how divorce lawyers do their work. It also emphasizes the variety of communities that shape standards of appropriate conduct. Insofar as the norms of these communities ensure that lawyers' day-to-day decisions are neither entirely idiosyncratic nor self-interested, our study reinforces the hope of law teachers and bar leaders that normative standards can be important in influencing what attorneys actually do. But our analysis also suggests that the norms that matter to lawyers are not only, or even mainly, the rules that the bar has formally adopted. Informal norms matter too, and they operate in the context of a wide variety of interpersonal relationships and interactions. Thus, our research should turn the discussion of professionalism away from a preoccupation with formal rules toward a focus on the actual forms of collegial control.

Highlighting collegial influences in informal communities of practice can also redirect the attention of organized professionals themselves, such as the leaders of national and state bar associations, to the locations and forms of influence that count so heavily in the decisions many lawyers make in practice. The ABA's Commission on Professionalism, for example, tacitly recognized the centrality of the issue of control over work, but ultimately pinned its hopes for "rekindling" lawyer professionalism on hortatory appeals to lawyers generally, enhanced law school training about professional ethics, strengthened disciplinary processes, and more serious supervision of lawyers' conduct by judges (1986: 12–15). A more textured analysis by the ABA of the localized character of collegial control and the forces that shape its form and content, as well as those that compete with and weaken it, might lead to more imaginative and potentially effective ways of enhancing such control.

The idea of collegial control draws particular attention to the vital significance of social networks and relationships in professional work. These relationships are largely informal, although specialized bar sections, law firms, or other employing organizations provide formal structures for them. Local groups of practitioners, law firms, and organized specialists serve as important reference points for individual judgments because attorneys repeatedly interact and identify with their members. These varied communities of practice can divide the bar by location, firm or employer, client characteristics, degree of specialization, and even gender. Efforts to advance collegial control over work must pay heed to these varied networks. Some of the most crucial questions for both advocates and critics of professional organization are about whether it is possible to harness and make more accountable the existing and highly varied forces of collegial control.

Recognition of the importance of social networks in professional work also encourages a view of professional conduct that is not so much a matter of conformity to rules as it is a product of discussion, deliberation, and reflective judgment (Gordon and Simon 1992). Schon (1983) offers the image of a "reflective practitioner" whose efforts at problem-solving draw not only on a body of knowledge but also on experience and insight. On the many occasions where rules require interpretation, the reflective practitioner looks to the practices of colleagues, to personal experience, and to general moral principles and values. A major challenge for professionals is to find ways to institutionalize such reflective judgments in practice and to organize and provide collegial support for making them.

Legal specialization creates one set of identities and communities of practice that could particularize and support deliberative judgment among lawyers. We observed in our research that experience with divorce clients and cases, and interactions with other divorce lawyers, helped to create the reasonable lawyer standard for divorce. As we also noted, however, this norm was not formalized. The efforts of divorce specialists to articulate norms of practice publicly and to link them to the general rules of professional responsibility provide a relatively recent innovation in family practice, one with potential utility for strengthening collegial influence in other areas of law as well. By clearly spelling out the often inchoate and "private" informal norms, such efforts may help to promote both public accountability and wider acceptance of the norms. Specialist organizations like the American Academy of Matrimonial Lawyers, through publication of their own standards of practice annotated with detailed examples of cases and judgments (1991), may be advancing deliberation and guiding judgment by examining the application of general rules in specific practice contexts.[12]

Wilkins (1990) makes a parallel point, arguing that "middle-level principles" are needed that will take practice context into account. The contextual factors that he notes include some of the key elements of the work setting examined in our research—law firms, client characteristics, and the subject-matter of the law. Practice can influence public definitions of professionalism through development of more nuanced formal rules that are based upon context. Wilkins cautions that his argument "is not an invitation to adopt a purely case-by-case approach to professional ethics," but that middle-level principles should "isolate and respond to relevant differences in social and institutional context" (1990: 516). To the degree that such specialized codes are relatively specific, reasonably consistent, and are grounded in the realities of practice, they may have somewhat greater potential for guiding crucial work decisions than the more general, frequently inconsistent, and less realistic bar rules.

Our analysis of divorce law practice suggests both the potential value of such middle-level principles but also their weaknesses. First, we have seen the limits of formal rules in providing day-to-day guidance to attorneys and must question what would make middle-level rules any more effective than general rules. Second, the utility of such rules may rest on increased specialization and restrictions on practice. Third, the development of such middle-level principles must take account of the varying economic resources and incentives of both lawyers and clients. Fourth, questions may arise about public accountability when middle-level rules emerge. And finally, such rules may fail to compete effectively with the powerful role of law firms in shaping lawyer choices. We take up each of these issues in turn in the following paragraphs.

Why should middle-level principles or rules matter more than the general bar rules that, as we have argued, are often vague, inconsistent, and subject to self-interested interpretation? The answer lies in part in whether the existing informal norms and localized expectations so crucial to everyday practices decisions evolve into such middle-level rules. But even if such rules were to express the understandings and values of particular communities of practice, their value may be questioned since rules themselves exert only weak influences on conduct. To the degree that the keys to collegial control in divorce practice rest on informal networks, then the virtue of middle-level principles would lie less in their creation and publication and more in their open discussion and implementation by groups of lawyers in various communities of practice. That is, it is through the social processes of deliberation about such principles and decision making in the context of day-to-day challenges of practice that lawyers give meaning to rules and translate them into common expectations about appropriate choices. Thus, the building of middle-level principles might be a far easier step than their institutionalization.

Also, enhancing specialist identities and strengthening the collegial relationships that give life to shared norms could result in pressures to restrict practice to specialists. Such a restriction would be likely to further limit competition, drive up costs, and diminish public access to legal assistance. Thus, efforts to advance collegial control through formal specialization may carry a high price of the sort that critics of the "professional project" have repeatedly warned. The effects of specialized codes will, however, depend on the strength of networks of social relationships to enforce them. Such networks may be lacking if many lawyers practicing in an area of law do not consider themselves specialists. As we have seen, nonspecialists, with different communities of practice and different perceptions of their roles, may contest the assumptions of specialists about the meaning of appropriate norms for their work.

An equally serious problem with setting standards for conduct that draw on the experiences of specialists is the likelihood that those standards would mirror most closely the experiences of lawyers with relatively affluent clients. We found that many decisions by lawyers were influenced by client resources—for example, the choices about how formally to pursue information or about how much time to devote to a case. On the one hand, standards of "best practice" that assume adequate time and resources may be useful targets of aspiration for all lawyers. On the other hand, such standards may be so far from the realities of practice that they become irrelevant for practitioners such as Henry Genrus, potentially creating risks for lawyers serving clients of limited resources.

One of the distinctive claims of the professional version of collegial work organization is that it is accountable to the public because of the transparency of its formal rules and methods of discipline. If we are correct that professional norms reside most importantly in local communities of practice, however, what happens to such accountability? It appears to be compromised when the most significant aspects of collegial control are confined to work organizations and localized communities of practices whose norms reflect the conditions of work and whose enforcement authority is limited.

Bringing the norms of practice to public light reveals additional problems in contemplating changes that promote professionalism. Indeed, if we return to two of the day-to-day challenges of divorce practice that we posed on the first page of this book—whether or not to represent an indigent client, and whether or not to represent a client's excessive and unrealistic demands—we see both the strengths and the weaknesses of one form of collegial control in particular. Responding to economic competition, law firms may refuse to allow their members to take on clients who may not be able to pay. At the same time, firms may insist that to keep business in the firm their lawyers must not challenge their affluent clients' unreasonable expectations. Indeed, one of the risks of collegial control is that it becomes increasingly localized in law firms whose highest priority may be their own economic viability. In this case, professionalism in practice not only becomes more particularized but also more closely identified with the self-interest of lawyers. The power of work organizations thus makes for strong collegial control but little public or wider professional accountability for the conduct that they encourage.

The organized bar has made only limited efforts to use formal rules to encourage law firms to accept responsibility for promoting deliberation and thoughtful choice in making professional judgments by their attorneys.[13] Such vague articulations of corporate responsibility for conduct as exist in bar rules do little to create an expectation of collective attention to articulating standards, to deliberating about firm lawyers' responsibilities, and to placing internal checks on their collective pursuit of self-interest. Even though our research reminds us of the limits of such formal rules in guiding individual conduct, there may be some symbolic value in requiring regular internal law firm discussions of obligations to the courts, clients, and bar rules.[14] The practice of making professional judgments in relation to group norms might also be advanced through new approaches to law school education and continuing legal education that focus on particularly difficult judgments in practice and model deliberative and collaborative processes for examining them.[15]

Deliberative discussion of middle-level principles of conduct might be less effective for shaping lawyer choices than changing the law itself, or the legal institutions in which lawyers practice. These have consequences both for the work that lawyers do and for the ways that lawyers define their roles and interact with clients (Harrington 1994). Indeed, law and legal institutions may have far more to do with lawyers' attitudes and behavior than the formal rules of professional conduct. The extent to which courts manage lawyers and processes, or cede control to them, helps to define the degree of discretion available to attorneys, furnishing important cues about how professional judgments should be made. Court efforts to mandate filing of property and earnings reports, set child support payment schedules, and require the use of mediation all appear to have affected how divorce lawyers conceive of their roles and responsibilities and make professional judgments. Professionalism in practice relates to the nature and demands of work, and the substantive law and court procedures influence that work. If we want lawyers to act in particular ways, then more attention might be paid to shaping the work they are required to do and the institutional settings in which they do it.

How then are lawyers to "rekindle professionalism" in the face of the inevitable weakness of formal bar rules to regulate law firms, highly differentiated and localized practices, and the limits of informal communities of practice as sources of collegial control? Our brief discussion suggests that they might do so by diversifying and grounding professional norms in varied forms of practice, by reinforcing and making more accountable collegial supports for attorneys' deliberative judgments, by enhancing peer communication and feedback, and by attending to the content of law and legal processes. But the problem of varying standards according to the resources of clients remains an intractable one. We hope that simply bringing this variance to light will help define part of the problem, if not its solution.

If professional organizations are to move beyond rhetoric and hollow rules to enhance professionalism, they will have to recognize the challenges posed by what we have called the "varieties of professionalism in practice." Would-be reformers must begin by acknowledging the centrality of the issues of the quality and substance of collegial control of professional work. Such recognition would help to ground and focus efforts to reinforce the collective and public accountability of lawyers. At the same time, skeptics must monitor such efforts to ensure that their major consequence is not simply enhancement of the prestige and incomes of practitioners. Meanwhile, we hope that social scientists will make their own contribution to this effort by remaining keen observers of the nature of professional decision making in disparate communities of practice.

APPENDIX

Studying Divorce Lawyers at Work

This examination of lawyer professionalism emerged out of a study of the day-to-day work of divorce attorneys in Maine and New Hampshire. In our proposal to the National Science Foundation for funding to support this research, we focused attention on "the range and causes of variation in the way lawyers carry out their work." We sought to explore the possibility that different legal procedures for divorce—for example, mandatory mediation in Maine and infrequent private mediation in New Hampshire—might affect divorce lawyering, as might differences in characteristics of individual attorneys, their firm organizations, their clienteles, and local legal cultures. Our book examines these core issues but employs an analytic framework of "professionalism" that emerged from the study.

Gathering the Data

Because of their accessibility and relative comparability, we chose to do our research in Maine and New Hampshire, contiguous, semirural New England states with similar 1990 populations of 1.2 and 1.1 million, respectively. Both states have small urban areas, and significant pockets

195

both of rural and urban poverty and prosperity, although in 1990 New Hampshire was growing more rapidly than Maine and had a higher per capita income. New Hampshire's per capita income in 1990 was slightly above the national average, while Maine's was slightly below it (U.S. Bureau of the Census 1994). The ratios of population to lawyers in the two states were virtually identical, and half the lawyers in each state practiced outside urban areas (Curran 1986).

In each state "no-fault divorce" laws had been passed, but the two states differed, as noted above, with regard to mediation. In addition, New Hampshire permitted marital fault to be a factor in awarding alimony and dividing property, whereas fault was excluded as a basis for such awards in Maine (Freed and Walker 1991). Both were equitable distribution common law states, but New Hampshire considered all property, whereas Maine confined consideration to marital property (Freed and Walker 1991).

Maine and New Hampshire are not representative states in the United States, but neither are they radically different with regard to law practice. For example, in the United States as a whole, 59 percent of private practitioners were in sole practice or in firms of up to five lawyers in 1991; in Maine and New Hampshire, the percentages were 60 and 62, respectively (Curran and Carson 1994). In these two states and in the United States as a whole, one-fifth of the lawyers were women. The ratio of population to lawyers was higher in Maine and New Hampshire (395/1 and 375/1) than in the United States overall (313/1).

Our initial sampling centered on counties—three of New Hampshire's ten counties and four of Maine's sixteen. We selected the counties to be demographically comparable with regard to population size, percent urban, and per capita income. In addition, we chose to represent different areas of the state that were said to be somewhat distinctive with regard to local legal cultures. Thus, in each state we chose, for example, a relatively rural and low-income county and a faster growing, more urbanized and higher-income county.

Our data came primarily from lengthy semistructured interviews with 163 divorce lawyers, conducted by the authors in 1990–1991. To select lawyers to interview, we sampled the 1989 divorce dockets of courts in the selected counties of the two states. In each court we recorded the names of the lawyers of record, developing a frequency distribution of their appearances. Then we sampled the list, taking all the lawyers with the most frequent representations, about half of those with moderate frequencies, and a few of those with lesser frequencies. In no case did we choose from the many lawyers who represented only one or two divorce clients a year in the sampled court. We supplemented (though largely reaffirmed) this list of active divorce lawyers with names identified by other attorneys and by court clerks.

Through this process we identified 178 divorce lawyers and arranged and completed interviews with 163 (92 percent): 88 in Maine and 75 in New Hampshire. The interviews varied from about half an hour to over three hours and averaged 90 minutes in length. All but one of the attorneys agreed to have the interview taped and transcribed. In the one exceptional case, the interviewer took notes and immediately dictated answers based on those notes that were then transcribed. Due to time pressures, we were not able to complete the full list of roughly 100 questions in all of the interviews. The interview questions are available at http://www.dartmouth.edu/~lmather/.

In arranging the interviews, we promised confidentiality to our respondents. Names and some identifying information have been changed in the reporting of the interviews to maintain that confidentiality. The variation in our sample of lawyers is summarized in Table A.1. We supplemented the lawyer interviews with informal interviews with court clerks, judges, and marital masters. In New Hampshire, marital masters handle nearly all of the divorces in the state, subject to what is typically routine approval by Superior Court judges. Interviews with the masters were tape-recorded and transcribed.

We also gathered data from a large sample (between one-quarter and one-half) of the docket records of divorce cases taken from the courts of the seven counties in Maine and New Hampshire. In Maine, we systematically sampled divorce dockets in each court used in our study for the years 1979, 1980, 1983, 1984, 1985, 1986, and 1988, while in New Hampshire, we sampled cases in 1980, 1984, and 1988. The larger Maine sample (4,790 cases compared with 2,001 in New Hampshire) was intended to bracket the beginning of mandatory divorce mediation (1984) and to reach back prior to the beginning of voluntary mediation around 1980. For most of the analysis reported in the book, we confine the comparisons to the data gathered from 1984 and later cases (2,958 Maine cases and 1,294 New Hampshire cases).

A group of student coders visited the courthouses and coded case information such as number and types of motions filed, court hearings and judicial orders, dates of filing and disposition, husband or wife as client, and lawyers' names in cases where parties were represented. The docket records reveal important facts about the aggregate practice of divorce law in these two states, facts that help us to understand the daily work of these divorce lawyers. They also tell something of the ways the lawyers we interviewed employ the legal system on behalf of their clients. By isolating within the docket samples the divorce cases handled by "our" 163 lawyers in 1984 and later, we were able to relate their accounts of decisions and behavior to actual patterns of practice. The docket data produced an average of 12 actual cases per lawyer for 157 of the 163 lawyers that we interviewed.

Analyzing and Making Sense of the Data

To analyze the data, we proceeded along several lines simultaneously. The interviews were first transcribed and then the close-ended questions

Table A.1 Characteristics of Sample of 163 Divorce Lawyers

	Number	Percent
State		
Maine	88	54.0
New Hampshire	75	46.0
Gender		
Female	53	32.5
Male	110	67.5
Years of Legal Practice before 1990		
30 or more	9	5.5
20–29 years	28	17.2
15–19 years	38	23.3
10–14 years	45	27.6
5–9 years	30	18.4
1–4 years	13	8.0
Size of Firm		
Sole	46	28.2
2 person	37	22.7
3–4 person	40	24.5
5–9 person	20	12.3
10 or more	20	12.3
Prestige of Law School		
State law school	59	36.2
(University of Maine or Franklin Pierce)		
Top 26 law schools	23	14.1
Other law schools	81	49.7
Degree of Specialization in Divorce		
Less than 25 percent of practice	53	32.5
25–49 percent of practice	52	31.9
50 to 74 percent of practice	25	15.3
75 percent or more of practice	33	20.2
Number of Active Divorce Cases (estimated)		
10 or fewer	23	14.1
11–20	41	25.2
21–30	25	15.3
31–50	28	17.2
51–90	20	12.3
91 and higher	20	12.3
Missing or uncertain	6	3.7
Self-described Social Class of Clientele		
Mostly upper-middle/	33	20.2
Upper-middle and middle class		
Mostly middle class/	62	38.0
"A cross-section"		
Mostly middle and working class/	68	41.7
Working class		
Hourly Rate in 1990		
Less than $80	19	12.6
$85–$95	36	22.1
$100–$110	51	31.3
$115–$125	33	20.2
$135 and higher	16	16.3
Variable rate or missing	8	4.5

were coded for analysis. These data along with the coded docket data were entered into SPSS, and a subset of docket data pertaining to our interviewees was aggregated and merged with the interview data for statistical analysis. Each of the authors read the roughly 7,000 pages of interview transcripts and sorted through themes, at times returning to questions or sets of questions for more systematic analysis, either by coding or by tabulating the frequency of recurring themes. When we created new variables for statistical analysis from the open-ended question responses, at least two of the authors (or an author and an assistant) coded the materials to check for reliability. We reconciled any differences in coding through discussion.

Since the argument presented in this book rests primarily on our interview data, it is important to address their strengths and weaknesses. We view the interview data in two different ways. At one level, the lawyers we interviewed were respondents whose answers can be analyzed both quantitatively and qualitatively for patterns and frequencies and for insights and examples. The interviews can also be understood at another level. That is, the attorneys were informants about their own work and that of their colleagues. These women and men had typically handled hundreds of divorce cases over years and were thoughtful and critical, as well as self-interested, observers of the world in which they worked. As respondents, the attorneys were reporting their understandings, perceptions, and beliefs about the divorce process, their senses of their roles in it. As informants, they offered observations of practice that helped to illuminate our understanding of a divorce lawyer's work and the ways that lawyers made sense of what they did.

Our friendly critics remind us of the need to be skeptical about the degree to which our data provide a window on actual practice. In fact, except where our evidence comes from court records of legal activity in cases, we have no direct evidence of how lawyers acted toward clients or toward one another. Thus, we are reluctant to report our data about practice with confident statements about numbers of lawyers who practice one way or another. And because the interviews relied on open-ended questions that led lawyers in very different directions, we cannot even be confident about the precise proportions of lawyers who speak with one voice or another about a particular topic. However, we think it reasonable to suppose that the accounts of attorneys capture much, if not all, of the range of behavior and of how differing approaches are understood. Thus, these accounts, we believe, address the central issues of divorce law practice and the major strategies for dealing with them, even if we cannot be certain precisely who and how often lawyers adopt one or another of these approaches.

A skeptical reader might also ask (as have we) whether we were hearing "professionally acceptable" responses to questions about how attorneys viewed and approached problems of practice—what we were "supposed to hear," not what they really believed or actually did. That is an important and complicated issue. We have considerable confidence that we were, in fact, hearing from most lawyers something close to their candid views of their own actions. This confidence derives in part from the fact that we heard widely divergent answers to our questions that were patterned by the characteristics of practice. Thus, if there was a single "right" or "best" answer, we did not hear it from everyone. In addition, our confidence is increased by the fact that not all lawyers responded in ways that flattered them or put their own conduct in the best light. Finally, our interview data, where we could check them against the data provided by a court's docket book, were generally consistent with the behavioral measures.

Our approach to these data combines interpretivism and more traditional structural and causal analysis. The interpretive elements emphasize the role of ideologies, norms, and identities in providing coherence and meaning to the work that lawyers do, and in providing a framework for interpreting and orienting "their choices according to an internalized world view that delimits but does not necessarily determine action" (Nelson and Trubek 1992b: 23). Cultural or interpretive approaches, as Silbey writes, "shift attention to the constitution and operation of social structure in historically specific situations rather than macro-sociological, transhistorical processes" (1992: 47). Our focus here is on the ways in which legal practice is constituted by the ideas, identities, shared knowledge, and material conditions of that practice (see Mather 1998 and Wendt 1998 for discussion of constitutive vs. causal analyses). Legal practice is also constituted by the law itself, and thus an interpretive perspective must also be one that "takes seriously the meaning and conceptions of law in the organization of legal practice" (Harrington 1994: 55).

The more traditional analysis attends to the social structures and processes that reinforce or create the ideas constituting practice. Structural and causal analysis can complement and strengthen interpretive analysis and help resolve a problem with much postmodern, interpretive thinking. D'Andrade argues that interpretive research "does not investigate the on-the-ground social processes by which power is used and maintained, but rather focuses on the interpretations of discourse to discover how power maintains its hegemony" (1995: 251). What is often missing is a theory of social structure and processes that explains how certain meanings come to have power (Taylor 1989). The nature of the economic exchange between lawyer and client, the material conditions of a lawyer's practice, the organization of relationships among lawyers, and professional socialization begin to provide elements of the theory that is needed here.

Ideas, norms, identities, and work settings thus not only constitute legal practice, but they also have behavioral consequences. They constrain lawyers' actions, provide reasons and incentives for action, and teach lawyers to behave in certain ways. Many of them operate on and through what we call communities of practice (see chapter 3). We consider the structural sources of variations in ideas, norms, and identities by looking primarily at variation in lawyers' work across different work settings and different personal and professional identities and secondarily through examination of significant changes in divorce law practice. Both approaches allow us to reach tentative conclusions about causal forces at work in current divorce law practice, such as the impact of law firm structures and growing specialization, the implications of new institutions such as mediation, or the consequence of increased numbers of women practitioners.

The discussion in the book ultimately moves between the margins of ideology and practice. Through our interview data, what we hear are lawyers depicting and rationalizing their conduct, but not necessarily describing it accurately. These accounts provide a window on the internal and public conversations that attorneys engage in about the nature, purpose, and meaning of their work. In this sense, these accounts tell us about the struggle to develop, modify, and sustain professional ideologies in the face of the uncertainties, shifting pressures, and contradictions of everyday practice. As ideology, these accounts reflect the set of assertions, arguments, and assumptions about how the world of divorce law practice works and the roles of the divorce lawyer in that world. And finally, as pictures of practice, these accounts describe the varied ways that attorneys respond to the demands of practice and translate ideology into behavior.

NOTES

Chapter 1

1. We discovered these particular communities through our research. Communities of practice, as we discuss them, are similar to some of the sites or "arenas" of professionalism described by Nelson and Trubek (1992a). We did not know what communities we would find in our research, just as "arenas of professionalism cannot be defined a priori, but must be determined based on empirical investigation" (Nelson and Trubek 1992a: 185).

2. Indeed, as Zacharias notes, "no term in the legal lexicon has been more abused than 'professionalism' " (1995: 1307). Even the American Bar Association's Commission on Professionalism has had to acknowledge what it calls the "elasticity" of the concept of legal professionalism (1986: 10).

3. For critics such as Johnson (1972), Larson (1977), and Abel (1988), the ideology of professionalism has simply served all along to justify and disguise the bar's monopoly over the legal marketplace. Professionals, in their view, are not virtuous, self-restrained experts serving society and monitoring the conduct of colleagues but rather members of self-interested groups using political, economic, and social power to limit competition and protect fees.

The doubts of both advocates and critics about the efficacy of professional control of lawyer conduct find reinforcement in other scholarship that raises questions about the utility of professional norms (Abel 1989); points to the increasing importance of large organizations to the practice of law (Galanter and Palay 1991); and challenges the idea of a unified legal profession (Heinz and Laumann 1982; Heinz, et al. 1998; Wilkins 1998). Most of this research on lawyers' pursuit of self-interest focuses on aggregate studies of the profession rather than on the practices of individual lawyers. According to one reviewer, for example, Abel and Lewis's massive cross-national comparative study of lawyers (1988) "is so concerned with the professional project defined as seeking income and status through market control ... that it does not concern itself much with what lawyers do. Instead it concerns itself a lot with who they are" (Shapiro 1990: 687). As a leading proponent of the professional project perspective, however, Abel has been well aware that "social scientists study the organization of professional work, not its content" (1985: 46), and he is one of those who has called for increased attention to studies of work and the workplace (1989: 14).

4. For a sampling of views about the problems of professionalism as seen at the state bar level, see, for example, Sullivan (1987); Frymire (1989); Abrams (1990); Greenwood (1991); and Armstrong (1994). Legal scholars, jurists, and lawyers reflecting on the problem include Burger (1993); Kronman (1993); Glendon (1994); and Zacharias (1995).

5. For example, Zacharias suggests that the problem of overzealousness in pursuit of clients' interests be addressed through codes "identifying subjects lawyers must discuss with clients," including "what an objectively 'fair' disposition of the case would be" and "the lawyers' own moral inclinations and any obligations to third-party or societal interests that the lawyers believe should be honored" (1995: 1359–1360).

6. A careful examination of the formal codes of professional responsibility leads some to conclude that such rules do more to define the conflicts at stake in discretionary judgments than to resolve them (Zacharias 1995; Feldman 1996). The codes set out at times mutually inconsistent expectations, a fact partly recognized in the Preamble to the American Bar Association's Model Rules. After asserting that the lawyer's multiple responsibilities are "usually harmonious," the Preamble acknowledges that "conflicting responsibilities are encountered," before concluding that it provides a framework for resolving those problems with "sensitive professional and moral judgment" (American Bar Association 1995: 6).

While many critics have described bar disciplinary rules as vague, inconsistent, and ineffective, these commentators nevertheless disagree on a solution. Simon (1998b), for example, proposes that lawyers follow a contextual approach, deciding on their own what actions will best promote justice, with a definition of justice that rests heavily on the legal merits of each case. In a *Stanford Law Review* symposium (Rhode 1999), concerns raised about Simon's position include its inattention to lawyers' personal moral judgments (Rhode 1999; Luban 1999; West 1999); to religious (Shaffer 1999) or racial (Alfieri 1999) identities; or to the organizational or social context of lawyers' practices (Rostain 1999).

7. Rosenthal (1974) and Flood (1991) emphasize the factual and legal uncertainty that help give rise to discretionary decision-making in day-to-day practice. But see Cain's (1979) assessment of the work of general practice lawyers, which, she argues, is frequently routine, with little room for lawyers to advise their clients about either ends or means.

8. The ABA too has pondered the impact of law firm management on both the quality of lawyers' work lives and on client services, although it

concludes optimistically that sound business management and good professional practice reinforce one another (American Bar Association 1991). But Trotter suggests that law firm profit-making does just the reverse: large New York law firms, he says, have created new professional standards for commercial practice that demand "that client files be overworked and that lawyers at all levels put in too many hours" (1997: 120).

9. Studies of the commitment of those involved in cause lawyering (Sarat and Scheingold 1998); the conscientiousness of many public defenders (Mather 1979; Flemming, Nardulli, and Eisenstein 1992); and the independence of early-twentieth century New York commercial lawyers (Gordon 1988) suggests that lawyers' actions cannot be attributed solely to self-interest since public service values do sometimes play a key role in their work.

10. But just as an impersonal or bleached out professionalism may be difficult to attain in practice, it can also provide some benefits as an ideal. For example, donning the professional mantle of a lawyer may help minority lawyers escape the harms of hostile racial stereotyping (Wilkins 1998: 145; Pue 1998: 129).

11. For other analyses of religious identity and legal professionalism, see Levinson (1993) on Jewish lawyers, and Shaffer (1999) on Christian lawyers.

12. But see Jack and Jack (1989), Harrington (1993), Hotel and Brockman (1994), Brockman (1996), and Sommerlad and Sanderson (1998) for research on gender differences among lawyers.

13. West (1988) also develops an argument for a distinctively female style of lawyering. See also Cahn (1992) and Mossman (1988). MacKinnon (1987) points to power differences between men and women, rather than to psychology or socialization, to explain women's concern for care over rights.

14. The complex picture of law practice that emerges from the research makes it clear that we cannot choose between the professional ideology, workplace, and personal accounts but rather that we must find ways to draw them together. Nelson and Trubek present a compelling argument for studying legal professionalism in the different arenas in which it is produced when they assert that "lawyer professionalism is not a fixed, unitary set of values, but instead consists of multiple visions of what constitutes proper behavior by lawyers" (1992a: 179). Wilkins (1990) also calls attention to the diversity of legal cultures in the United States, each with its own normative approach to professional conduct.

15. Such an emphasis on collegial identities and standards lies at the heart of the analysis done by those who helped to pioneer the social scientific study of the professions. Goode (1957), for example, saw professions as unified groups that grew naturally from the development of abstract and specialized knowledge and contributed altruistically to the public good (Freidson 1994: 13). Altruism was achieved through professional identity that helped to transform conceptions of self-interest to make them compatible with service. Thus, professional identity generally provided guidance for the choices of individual practitioners.

16. Handler noted that there was "sharp conflict" between the official ABA position about the propriety of certain conduct and the position of the local "Prairie City" bar, which did not regard the conduct as unprofessional (1967: 138–139).

Chapter 2

1. Throughout the book we have on occasion edited the interview extracts slightly to improve clarity and readability. For example, we often removed gratuitous phrases such as "you know," "uh," "hmm," and so forth.

2. The names of lawyers portrayed in this chapter are fictitious, and non-essential details about them have been altered to preserve confidentiality.

3. By "specialist" here we mean that 50 percent or more of the attorney's law practice involves divorce cases.

Chapter 3

1. In addition, some lawyers create and participate in local, state, and national organizations—such as the American Academy of Matrimonial Lawyers—to help define, reinforce, and sustain their views of practice and of their professional roles and obligations (see Tobol 1996).

2. This division between lawyers and nonlawyers is, of course, strongly reinforced by the formal rules of the bar that prohibit "unauthorized practice of law" by nonlawyers, sharing of fees with nonlawyers, and partnerships between lawyers and nonlawyers. See Model Rule 5.5 (American Bar Association 1995). See also Freidson (1994: 204) for a discussion of such formal rules.

3. These data come from our total sample of 6,791 docket records of divorce cases in the two states (see appendix for details). These data also show that two-lawyer divorces occur in 38 percent of Maine and 46 percent of New Hampshire cases. Other studies show even lower rates of lawyer representation in divorce. Goerdt (1992: 48) reports that in the 16 urban courts that he studied, fewer than half the parties in divorce cases have any lawyers, and in some jurisdictions the most common pattern may be for both parties to be without representation. Goldschmidt (1997) similarly reports data showing *pro se* litigants in the majority of domestic relations cases in courts in Arizona and California. Pearson (1993: 282) found two-attorney representation in only 32 percent of divorces with children in Los Angeles County in 1990.

4. In our sample of lawyers, those reporting largely upper-middle-class clients faced *pro se* opponents in 22 percent of their docketed cases, while those attorneys with largely working-class clients faced unrepresented parties in 37 percent of their cases. The fact that these frequencies of single-lawyer cases for our sample of attorneys are considerably lower than that in the dockets as a whole suggests that the attorneys we interviewed (generally, those doing substantial divorce work) tend more often to be involved in two-lawyer divorces than lawyers who do just occasional divorce cases.

5. Goldschmidt (1997) found considerable variation in judicial policies toward *pro se* litigants, ranging from specific help, to some relaxation of court rules, to active assistance to the *pro se* party, in order to level the playing field.

6. Mediation in Maine provides attorneys a useful substitute in such cases. Many Maine lawyers reported finding a mediator's assistance useful because they then felt that someone was overseeing the interests of the other party, leaving them free to concentrate on representing their clients. In New Hampshire, we were told, lawyers could anticipate somewhat greater scrutiny in court of stipulated agreements involving only one lawyer. Marital masters

(experienced family law attorneys appointed for three-year terms to act as judges in marital matters in New Hampshire) acknowledged in interviews that they paid much closer attention to agreements involving only one attorney in order to be certain that unrepresented parties understood their rights and were treated fairly.

7. In 1990, New Hampshire's professional conduct code closely resembled that of the American Bar Association's Model Rules of Professional Conduct, while Maine's was much more a hybrid set of rules that departed substantially from the Model Rules.

8. At the time of our study, Maine had an Office of Bar Counsel whose lawyers acted as prosecutors to screen, investigate, and then prosecute complaints in adversarial proceedings before three-person panels of the Grievance Commission, one-third of whose members were nonlawyers. In New Hampshire at that time, the Professional Conduct Committee of the Supreme Court had 16 members, with representation from each of the 10 counties. The PCC administrator (a lawyer) screened complaints about lawyer misconduct, docketed those with a claim alleging violation of bar rules, and oversaw a process of investigations and informal hearings carried out by individuals and panels from the Committee. In each state, lawyers were asked to respond in writing to complaints that passed through the initial screening process. Their responses typically were shared with complainants. Both states had entirely separate committees to handle complaints about fees—the Fee Arbitration Commission in Maine and the Fee Dispute Resolution Committee in New Hampshire.

9. Bar Counsel in Maine (Davis 1991: 225) reports that 83 percent of the complaints were dismissed in 1990. Similarly, Trevethick reports for New Hampshire that 81 percent of complaints against divorce attorneys were dismissed without a hearing, and that 12.5 percent of the divorce complaints led to findings of misconduct (1995: 19). See also Abel (1989: 145).

10. One of the most frequently reported instances of defensive practice was the "CYA Letter," a letter confirming that the lawyer had advised the client not to accept a settlement agreement that the client wanted to accept (see chapter 5).

11. The Preamble of the Model Rules points out that lawyers face conflicting responsibilities in their law practices and goes on to say that: "Virtually all difficult ethical problems arise from conflict between a lawyer's responsibilities to clients, to the legal system, and to the lawyer's own interest in remaining an upright person while earning a satisfactory living." (American Bar Association 1995).

12. See, for example, Maine Bar Rule 3.4(c)(1): "Notwithstanding the consent of each affected client, a lawyer may not simultaneously represent, or continue to represent, more than one client in the same matter or group of substantially related matters when the matter or matters are the subject of litigation or any other proceeding for dispute resolution and the clients are opposing parties" (Maine Bar Rules 1994). Both states' rules on conflict of interest track closely, though not identically, the ABA Model Rule 1.7 (American Bar Association 1995).

13. Some of these lawyers appearing in our dockets with only one or two divorce clients may in fact be regular divorce practitioners in neighboring counties, but they only infrequently handle divorce in the counties we sampled. The greater percentage in New Hampshire than in Maine of lawyers

doing occasional divorces most likely results from the fact that we sampled fewer years and cases in New Hampshire and thus there was less chance for repetition. In addition, because of the borders with Maine, Massachusetts and Vermont, more out-of-state lawyers appeared in the New Hampshire dockets.

14. Sarat and Felstiner (1995) also discuss the reasonable divorce lawyer. For a discussion of reasonableness in a different legal context, that of legal assistance programs, see Katz (1982: 56–59).

15. Such colorful references to *un*reasonable lawyers, those who increased rather than resolved case conflicts, were cited by over 80 percent of the attorneys we interviewed.

16. This pattern of women attorneys disproportionately representing female clients existed regardless of specialization and was also evident in our larger docket sample of divorce cases from 1984 to 1988. Women lawyers represented wives in 70 percent of their cases, while male lawyers represented wives in only 51 percent of their cases.

17. Variations in firms tended to reflect the different communities of practice—divorce specialists, general practitioners and clinic lawyers, corporate law, insurance defense, and personal injury. Since our research did not focus on law firm cultures, we may have missed variations in them within areas of practice. That is, we did not try to interview all members of law firms or ask the lawyers whom we interviewed about their law firms.

18. New Hampshire has a unified bar so that all lawyers are required to belong to the New Hampshire Bar Association. Maine's bar, by contrast, is not unified. In 1990, 64 percent of all Maine lawyers belonged to the Maine State Bar Association. Of course, in smaller states such as Maine and New Hampshire, these identities may be more powerful than in larger states such as California or New York, where local—e.g., Los Angeles or New York City— bar associations may provide the equivalent networks.

19. $\chi^2 = 5.92$ with 2 d.f.; p=.05 (n=136). This difference holds up under a variety of controls for divorce specialization, class of clientele, and gender of lawyer.

20. We coded from the docket books the presence or absence of various kinds of legal activity by one or both parties suggesting legal dispute. An inclusive list of the motions coded in at least one of the two states follows: motions to amend, for temporary custody, for temporary support, payment of attorney's fees, appointment of guardian *ad litem*, for protection from abuse, to compel discovery, for contempt, to reconsider, to modify, for findings of fact, for clarification, for counseling, for payment of child support through Human Services, for conditional default; and memoranda in support of arguments, requests for production of documents or interrogatories, objections filed, and answers to motions. We recognize that these motions are not necessarily indicative of formal legal contest in every instance, but they do provide a rough aggregate measure of formal adversarial actions.

21. The percentage of New Hampshire lawyers who identified client control as a key difference among divorce lawyers was nearly twice the percentage of Maine lawyers who did. $\chi^2 = 4.96$ with 1 d.f.; p = .03 (n=163).

22. In New Hampshire, courts are county-based so that the "local legal community" is defined by repeated practice within the county court. In Maine, divorces are heard both in Superior Court (county-based) and District Court (based on smaller geographic units, not always county-based). Since

most divorce work was in the District Court, common practice in these courts defined the local communities.

23. The number of contested motions per case in Maine varied from 0.27, 0.42, and 0.57 motions per case in three rural district courts to 0.74 and 0.98 motions per case in two more urban courts. Similar variability was found across counties in New Hampshire.

24. Attorneys in the three southern counties were significantly more likely than those in the other four counties to specialize in divorce law, to report an upper-middle-class clientele, to charge a higher hourly rate, and to resolve fewer of their cases in less than 10 hours.

25. In their discussion of criminal courts as communities of practice, Eisenstein, Flemming, and Nardulli (1988: 22–54) show how court communities shape practitioners' identities, lead to common beliefs about interpersonal relations and about how cases should be processed, and reflect the special language, culture, and history of the court. For a detailed analysis of communities of practice in the context of social learning theory, see Wenger (1998).

Chapter 4

1. Abel criticizes Abbott's theory for precisely the difficulty in ascertaining "what professionals know and how they are using that knowledge" (Abel 1995: 11).

2. Heinz and Laumann's (1982: 65, 67) research among Chicago lawyers discovered that divorce lawyers were the lowest among six specialties in describing their work as requiring professional expertise that an educated layman or paraprofessional could not easily undertake.

3. Heinz and Laumann's (1982: 103) study of the Chicago bar found that divorce law was ranked the lowest on "intellectual challenge" of 30 specialties by a panel of law professors.

4. See Harrington (1994) and Shamir (1995) for analyses of *intra*professional competition in the area of administrative law.

5. The interview question read as follows: "I have here a list of six items that you may or may not consider important in the day-to-day practice of divorce law. I would like you to rate the importance of each item on a scale of one to five, with one meaning "not important" and five meaning "essential," in your opinion, to the practice of divorce law. The items are: "being a sensitive listener to the client"; "being an expert in divorce law"; "being a skillful negotiator"; "being a skillful litigator"; "knowing the other lawyers"; and "knowing the judges' idiosyncrasies." This list of skills was distilled from O'Gorman's (1963) classic study of divorce lawyers and other more recent research on lawyers, such as that of Heinz and Laumann (1982).

6. That divorce lawyers as a whole shared a view that these were the two most important skills is underscored by the fact that the standard deviations for these two items were far lower than the others: 0.85 for sensitive listening and 0.74 for negotiation, in contrast to standard deviations of 1.0 and higher for the other four skill ratings.

7. We also asked lawyers whether they could suggest additions to this list of six skills, but most did not, commenting that the list was quite complete. The few suggestions we did hear did *not* involve formal legal knowledge but instead were qualities learned through day-to-day experience in representing

clients getting divorced. These qualities or "skills" included "patience," "being an organized person," "an understanding of what is happening in the real world," "common sense," "solving practical problems," and "having a strong nervous system."

8. This argument is consistent with the call for a more "client-centered" practice in lawyering (Binder and Price 1977). In this view, listening promotes client autonomy in decision making, since only if the lawyer has elicited the relevant facts can clients understand the alternatives. On the other hand, emphasis on the information lawyers gain through careful listening to clients also is consistent with the opposite, traditional model of lawyer-dominated decision-making (Rosenthal 1974), since it helps lawyers to have the relevant information necessary to pursue goals in attaining case outcomes.

9. A side benefit of sensitive listening that was mentioned by at least one lawyer was its role in attracting new clients. In this view, listening is "very important from the perspective of you are a very sought-after attorney in the community."

10. O'Gorman (1963) and Kressel (1985) found similar variation in their studies of divorce lawyers.

11. Sarat and Felstiner (1995) report that the divorce lawyers they observed responded to clients' narratives of marriage failure with either evasion or by changing the subject, and that the lawyers worked hard to focus their efforts on the legal side of the divorce.

12. When lawyers described their responses to a client's need for emotional as well as legal counseling, about a quarter said they strongly discouraged clients from talking about personal or emotional issues, half indicated some tolerance for listening to them for limited periods of time, and another quarter saw hearing about and responding to such issues as an inevitable and important part of their practices. These answers came when we asked lawyers, "What do you typically do when you face a situation where your client wants to talk about his or her personal problems and wants or needs emotional counseling as much as legal advice?" We coded their responses according to whether they said they completely discouraged such talk; they accepted some discussion of personal issues but then cut it off; or they expressed a full willingness to listen.

13. For example, when faced with demands from their clients for personal or emotional help, over 80 percent of the lawyers we interviewed said that they would refer clients to some type of counseling. Some lawyers said they would even make counseling a condition of their continuing with the case, believing that unless the client received such assistance their legal representation would not be effective.

14. We asked a little over half of our respondents explicitly, "What are the most important qualities of an effective negotiator?"

15. The questions were as follows: "Would you say that you *encourage* your divorce clients to do at least some of the negotiating with their spouses, that you *permit* them to do so, or that you *discourage* your clients from doing any negotiating?" and "Under what circumstances, if any, do you encourage or discourage your client from negotiating with the other party?" (n=154).

16. Maine divorce lawyers came to recognize, for example, that a mediator could provide a patient and sympathetic listener for clients' tales of despair or anger at the marital breakdown, thus relieving them of some of the

burden of listening. The mediation process also assisted in direct and efficient communication between attorneys and parties by putting them all in the same room. Lawyers usually welcomed the help of mediators in resolving disputes over personal property and visitation that most found frustrating diversions from the use of their legal skills.

17. New Hampshire's ban on lawyers as mediators changed after our research was completed. The New Hampshire Marital Mediator Certification Board was established in the early 1990s. In Maine, by contrast, lawyers regularly acted as mediators although the vast majority of mediators in the Court Mediation Service that did court-based divorce mediation had no legal training.

18. In our interviews, about a fifth of New Hampshire lawyers reported they had never had a client who had been involved in divorce mediation, and just over half reported having only between one and five clients who had used mediation

19. These themes reflect the national pattern of development of court-related mediation in family cases, with mandatory mediation typically confined to areas that lawyers view as nonlegal and not within their special purview as legal experts—custody and visitation. Maine's mandatory mediation on all issues within the divorce is clearly a minority approach (McEwen, Rogers, and Maiman 1995).

20. The mean rating of negotiation skill was 4.37 for lawyers with middle- or upper-middle-class clients and 4.14 for lawyers with mainly working-class clients (F=3.59 with 1 and 154 d.f.; p=.06; n=156).

21. $\chi^2 = 7.07$ with 2 d.f.; p = .03.

22. The mean rating of litigation skill was 3.82 for lawyers with middle- or upper-middle-class clients and 3.48 for lawyers with mainly working-class clients (F=4.26 with 1 and 154 d.f.; p=.04; n=156).

23. Our research thus supports Chambers's comment that "attorneys might well discuss the final negotiation differently, and the negotiation might have a different 'meaning' to clients, if the lawyer and client expected that the client was going to do the negotiating directly with the unrepresented spouse" (1997: 225).

24. The linear relationships between specialization and the importance of expertise was significant (p=.01). A similar linear relationship appeared between specialization and the importance of litigation skills (p=.06).

25. In this chapter, nonspecialists are defined as those with divorce as less than 50 percent of their practice, and specialists are those with 50 percent or more. Obviously, the terms are not dichotomous, since in reality there is a continuum of specialization.

26. F=6.23 with 1 and 154 d.f.; p=.01 (n=156).

27. The standard deviation on the importance of "sensitive listening" was 0.59 for the women compared with 0.93 for the men (n=51 for women and n=106 for men).

28. By contrast, some of the male general practice lawyers described listening to clients as something that needed to be done, but that lacked importance. "It's not anything that becomes part of the case," noted one lawyer, while another said, "there's no skill involved, just listen and agree when you can get away with just doing that." A third explained his low rating for sensitive listening: "to do your job you could be a cold-hearted bastard."

29. We asked, "If you had the choice, would you like to increase, decrease, or keep the same proportion of your practice devoted to divorce?"

30. $\chi^2 = 4.76$ with 2 d.f.; $p = .09$ (n=123).

Chapter 5

1. Rule 2.1 (American Bar Association 1995).

2. Rule 1.16 (a) (3) (American Bar Association 1995).

3. Rule 1.2 (a) (American Bar Association 1995). Similarly, according to Rule 1.4 (b), "A lawyer shall explain a matter to the extent reasonably necessary to permit the client to make informed decisions regarding the representation."

4. Another defender of this view argues, in a famous article entitled "The Lawyer as Friend" that "it is not only legally but also morally right that a lawyer adopt as his dominant purpose the furthering of his client's interests—that it is right that a professional put the interests of his client above some idea, however valid, of the collective interest" (Fried 1976: 1066). What Fried (1976) defines as a friendship between lawyer and client, Simon (1978) in contrast, sees as akin to prostitution, since *money* provides the basis on which the lawyer adopts the client's interests as his own, and since the relationship lacks the qualities of genuine friendship.

5. For research showing lawyer domination over clients in decision making in criminal defense, see Blumberg (1967), Skolnick (1967), Flemming (1986), and Mather (1979); in legal services, see Hosticka (1979); in family law, see O'Gorman (1963), Erlanger, Chambliss, and Melli (1987), Mather, Maiman, and McEwen (1995); and in personal injury law, see Rosenthal (1974). Many of these studies also describe variation in decision making, in which some lawyers exercise less control than other lawyers over clients. See, for example, Skolnick (1967), Flemming (1986), and Mather (1979) on public defenders who follow their clients' wishes. In the area of public interest law, Olson (1984) depicts great client participation in disability rights litigation in contrast to Kluger's (1976) study of lawyer-dominated school desegregation litigation. Kritzer (1998a) presents a "mixed" picture of contingent fee lawyers with regard to lawyers' control over clients, while Sarat and Felstiner (1995) suggest considerable client resistance against control by divorce lawyers.

6. Other factors that affect lawyers' control over clients include the relative bargaining power of lawyers and clients, organization of legal practice (e.g., solo or firm, public defender or private attorney), client characteristics, and fee arrangements or market position of lawyers (Olson 1984; Flemming 1986; Gordon 1988; Abel and Lewis 1995).

7. We asked, "From your experience would you say that marital clients are generally similar to or different from other types of clients?" Sixty-one percent said they were different (n=112). However, many of those who responded that divorce clients were similar added the qualification that, as people, divorce clients were similar, but they *acted* differently because of their divorce. See also Erlanger, Chambliss, and Melli (1987) and Sarat and Felstiner (1995) on the emotional and stressful state of divorce clients.

8. One divorce specialist argued, for example, that "husband's issues are very different generally than wives' issues. You're doing damage control in different areas." When we asked attorneys whether they had a preference for

husbands or wives as divorce clients about two-thirds of both male and female attorneys said they had none. Of those who did have a preference, it was overwhelmingly for wives. Women as divorce clients presented particular kinds of feminist issues, involving their status in the marriage and their need for empowerment and growth that appealed to some lawyers, especially women. As one who preferred wives as clients explained, "Women generally probably suffer the most because of divorce . . . [I like] working with women who are sort of discovering themselves and their own potential and having to become self-sufficient and self-reliant. Those are issues that are important to me." In contrast, male attorneys who preferred wives as clients were slightly more likely than women attorneys to base their preference either on the better chance of winning or on the perceived ease of client control with wives as clients.

9. Reporting on an earlier generation of divorce lawyers operating in a fault-based system of divorce, O'Gorman showed how attorneys transformed their clients' failed marriages to fit the narrow legal requirements of fault. In this system, a spouse became either a transgressor or a victim, so as to create the legal basis for a divorce. And it was partially due to lawyers' dissatisfaction with fault-based divorce that state laws changed to embrace no-fault (Jacob 1988). In a no-fault divorce system, lawyers must redefine their clients' problems in ways that remove blame and responsibility for the marital breakdown in order to fit the legal framework.

10. Popular accounts often depict divorce lawyers as gladiators who escalate conflict (see, e.g., Couric 1992). Most social scientific studies of divorce practice portray them as focused on moderating client demands and trying to "cool out" their clients (see, e.g., Griffiths 1986; Erlanger, Chambliss, and Melli 1987; Ingleby 1988; Gilson and Mnookin 1994; and Sarat and Felstiner 1995).

11. The questions were: "In representing clients, how often would you say that you find yourself in the position of encouraging the client to take a stronger stand on issues? How often by comparison do you have to encourage the client to soften his or her stand in order to accept a compromise? Which happens more frequently?" Nearly half of our lawyers (46 percent) said that the need to "soften" a client's position was more common in divorce; 17 percent said that "hardening" the client's position was more common; while the remaining 37 percent said that the answer depended on other factors—with the client's gender being most frequently mentioned. Consistent with their gendered perceptions of divorce clients, some lawyers explained that they often had to encourage their female clients to be more assertive of their legal rights but had to persuade their male clients to accept a compromise. Other lawyers said the dimension was not gender-related but instead was based on guilt over the divorce. The spouse who felt most responsible for the marital break-up was less willing to claim legal entitlements, while the "innocent" spouse, seeking revenge through the divorce process, needed to have expectations lowered.

12. Only about half of the 163 lawyers we interviewed were asked whether or not they screened clients. Of those, 93 percent replied that they did screen clients in divorce.

13. Some lawyers referred not to problem clients but to specific issues that they hesitated to take on. These issues included sexual abuse of children (although one attorney commented that "alleged [child abuse] doesn't bother

me [but] if the party is the abuser, I probably wouldn't handle that") and batterers in domestic violence situations ("It is a matter of ideology"). Some lawyers expressed a particular distaste for bitter fights over child custody. One attorney noted, "I don't mind fighting about property," but she would refuse to represent a client in a custody battle. Lawyers' personal values thus also played a role in the screening process.

14. $F = 5.57$ with 1 and 146 d.f.; $p = .02$; $n = 148$.

15. Of those most specialized in divorce, 46 percent have 15 percent or more of their docketed clients as recycled clients, whereas only 18 percent of the remaining lawyers had that many recycled clients. $\chi^2 = 10.9$ with 3 d.f.; $p = .012$ ($n = 153$). Lawyers with upper-middle-class clienteles are also more than twice as likely to appear as second lawyers. $\chi^2 = 9.39$ with 2 d.f.; $p = .009$ ($n = 153$).

16. In this section and those following, we draw primarily on lawyers' responses to questions about how they would handle the following situations: "Your client and the other party reach a tentative agreement that you believe sells your client short"; and "Your client seems more interested in trying to get back at the other party so that he or she makes unreasonable demands."

17. Chapter 6 discusses the legal framework for divorce in Maine and New Hampshire in greater detail—and the differences between that framework and what Sarat and Felstiner (1995) report about California and Massachusetts.

18. Research in other areas of law besides divorce also shows specialist lawyers in effect creating the law through their local patterns of negotiation and setting of client expectations. See, for example, Suchman and Cahill (1996) on law in Silicon Valley, Atleson (1989) on labor-management law, and Engel (1984) on personal injury law.

19. About 40 percent of our lawyers mentioned references to the judge, the court, or the law in response to hypothetical situations involving conflict with unreasonable clients or clients who wanted to sell themselves short.

20. A few lawyers said they would refer to mediators or guardians *ad litem* as other third parties who, like the judge, would reject a client's unreasonable position. Some also suggested that clients with unrealistic demands seek a second legal opinion.

21. About 20 percent of the lawyers we interviewed commented on delay as a tactic used in negotiating with clients.

22. As a tactic for responding to unreasonable clients, the increase in fees or additional expense was mentioned by about 25 percent of our interviewees.

23. Gilson and Mnookin (1994: 524) argue that the client always pays a price for switching lawyers, since a new lawyer must invest time in learning about the facts and law in the client's case. Cf. Felstiner and Sarat (1992) on the client's choice to exit.

24. Our interviewees also referred to variation across the divorce bar on this point. Most lawyers claimed that they set their client's expectations and insisted on reasonable dispositions, but a small number (one estimate was "5 to 10 percent") were described by their peers as client-driven hired guns.

25. $\chi^2 = 16.58$ with 3 d.f; $p = .001$ ($n = 144$).

26. Gilson and Mnookin use market analysis to explain the penalty imposed on lawyers who abandon a cooperative, reasonable reputation "by turning into a gladiator at the request of an opportunistic client" (1994: 525).

27. We recognize that our picture of these relationships has been drawn only by lawyers. Without client perspectives to provide balance, this picture must remain incomplete and tentative.

28. According to critics of the hired gun role for lawyers, a role-differentiated morality for lawyers is impossible because lawyers must apply their engaged moral judgment in practice (Postema 1980), and thus they cannot avoid personal responsibility for allowing client interests to override competing values (Luban 1988; Rhode 1985).

29. Drawing on research on personal injury case settlements, Kritzer (1998a: 814) argues that lawyers in contingent-fee practices manage clients' expectations because the strategy results in smoother case settlements, more satisfied clients, and more client referrals for future business.

Chapter 6

1. The principle of accountability for lawyers provides an alternative to the dominant view of partisan advocacy. Simon (1998b) describes this alternative as the "Public Interest" view, in which lawyers behave according to the substantive purposes of the law. Atkinson (1995) terms this alternative the "Officer of the Court" approach, in which private representations are pursued according to public values and norms, in contrast to advocacy based solely on the private interests of one's client.

2. Our findings on this point support Landon's (1990) research on how lawyers in rural communities avoided excessive zeal and thereby redefined the meaning of zealous advocacy.

3. N = 136 attorneys.

4. In this respect, our findings are inconsistent with those of Sarat and Felstiner (1995: 112), who found divorce law to be unpredictable and disorderly and divorce negotiations typified by adversarial, "hard bargaining." Several points could explain the difference between the findings. The time period of the studies was different. Sarat and Felstiner's research was conducted in the mid-1980s. Our research was done in 1990–1991, after the introduction of child support guidelines, that, according to our interviewees, significantly reduced adversarial conflict in divorce. Patterns of judicial decision making in the courts in California and Massachusetts may in fact have been less predictable than those in New Hampshire and Maine. Finally, the research methods of the two studies differed. In the recorded conversations with clients, Sarat and Felstiner's lawyers emphasized the unpredictability of law but may have done so partly as a strategy of client control. In describing the process to us, the lawyers we interviewed may have overemphasized the predictability of the process and their norms of orderly cooperation. Most important, perhaps, were the income differences between divorce clients in the two studies. Two-lawyer divorces (which comprised Sarat and Felstiner's sample) tended to involve wealthier clients than the more typical divorces involving only one lawyer, and their field sites in California and Massachusetts were somewhat wealthier communities than the average towns and cities we studied in New Hampshire and Maine.

5. Gifford's (1985) distinction between competitive and integrative bargaining is somewhat similar to Kritzer's (1991) distinction between concessions-oriented and consensual bargaining.

6. N = 146 attorneys.

7. Empirical studies of plea bargaining in some criminal courts portray a world in which "everyone knows what a case is worth" and hence there is no point in playing a concessions-oriented negotiation game (Heumann 1978; Feeley 1979; Mather 1979). In other criminal courts, however, plea bargaining is more adversarial (see Eisenstein and Jacob 1977; Utz 1978; and Flemming, Nardulli, and Eisenstein 1992).

8. A New Hampshire divorce attorney described the change in property division: "New Hampshire probably since about 1984 has undergone changes in its divorce statutes with regard to property division. They've certainly tried to standardize . . . how a judge or a master should view a domestic case in a division of property and a division of pension rights." A marital master referred to how the property statutes have "tightened up and taken away some of my discretion." In a 1983 decision, the New Hampshire Supreme Court clarified the presumption of a 50–50 split of property in a no-fault divorce and set specific guidelines for property distribution.

9. The Child Support Enforcement Amendment provided financial incentives for states to expand their collection efforts and to increase the amounts awarded for support. In New Hampshire, these federal funds resulted in expansion of the number of marital masters for the state.

10. The New Hampshire guidelines followed a percent of income model, and the Maine guidelines followed an income share model, but they were similar in presenting mandatory mathematical formulas to judges for calculating support amounts (Elrod and Walker 1994).

11. We asked lawyers, "What has been the effect of introducing child support guidelines on the way you handle divorce cases?" (n=123).

12. See Racusin et al. (1989) for empirical support of the importance of legal presumptions of shared custody on actual custody awards in Vermont and New Hampshire.

13. Contrary to popular belief, alimony has never been common in divorce, and judges typically distribute ongoing financial help through child support rather than through alimony. In 1989, only 16 percent of ever-divorced women in the country had been awarded alimony payments and even those were usually for only a short period of time (U.S. Bureau of the Census 1994).

14. Unlike Maine, which distinguished between marital and nonmarital property by statute, New Hampshire considered all property owned by either party to be subject to division by the court; however, the fact that the property may have originated from one side could justify redistribution back to that party.

15. Gilson and Mnookin (1994) apply game theory to divorce and show how the payoff structure provides gains to both divorcing parties from cooperation. Cooperation is beneficial in divorce bargaining because of shared parental interests in the well-being of their child, shared interests in reducing transaction costs, and because of "differences in relative values that they may attach to different assets or activities" (Gilson and Mnookin 1994: 542).

16. Unlike the vast majority of lawyers we interviewed who preferred to initiate settlement negotiations with an offer fairly close to what they saw to be a fair outcome, four attorneys said they preferred to open with somewhat extreme offers of settlement. Each of these four referred to the ultimate need to compromise as justification for starting with a high position. Not surpris-

ingly, three of the four attorneys had clienteles that were upper-middle or upper class, and the fourth had a middle-class clientele.

17. Criminal cases with less at stake in terms of possible punishment were often settled by implicit plea bargaining, in contrast to serious cases whose disposition was more likely settled by explicit plea bargaining or adversary trial (Heumann 1978; Mather 1979).

18. We asked lawyers, "In general, would you say that in a divorce negotiation that you would rather make the first settlement offer, wait for the other party to make the first offer, or that it doesn't really matter? Why?" Responses included 19 percent who preferred to go first, 21 percent who preferred to wait, 31 percent who said "it depends," and 29 percent who said it didn't matter (n = 157).

19. According to the New Hampshire report, 93 percent of women lawyers (and even 59 percent of the men in New Hampshire) believed there was an old boy network in the state bar; female lawyers were also almost three times more likely than men to perceive that women were treated differently, for example, in levels of respect, promotion, and pay (Shanelaris and Luneau 1998). Gender bias task forces in other states document attorneys' perceptions of similar problems for women in the legal profession (see, e.g., Swent 1996; and Bowman and Schneider 1998).

20. Other research on women attorneys hints at a possible cohort effect at work for the first generation of women in the legal profession. Women who entered the bar during the 1970s and first encountered the hostile attitudes of their peers may have responded with even more aggressive advocacy than their male colleagues (see Hotel and Brockman 1994; Epstein et al., 1995; Brockman 1996). Just as we heard several women divorce specialists described as especially "tough" and "difficult," the *California Lawyer* magazine labeled a woman divorce attorney there as one of the "most aggressive, toughest divorce practitioners in the state." The article explained that this lawyer's "aggressive lawyering wasn't so much a choice as it was a survival technique when she began her practice 25 years ago. 'There were very few female lawyers, and male attorneys talked to me in a very demeaning way,' she says. 'I either had to get tough or give up' " (Goodwin, Kaae, and Weeks 1998: 42).

21. In response to the question, "How, if at all, does your negotiation style vary with the identity of the attorney on the other side?" 70 percent said yes, they would match the behavior of their opponent with more adversarial negotiations, 15 percent said, yes, they would vary their behavior by negotiating less, and going to court instead, and 15 percent said no, they tried not to change their behavior (n = 138).

22. For example, "I might write this long letter . . . if I don't think the lawyer is educating the client properly on the other side . . . to educate the other client about why they are not hearing from their lawyer."

23. In its published 1991 report, the American Academy of Matrimonial Lawyers lamented the lack of adequate guidance provided by the bar rules defining zealous advocacy. The Academy also criticized zealous representation as "not always appropriate" in family law matters (American Academy of Matrimonial Lawyers 1991: 3). The Academy's guidelines articulate formally the standards developed informally by specialists in family law.

Chapter 7

1. Canon 32 of the outdated Canons of Ethics, adopted by the American Bar Association in 1908, generally exhorted that "a lawyer will find his highest honor in a deserved reputation for fidelity to private trust and public duty, as an honest man and as a patriotic and loyal citizen," (American Bar Association 1969).

2. Model Code of Professional Responsibility, EC 2–25 (American Bar Association 1979).

3. Model Rules of Professional Conduct (American Bar Association 1995).

4. Model Rules of Professional Conduct (American Bar Association 1995).

5. See, for example, Nacht et al. (1990); Coulter (1991); Bennett (1994); Reed (1996); Newberry (1996); Jones (1999).

6. Unlike such countries as Great Britain and Israel, the U.S. government no longer provides free legal assistance for low-income divorce clients through its legal services program. To fill the void, states have made widely varying attempts to enlist private attorneys to handle such matters on a pro bono basis.

7. In Maine, the Volunteer Lawyers Project has operated since 1983, with funding both from the state legal services program and from the Maine Bar Foundation, supported largely through the IOLTA (Interest on Lawyer Trust Accounts) program. In 1990, 73 percent of active Maine lawyers participated in the Volunteer Lawyer Project, with a slightly lower percentage (about 55 percent) agreeing to accept up to three cases a year according to subject area and lawyer expertise (Maine Commission on Legal Needs 1990: 44, 49). In New Hampshire, the state bar association operates both a Pro Bono Referral System and a Reduced Fee Service. In 1990, 34 percent of active, in-state New Hampshire attorneys accepted pro bono referrals (data obtained from New Hampshire Bar Association). Data are not available on attorneys' participation in the reduced fee program. Participation rates in the formal pro bono programs of Maine and New Hampshire do not appear to be comparable because the Maine data show those who "agreed" to accept cases, not those who actually did.

8. $\chi^2 = 3.50$ with 1 d.f.; p=.06 (n=155).

9. $\chi^2 = 4.98$ with 2 d.f.; p=.08 (n=155).

10. $\chi^2 = 5.98$ with 1 d.f.; p=.015 (n=154).

11. $\chi^2 =12.78$ with 2 d.f.; p=.002 (n=154).

12. The Maine Commission on Legal Needs recognized this common practice among lawyers in the state in 1990, estimating that in 35 percent of the instances where low-income people received legal help outside of the formal system in the state, no fee or a reduced fee was charged (Maine Commission on Legal Needs 1990: 43).

13. Of the lawyers with upper-middle-class clients, only 7 percent indicated that as many as one-fifth of their divorce cases concluded in 10 hours or under, while 52 percent of lawyers with working-class clients reported that at least half of their cases were billed at 10 or fewer hours.

14. According to Freidson, "an overwhelming caseload combined with a poverty of resources by which to handle it will at least discourage if not destroy both the inclination and the capacity to do good work" (Freidson 1994: 211).

15. These problems may have been compounded by the fact that our interviews occurred in 1990 and 1991, near the height of the economic downturn in northern New England.

16. This relationship is not statistically significant. $\chi^2 = 4.14$, with 2 d.f.; p =.13 (n=150).

17. One of those justified his willingness to use the court with other obligations that competed with loyalty to the client: "I don't hesitate in the least. I give them plenty of opportunities, but I have three children. They are always saying to me, 'Well, I've got three kids, and I've got to do this.' Well, I've got them too. I did the work."

18. Comment [5] under Rule 1.5 (American Bar Association 1995).

19. Seven of the eight attorneys with this response had working-class clienteles, while one reported a mixed or middle-class client base.

20. We asked lawyers about the kinds of problems they encountered in collecting fees, and the ways they dealt with those problems. Withdrawal was one of several tactics they described.

21. Model Code of Professional Responsibility, EC 2–32 (American Bar Association 1979).

22. The new Model Rules of Professional Conduct permit a lawyer to withdraw if

(4) the client fails substantially to fulfill an obligation to the lawyer regarding the lawyer's services and has been given reasonable warning that the lawyer will withdraw unless the obligation is fulfilled;

(5) the representation will result in an unreasonable financial burden on the lawyer or has been rendered unreasonably difficult by the client; Rule 1.16 (b) (American Bar Association 1995).

23. Maine Bar Rules 3.5 (c) (6) (Maine Bar Rules 1994).

24. In our interviews, lawyers identified four primary causes of "out of control cases," that is, ones with unusually high costs: party vindictiveness and stubbornness; complexity of property issues; the behavior of other lawyers; and increased procedural demands by courts or court inefficiency. None of these implicate their own actions or suggest that they share any responsibility for high costs. Indeed, these portraits emphasize how little lawyers believe they can control the costs of the case that can be driven up by an unreasonable client, a resistant spouse on the other side, a Rambo opposing lawyer, or waiting in an overcrowded court.

25. Only 6 percent of the lawyers we interviewed reported asking for no retainer. Over one half (55 percent) indicated that their retainers were flexible—depending on client or case—while 39 percent said that their retainers were fixed and unchanging. These policies—unlike the size of the retainers—were not related to resources of clients but were related to lawyer's gender. Women were almost twice as likely as men to report having fixed retainers χ^2 =9.62 with 2 d.f.; p=.008 (n=161).

26. A recent *New York Times* article similarly points to the impact of firm policies in producing a nationwide decline in pro bono work among the most successful firms (Winter 2000).

27. Some sole practitioners said they delegated the unsavory task of bill collection to their secretaries. As one lawyer exclaimed, "Thank God, I've got

Darlene. I don't really follow that too much anymore." Another attorney admitted a degree of ignorance about collection problems, "I don't do it. I have a secretary who does."

Chapter 8

1. Some identify the idea of "calling" with that of a profession and argue that it offers as well a sense of virtue through work and thus provides "an identity and hence a meaningful place in the world" (Kronman 1993: 370). Freidson also makes this point: "Professionals develop intellectual interest in their work, so they are concerned with extending and refining it and they believe in its value to society. They do not merely exercise a complex skill, but identify themselves with it" (1994: 200).

2. Much of this writing tacitly assumes that professional work is satisfying to its practitioners. The very qualities that some see as defining the professions distinctively—such as control over one's work (Ritzer 1972; Freidson 1994) as well as its public prestige and financial rewards—are consistent with that assumption. Even those who take a more critical view of the "professional project" (Larson 1977; Abel 1989; Nelson and Trubek 1992a,b;) seem to take for granted that the work of professionals yields significant rewards. This assumption is consistent with research evidence about job stress and dissatisfaction that makes clear that white collar and professional workers find their work more meaningful and rewarding and less stressful than do blue collar workers, in part, because of the degree of control workers have over the labor process (Ritzer 1972: 186).

3. In New Hampshire in 1989, for example, the median income for lawyers in domestic relations law was $37,000, the lowest of any legal specialty and a sharp contrast with the median income of $51,000 for all attorneys in the state that year (New Hampshire Bar Association 1990: 11). Surveys of attorneys in Ohio, Texas, and Michigan similarly show that family law ranks the lowest or second lowest in median annual income out of 24 different legal specialties (New England School of Law 1999).

4. For a more general discussion of the role of organizational context in shaping professional work, see Freidson (1994: 206–214.)

5. The American Bar Association's Young Lawyers' survey and others like it focus on working conditions more than on the character of the work itself. Thus, long hours, political intrigue and backbiting, limited advancement opportunities, and so on are the focus of attention. The survey did examine the importance of "intellectual challenge" to job satisfaction, but appears to have probed little into the nature of the work that lawyers do (Goldberg 1990). In more recent research, Heinz, Hull, and Harter (1999: 736) report high levels of satisfaction among lawyers, with 84 percent of Chicago lawyers either satisfied or very satisfied. Their conclusions contrast with the earlier study by the Young Lawyer's Division of the American Bar Association that found only 33 percent of young lawyers very satisfied with their jobs and 19 percent dissatisfied (Goldberg 1990). See Heinz, Hull, and Harter (1999) for a review of research on job satisfaction among lawyers.

6. In recent bar assessments of lawyer unhappiness, sole practitioners receive only a token nod in the acknowledgment of their "isolation" from circles of professional support (American Bar Association 1991: 8). A 1994 survey of the California bar reveals that sole practitioners are more likely to be sat-

isfied with choice of law as a career (32 percent) than law firm associates (23 percent) and in-house counsel (27 percent) but less satisfied than law firm partners (36 percent) and government lawyers (43 percent) and legal services or public interest lawyers (45 percent) (Rand Institute for Civil Justice 1995). Heinz, Hull, and Harter report higher levels of both "very satisfied" and "very dissatisfied" lawyers in sole practice than in large law firms (1999: 744).

7. The need to reconcile the potential contradictions between these reference points is one of the central challenges to traditional notions of professionalism that deny a substantial role to consumers and vest judgments about quality of work in the professional and in her colleagues.

8. Dissatisfied clients pose a particular problem for lawyers in contingent fee practice (see Kritzer 1998a).

9. These responses were coded from the answers to two questions about how lawyers judged their success generally and in divorce cases in particular. All the answers to questions about the lawyer's criteria for judging success in divorce cases or as lawyers generally were read and coded in terms of the criteria the lawyers indicated that they employed. A lawyer could mention several criteria (such as client satisfaction, referral rates, respect of peers, and satisfactory income) and thus could be counted more than once.

10. Heinz, Hull, and Harter (1999: 750) found that lawyers' "personal control over the circumstances of their work" relates significantly to higher job satisfaction.

11. Our analysis here is based on coding of lawyers' answers to one question about their perception of their role ("What do you consider to be your primary responsibility in representing divorce clients?") and one question about their own satisfaction with their work ("What aspect of your work as a lawyer do you enjoy the most?"). Answers to these two questions were coded independently by two of the authors, and disagreements were resolved by discussion. In essence, each answer was scored 1 or 3, depending on whether it was exclusively legal-craft-oriented or client-adjustment-oriented, and 2 if it involved both orientations. The average of the two scores was computed, and the scores divided into three groups: legal-craft-oriented lawyers (1–1.50), mixed-types (1.51–2.50), and client-adjustment-oriented lawyers (2.51-3.00). When an answer to one question was missing or uncodable, the answer to the other served as the score for this variable. In two cases, codable answers were unavailable for both questions. In both instances, we estimated the score on this variable by similarly coded responses to a question about what the lawyer liked least about law practice.

12. Naming these different orientations is difficult without implicitly criticizing one or the other (cf. Krauskopf 1994). Legal-craft attorneys do not ignore their clients nor do client-oriented lawyers neglect the law. Instead, lawyers tend to emphasize one or another aspect of the practice. The variation between craft and client orientation closely resembles the distinction that O'Gorman (1963) identified among New York matrimonial lawyers over 30 years ago. He differentiated among problem-, people-, and money-oriented attorneys. The first two of his categories parallel our legal-craft- and client-adjustment-oriented categories. We distinguished, however, those lawyers interested in solving people's problems from those focused on legal problems and processes and found money-orientation never to be exclusive and to overlap these other categories.

13. Of course, some of those attorneys most committed to client adjustment also enjoyed and thought courtroom advocacy necessary. For them, the formal legal process was an important way to help empower clients and secure for them a better future.

14. Analysis of gender, specialization, and role orientation in this chapter is slightly revised from our earlier presentation in Maiman, Mather, and McEwen (1992) in order to correct some coding errors and use a different measure of specialization.

15. A logit analysis of five independent variables on the role orientation score reveals that specialization, gender, and class of clientele are statistically significant predictors of role orientation (defined as either legal-craft oriented or mixed/client-adjustment oriented), while control variables (age and the state the lawyer practiced in) are not.

16. To the extent that such gender differences exist, they may result not from socialization or psychological dynamics as Gilligan (1982) and Chodorow (1978) suggest, but rather from differences in power and domination (MacKinnon 1987). According to MacKinnon, the distinctively "female" attributes of caring and nurturance so celebrated by "difference feminists" are simply the product of the systematic domination and subordination of women that leaves women no other social role besides that of care (1987: 39). Other observers of women in the legal profession who have expressed skepticism about the likelihood of women's transformative potential include, for example, Mossman (1988), Epstein (1990, 1993), and Harrington (1993).

17. As shown in chapter 2, Andrea Wright exemplified this combination of a strong client orientation to clients and vigorous legal advocacy. Or, as Epstein writes, "One may be caring toward a client in the office, but ruthless against an opposing attorney in the courtroom" (1990: 320).

18. Financial rewards clearly were not the primary justification for doing the work among the lawyers we interviewed. Few either showed or celebrated the financial rewards of their practices. Some, in fact, responded "not the money" when asked about how they evaluated their own success as lawyers. Others—only about 15 percent—indicated that "money," "making a living," or "being able to support a family" were among the criteria they used to evaluate their own work.

19. The Family Law Section of the American Bar Association was established in 1957 and experienced its greatest growth during the decade from 1976 to 1987, when it expanded from 5,000 to nearly 16,000 members (telephone conversation with Gerry Caulfield of the American Bar Association, Chicago, June 12, 1991). Note that this decade of growth followed the no-fault divorce reforms of the 1970s and the leveling off of the growth in divorce rates.

20. Membership in the Academy is by invitation only and requires at least 10 years of divorce law experience and a concentration of at least 75 percent of a lawyer's practice in matrimonial law (with some exceptions). In its brochure, the Academy defines its mission in the following terms: "To encourage the study, improve the practice, elevate the standards and advance the cause of matrimonial law, to the end that the welfare of the family and society be preserved." Through its work, the Academy claims, it has "set the standard for the rest of the matrimonial bar" and "improved the quality of family law practice in general throughout the country for lawyers and litigants alike."

Chapter 9

1. See, for example, Van Hoy's (1993) description of the political struggle in the ABA over issues of professionalism. Indeed, some critics suggest abandoning the idea of professionalism because of the way professions reinforce hierarchy, exclusion, and elitism (Illich et al. 1978; Derber, Schwartz, and Magrass 1990).

2. Johnson (1972: 45–47) distinguishes among different types of occupational control: collegiate (which includes professionalism as a "subtype"), control by powerful consumers such as individual or corporate patrons, and control by intermediaries between producers and consumers such as capitalist entrepreneurs and the state. See also Freidson (1994). Although Johnson (1972: 45) employs the term "collegiate control" in discussing professionalism, he sees "collegiate control" as "exemplified by the emergence of autonomous occupational associations" (1972: 45). Our concept of collegial control rests on the norms of informal associations and loosely defined communities, as well as on those of formal associations.

3. In 1991, the Hillsborough County Women's Bar Association was formed in New Hampshire. The group held monthly meetings, with about 75 members. Meetings included casual discussions and formal programs three or four times a year. Women lawyers in a neighboring county later formed the Merrimac County Women's Bar Association. In 1998, the statewide New Hampshire Women's Bar Association was formed and replaced the two county organizations.

In Maine, women lawyers were active in the Status of Women Attorneys Committee, which was formed in 1983. That committee became a Section of the Maine State Bar Association in 1995.

4. Other forms of collegial control over work might include to some extent guilds, unions, worker subcultures, and collective ownership by employees. The power of collegial control in a "nonprofessional" setting is perhaps best exemplified in policing. In this case, police subcultures appear to compete and collude with bureaucratic leadership to guide the conduct of police officers (Skolnick 1994). It is our view that the study of professions such as law will be enriched by serious comparisons with other occupations, where varying forms of collegial control operate. For discussion of occupational subcultures, see Rothman (1987: 40–59).

5. A complete examination of this argument would require longitudinal research on changes in collegial control over time. Here we draw on what is in effect cross-sectional research to speculate about how differences at the microlevel in the various communities of practice may reflect macrolevel changes in the profession.

6. Prior to the sharp increases in divorce rate and volume, only a handful of lawyers specialized in divorce or matrimonial law. For example, in his pioneering study of matrimonial lawyers in New York during the late 1950s, O'Gorman found that a small minority of those attorneys doing divorce cases were "specialized" (1963: 65–80). Writing about Chicago in roughly the same period, Carlin quoted one of his respondents as saying that "there are about twelve specialists in divorce law in Chicago" (1962: 95). Although no precise comparisons are possible, it is clear that specialization in family law has increased significantly in the intervening years. For example, we found

that there were at least two dozen divorce specialists in 1990 in Portland, Maine, an urban area with one-twentieth the population that Chicago had in 1960.

7. The Model Rules of Professional Conduct as recently amended (American Bar Association 1995) permit attorneys to "state that the lawyer is a 'specialist,' practices a 'specialty,' or 'specializes in' particular fields...." (Comment, Rule 7.4), and they acknowledge certification of specialization by appropriate regulatory bodies. The earlier Model Rules and Model Code prohibited lawyers from claiming to be specialists, except in states where formal certification procedures existed or in reference to admiralty, patent and trademark law. For a general discussion of specialization, see Ariens (1994) and for an argument on behalf of acknowledging specialization more fully in legal education and practice, see Kritzer (1998b: 209–216).

8. Between 1947 and 1990, the percentage of sole practitioners among private practice attorneys dropped from 69 percent to 45 percent. At the other end of the scale, by 1990, 25.6 percent of private attorneys were in firms of 21 or more lawyers, up from 13.4 percent only a decade earlier (Curran and Carson 1994).

9. This perspective on the significance of firm organization for practice suggests that staff lawyers in salaried positions working for government or businesses—also a growing area of legal practice—face different pressures on their professional roles. For these lawyers, independence may remain an issue because their employers are their clients, making independent judgment more difficult (Spangler 1986). However, they do not face the problem of competing loyalties to firm or to client that could lead to overbilling when client pockets are deep or to restricted service or withdrawal when they are shallow.

10. Indeed, Abel argues that "the large law firm has come to symbolize law practice, both inside and outside the profession" (1989: 235).

11. Cf. Fineman (1991) who argues that the claims of equality fall far short of reality.

12. Other efforts to create more specialized, middle-level codes include the work of the New York State Trial Lawyers Association, which in 1975 approved a Code of Professional Responsibility for Matrimonial Lawyers according to Gillers and Simon, who then include the short text in their volume (1992: 515–518). In addition, a Special Committee of the ABA appointed in 1964 prepared Standards for Criminal Justice that have been revised several times (American Bar Association 1993). They provide detailed standards for prosecutors and defense lawyers.

13. Model Rules 5.1 to 5.7 explicitly relate to "Law Firms and Associations," but they impose no collective obligation on firms for deliberation with respect to professional responsibility or ethical conduct (American Bar Association 1995). In essence, the Rules appear to presume lawyers to be independent practitioners and generally ignore collegial and organizational pressures and responsibilities. The one possible exception is Rule 5.1 (a) that states that "a partner in a law firm shall make reasonable efforts to ensure that the firm has in effect measures giving reasonable assurance that all lawyers in the firm conform to the Rules of Professional Conduct" (American Bar Association 1995). This minimal standard emphasizes conformity rather than judgment and provides no guidance regarding the content of such efforts. A recent *ABA Journal* story describes a New York bar rule that holds law firms accountable for the same conduct as individual attorneys. In ad-

dition, it requires firms to "supervise the work of lawyers and nonlawyers alike, and maintain an effective system for checking conflicts of interest" (Hansen 1998: 24).

14. Such a rule could have more than symbolic value to the extent that it would entail possible financial liability for firms. See Ramos (1994) for discussion of malpractice insurance as a vehicle for regulating the professional conduct of lawyers.

15. For example, Continuing Legal Education (CLE) programs might take on a somewhat different focus if some of them were aimed at collegial discussion of important issues of practice. CLE may indeed be one of the organized activities that most effectively brings together practitioners with similar interests and practices from different firm settings and varied clienteles. Utilizing such opportunities less for the transmission of expert technical knowledge and more for guided, collective discussions of problems of practice might promote both collegial norms and control. The organized bar might also examine ways of extending peer support to deliberation about difficult professional decisions of practice. Currently, models exist to provide peer assistance to lawyers in need of help with law office management or substance abuse problems. Such assistance appears to be premised implicitly on a recognition that many lawyers are practicing on their own and may need the organized support of colleagues. An even more radical suggestion would be for some kind of peer review of lawyer performance that provides a context for reflections about practice style and decisions. Lawyers in sole practice or small firms may find it very difficult to gain perspective on their work, and members of large firms may be insulated from the judgments of lawyers outside the firm. Bar efforts to provide aid and information on performance could enhance and strengthen peer controls but would be very difficult to organize, especially among professional competitors.

REFERENCES

Abbott, Andrew. 1988. *The System of Professions: An Essay on the Division of Expert Labor*. Chicago: University of Chicago Press.

Abel, Richard L. 1985. "Comparative Sociology of Legal Professions: An Exploratory Essay." *American Bar Foundation Research Journal* 1985:5–79.

———. 1988. "United States: The Contradictions of Professionalism." In *Lawyers in Society: The Common Law World*, edited by Richard L. Abel and Philip S. C. Lewis. Berkeley: University of California Press.

———. 1989. *American Lawyers*. New York: Oxford University Press.

———. 1995. "Revisioning Lawyers." Pp. 181–243 in *Lawyers in Society: An Overview*, edited by Richard L. Abel and Philip S. C. Lewis. Berkeley: University of California Press.

Abel, Richard L., and Philip S. C. Lewis. 1995. "Putting Law Back into the Sociology of Lawyers." Pp. 281–330 in *Lawyers in Society: An Overview*, edited by Richard L. Abel and Philip S. C. Lewis. Berkeley: University of California Press.

Abel, Richard L., and Philip S. C. Lewis (Eds.). 1988. *Lawyers in Society*. 3 vols. Berkeley: University of California Press.

Abrams, Roger I. 1990. "Lawyer Professionalism and Legal Education." *Florida Bar Journal* 64:67–68.

Alfieri, Anthony V. 1999. "(Er)Race-Ing an Ethic of Justice." *Stanford Law Review*, 51:935–955.

American Academy of Matrimonial Lawyers. 1991. *Bounds of Advocacy: American Academy of Matrimonial Lawyers Standards of Conduct.* Chicago: American Academy of Matrimonial Lawyers.

American Bar Association. 1969. *ABA Canons of Professional Ethics.* Chicago: American Bar Association.

———. 1979. *ABA Model Code of Professional Responsibility.* Chicago: American Bar Association.

———. 1986. *In the Spirit of Public Service: A Blueprint for the Rekindling of Lawyer Professionalism.* Chicago: American Bar Association.

———. 1991. *The Report of At the Breaking Point: A National Conference on the Emerging Crisis in the Quality of Lawyer's Health and Lives, Its Impact on Law Firms and Client Services.* Chicago: American Bar Association.

———. 1993. *ABA Standards for Criminal Justice: Prosecution Function and Defense Function.* 3d ed. Chicago: American Bar Association.

———. 1995. *ABA Model Rules of Professional Conduct.* Chicago: American Bar Association.

Ariens, Michael. 1994. "Know the Law: A History of Legal Specialization." *South Carolina Law Review* 45:1003–1061.

Armstrong, Walter P. 1994. "Professionalism: What Lies Ahead?" *Tennessee Bar Journal* 30:12–17.

Atkinson, Rob. 1995. "A Dissenter's Commentary on the Professionalism Crusade." *Texas Law Review* 74:259–343.

Atleson, James B. 1989. "The Legal Community and the Transformation of Disputes: The Settlement of Injunction Actions." *Law and Society Review* 23:41–73.

Auerbach, Jerold. 1976. *Unequal Justice: Lawyers and Social Change in Modern America.* New York: Oxford University Press.

Bennett, Joel P. (Ed.). 1994. *Flying Solo: A Survival Guide for the Solo Lawyer.* Chicago: American Bar Association.

Binder, David, and Susan Price. 1977. *Legal Interviewing and Counseling: A Client-Centered Approach.* Saint Paul, Minn.: West Publishing Company.

Blumberg, Abraham S. 1967. "The Practice of Law as a Confidence Game: Organizational Cooptation of a Profession." *Law and Society Review* 1:15–39.

Bogoch, Bryna. 1997. "Gendered Lawyering: Difference and Dominance in Lawyer-Client Interaction." *Law and Society Review* 31:677–712.

Bowman, Cynthia Grant, and Elizabeth Schneider (1998). "Feminist Legal Theory, Feminist Lawmaking, and the Legal Profession." *Fordham Law Review* 67:249–271.

Brockman, Joan. 1996. "Reluctant Adversaries in the Adversarial System." Annual Meeting of the Law and Society Association. Glasgow, Scotland.

Burger, Warren E. 1993. "The Decline of Professionalism." *Yale Law Journal* 22:590–613.

Cahn, Naomi. 1992. "Styles of Lawyering." *Hastings Law Journal* 43:1039–1069.

Cain, Maureen. 1979. "The General Practice Lawyer and the Client: Towards a Radical Conception." *International Journal of the Sociology of Law* 7:331–354.

Carlin, Jerome. 1962. *Lawyers on Their Own.* New Brunswick, N.J.: Rutgers University Press.

————. 1966. *Lawyers' Ethics—A Survey of the New York City Bar*. New York: Russell Sage Foundation.

Chambers, David L. 1997. "25 Divorce Attorneys and 40 Clients in Two Not So Big but Not So Small Cities in Massachusetts and California: An Appreciation." *Law and Social Inquiry*, 22:209–230.

Chodorow, Nancy. 1978. *The Reproduction of Mothering: Psychoanalysis and the Sociology of Gender*. Berkeley: University of California Press.

Church, Thomas. 1985. "Examining Local Legal Culture." *American Bar Foundation Research Journal*, 1985: 499–518.

Coulter, Charles R. 1991. *Practical Systems: Tips for Organizing Your Law Office*. Chicago: American Bar Association.

Couric, Emily. 1992. *The Divorce Lawyers: The People and Stories Behind Ten Dramatic Divorce Cases*. New York: St. Martin's Press.

Crowley, Robert, et al. 1996. "Report of the Maine Commission on Gender, Justice and the Courts."

Cunningham, Clark D. 1989. "The Tale of Two Clients: Thinking About Law as Language." *Michigan Law Review* 87:2459–2494.

Curran, Barbara A. 1986. "American Lawyers in the 1980s: A Profession in Transition." *Law and Society Review* 20:19–53.

Curran, Barbara A., and Clara N. Carson. 1994. *The Lawyer Statistical Report: The U.S. Legal Profession in the 1990's*. Chicago: American Bar Foundation.

D'Andrade, Roy. 1995. *The Development of Cognitive Anthropology*. Cambridge: Cambridge University Press.

Davis, J. Scott. 1991. "Bar Counsel's 1990 Annual Report." *Maine Bar Journal* 6:218–227.

Derber, Charles, William A. Schwartz, and Yale Magrass. 1990. *Power in the Highest Degree: Professionals and the Rise of a New Mandarin Order*. New York: Oxford University Press.

Dingwall, Robert. 1976. "Accomplishing Profession." *Sociological Review* 24: 331–349.

Eisenberg, Melvin A. 1976. "Private Ordering Through Negotiation: Dispute Settlement and Rulemaking." *Harvard Law Review* 89:637–681.

Eisenstein, James, Roy B. Flemming, and Peter F. Nardulli. 1988. *The Contours of Justice: Communities and Their Courts*. Boston: Little, Brown and Company.

Eisenstein, James, and Herbert Jacob. 1977. *Felony Justice: An Organizational Analysis of Criminal Courts*. Boston: Little, Brown.

Ellmann, Stephen. 1987. "Lawyers and Clients." *UCLA Law Review* 34:717–779.

————. 1993. "The Ethic of Care as an Ethic of Lawyers." *Georgetown Journal of Legal Ethics* 81:2665–2726.

Elrod, Linda D., and Timothy B. Walker 1994. "Family Law in the Fifty States." *Family Law Quarterly* 27:515–745.

Engel, David M. 1984. "The Oven Bird's Song: Insiders, Outsiders, and Personal Injuries in an American Community." *Law and Society Review* 18: 551–582.

Epstein, Cynthia Fuchs. 1990. "Faulty Framework: Consequences of the Difference Model for Women in the Law." *New York Law School Law Review* 35:309–336.

————. 1993. *Women in Law*. 2d ed. Urbana: University of Illinois Press.

————. et al. 1995. "Glass Ceilings and Open Doors: Women's Advancement in the Legal Profession." *Fordham Law Review* 64:291–449.

Erlanger, Howard S., Elizabeth Chambliss, and Marygold S. Melli. 1987. "Participation and Flexibility in Informal Processes: Cautions from the Divorce Context." *Law and Society Review* 21:585–604.

Federle, Katherine Hunt. 1994. "Looking for Rights in All the Wrong Places: Resolving Custody Disputes in Divorce Proceedings." *Cardozo Law Review* 15:1523–1566.

Feeley, Malcolm M. 1979. *The Process is the Punishment.* New York: Russell Sage Foundation.

Feldman, Heidi Li. 1996. "Codes and Virtues: Can Good Lawyers Be Good Ethical Deliberators?" *Southern California Law Review* 69:885–948.

Felstiner, William L. F., and Austin Sarat. 1992. "Law and Strategy in the Divorce Lawyer's Office." *Law and Society Review* 20:93–134.

Fineman, Martha A. 1991. *The Illusion of Inequality: The Rhetoric and Reality of Divorce Reform.* Chicago: University of Chicago Press.

Flemming, Roy B. 1986. "The Client Game: Defense Attorney Perspectives on Their Relations with Criminal Clients." *American Bar Foundation Research Journal* 1986:253–277.

Flemming, Roy B., Peter F. Nardulli, and James Eisenstein. 1992. *The Craft of Justice: Politics and Work in Criminal Court Communities.* Philadelphia: University of Pennsylvania Press.

Flood, John. 1991. "Doing Business: The Management of Uncertainty in Lawyers' Work." *Law and Society Review* 25:41–71.

Frankel, Marvin E. 1975. "The Search for Truth: An Umpireal View." *University of Pennsylvania Law Review* 123:1031–1059.

Freed, Doris Jonas, and Timothy B. Walker. 1991. "Family Law in the Fifty States: An Overview." *Family Law Quarterly* 24:309–405.

Freedman, Monroe. 1966. "Professional Responsibility of the Criminal Defense Lawyer: The Three Hardest Questions." *Michigan Law Review* 64: 1469–1484.

Freidson, Eliot. 1994. *Professionalism Reborn: Theory, Prophecy and Policy.* Chicago: University of Chicago Press.

Fried, Charles. 1976. "The Lawyer as Friend: The Moral Foundations of the Lawyer-Client Relation." *Yale Law Journal* 85:1060–1089.

Frymire, Richard L. 1989. "A Report on Lawyer Professionalism." *Kentucky Bench and Bar* 53:19–21.

Galanter, Marc. 1984. "Words of Deals: Using Negotiation to Teach about Legal Process." *Journal of Legal Education* 34:268–276.

Galanter, Marc, and Thomas Palay. 1991. *Tournament of Lawyers: The Growth and Transformation of The Big Law Firm.* Chicago: University of Chicago Press.

Genn, Hazel. 1987. *Hard Bargaining: Out of Court Settlement in Personal Injury Actions.* Oxford: Clarendon Press.

Gibeaut, John. 1997. "Avoiding Trouble at the Mill: A Lengthy Client List Guarantees Success, Right? Not Necessarily. Ethics and Malpractice Problems Can Plague a High Volume Practice." *ABA Journal* 83:48–52.

Gibeaut, John, and James Podgers. 1998. "Feeling the Squeeze: Commission Appointed to Assess Threat from Accountants." *ABA Journal* 84:88.

Gifford, Donald G. 1985. "A Context-Based Theory of Strategy Selection in Legal Negotiation." *Ohio State Law Journal* 46:41–94.

Gillers, Stephen, and Roy D. Simon, Jr. 1992. *Regulation of Lawyers: Statutes and Standards with Recent Supreme Court Decisions*, 1992 Edition. Boston: Little, Brown.

Gilligan, Carol. 1982. *In a Different Voice: Psychological Theory and Women's Development*. Cambridge: Harvard University Press.

Gilson, Ronald J., and Robert H. Mnookin. 1994. "Disputing Through Agents: Cooperation and Conflict Between Lawyers in Litigation." *Columbia Law Review* 94:509–566.

Glendon, Mary Ann. 1994. *A Nation Under Lawyers*. New York: Farrar, Straus and Giroux.

Glick, Paul. 1975. "A Demographic Look at American Families." *Journal of Marriage and the Family* 37:15–26.

Goerdt, John. 1992. *Divorce Courts: Case Management, Case Characteristics, and the Pace of Litigation in 16 Urban Jurisdictions*. Williamsburg, Va.: National Center for State Courts.

Goldberg, Stephanie Benson. 1990. "One In Five Lawyers Dissatisfied: Lawyers Are Burned Out but Not Leaving, Survey Says." *ABA Journal* 76:36.

Goldschmidt, Jona. 1997. "How Are Judges and Courts Coping with Pro Se Litigants?: Results from a Survey of Judges and Court Managers." Annual Meeting of the Law and Society Association. St. Louis, Mo.

Goode, William J. 1957. "Community Within a Community: The Professions." *American Sociological Review* 22:194–200.

———. 1993. *World Changes in Divorce Patterns*. New Haven: Yale University Press.

Goodwin, Tema, Jennifer Kaae, and Janet Weeks. 1998. "The Divorce Duelers: Ten of the Toughest Marriage-Splitting Attorneys in California." *California Lawyer*, August, 41–47, 87.

Gordon, Robert W. 1988. "The Independence of Lawyers." *Boston University Law Review* 68:1–83.

Gordon, Robert W., and William H. Simon. 1992. "The Redemption of Professionalism." Pp. 230–258 in *Lawyers' Ideals/Lawyers' Practices*, edited by Robert L. Nelson, David M. Trubek, and Rayman L. Solomon. Ithaca, N.Y.: Cornell University Press.

Greenwood, Pamela T. 1991. "Is Lawyer Professionalism Alive and Well in Utah?" *Utah Bar Journal* 4:4–5.

Griffiths, John. 1986. "What Do Dutch Lawyers Actually Do In Divorce Cases?" *Law and Society Review* 20:135–175.

Hagan, John, and Fiona Kay. 1995. *Gender in Practice: A Study of Lawyers' Lives*. New York: Oxford University Press.

Halliday, Terence C. 1987. *Beyond Monopoly: Lawyers, State Crises, and Professional Empowerment*. Chicago: University of Chicago Press.

———. 1999. "The Politics of Lawyers: An Emerging Agenda." *Law and Social Inquiry* 24:1007–1011.

Handler, Joel. 1967. *The Lawyer and His Community: The Practicing Bar in a Middle-Sized City*. Madison: University of Wisconsin Press.

Hansen, Mark. 1998. "Taking a Firm Hand in Discipline: New York Ethics Rules Pinpoint Law Firms—Some Say More States Should Follow." *ABA Journal* 84:24.

Harrington, Christine B. 1994. "Outlining a Theory of Legal Practice." Pp. 49–70 in *Lawyers in a Postmodern World: Translation and Transgres-*

sion, edited by Maureen Cain and Christine B. Harrington. New York: New York University Press.

Harrington, Mona. 1993. *Women Lawyers: Rewriting the Rules.* New York: Penguin Books.

Haskell, Paul G. 1998. *Why Lawyers Behave as They Do.* Boulder, Colo.: Westview Press.

Heinz, John P., et al. 1998. "The Changing Character of Lawyer's Work: Chicago in 1975 and 1995." *Law and Society Review* 32:751–775.

Heinz, John, K. E. Hull, and A. A. Harter. 1999. "Lawyers and Their Discontents: Findings from a Survey of the Chicago Bar." *Indiana Law Journal* 74:735–758.

Heinz, John, and Edward Laumann. 1982. *Chicago Lawyers: The Social Structure of the Bar.* New York and Chicago: Russell Sage Foundation and American Bar Foundation.

Heumann, Milton. 1978. *Plea Bargaining: The Experiences of Prosecutors, Judges, and Defense Attorneys.* Chicago: University of Chicago Press.

Hosticka, Carl J. 1979. "We Don't Care What Happened: We Only Care About What is Going to Happen: Lawyer-Client Negotiations of Reality." *Social Problems* 26:599–610.

Hotel, Carla, and Joan Brockman. 1994. "The Conciliatory-Adversarial Continuum in Family Law Practice." *Canadian Journal of Family Law* 12:11–36.

Hughes, Everett C. 1962. "Good People, Dirty Work." *Social Problems* 10(Summer):3–11.

Illich, Ivan, et al. 1978. *Disabling Professions.* Boston: M. Boyars.

Ingleby, Richard. 1988. "The Solicitor as Intermediary." Pp. 43–55 in *Divorce Mediation and the Legal Process,* edited by Robert Dingwall and John Eekelaar. London: Oxford University Press.

———. 1992. *Solicitors and Divorce.* Oxford: Clarendon Press.

Jack, Rand, and Dana Crowley Jack. 1989. *Moral Vision and Professional Decisions: The Changing Values of Women and Men Lawyers.* New York: Cambridge University Press.

Jacob, Herbert. 1988. *Silent Revolution: The Transformation of Divorce Law in the United States.* Chicago: University of Chicago Press.

Johnson, Terence C. 1972. *Professions and Power.* London: Macmillan.

Jones, Nancy Byerly. 1999. *Easy Self-Audits for the Busy Law Office.* Chicago: American Bar Association.

Katz, Jack. 1982. *Poor People's Lawyers in Transition.* New Brunswick, N.J.: Rutgers University Press.

Kelly, Michael J. 1994. *Lives of Lawyers.* Ann Arbor: University of Michigan Press.

Kluger, Richard. 1976. *Simple Justice.* New York: Alfred Knopf.

Krauskopf, Joan. 1994. "Touching the Elephant: Perceptions of Gender Issues in Nine Law Schools." *Journal of Legal Education* 44:311–340.

Kressel, Kenneth. 1985. *The Process of Divorce: How Professionals and Couples Negotiate Settlements.* New York: Basic Books.

Kritzer, Herbert M. 1991. *Let's Make A Deal.* Madison: University of Wisconsin Press.

———. 1998a. "Contingent-Fee Lawyers and Their Clients: Settlement Expectations, Settlement Realities, and Issues of Control in the Lawyer-Client Relationship." *Law and Social Inquiry* 23:795–821.

————. 1998b. *Legal Advocacy: Lawyers and Nonlawyers at Work*. Ann Arbor: University of Michigan Press.

Kritzer, Herbert M., and Frances Kahn Zemans. 1993. "Local Legal Culture and the Control of Litigation." *Law and Society Review* 27:535–557.

Kronman, Anthony T. 1993. *The Lost Lawyer*. Cambridge, Mass.: Belknap Press.

Landon, Donald D. 1990. *Country Lawyers: The Impact of Context on Professional Practice*. New York: Praeger.

Larson, Magali Sarfatti. 1977. *The Rise of Professionalism*. Berkeley: University of California Press.

Lee, Robert G. 1999. *Firm Views: Work of and Work in the Largest Law Firms*. Research Study #35. London: The Law Society.

Levinson, Sanford. 1993. "Identifying the Jewish Lawyer: Reflections on the Construction of Professional Identity." *Cardozo Law Review* 14:1577–1612.

Linowitz, Sol M. 1994. *The Betrayed Profession: Lawyering at the End of the Twentieth Century*. New York: Scribner.

Luban, David. 1988. *Lawyers and Justice: An Ethical Study*. Princeton, N.J.: Princeton University Press.

————. 1999. "Reason and Passion in Legal Ethics." *Stanford Law Review*, 51:873–903.

MacKinnon, Catherine A. 1987. *Feminism Unmodified: Discourses on Life and Law*. Cambridge: Harvard University Press.

Maiman, Richard J., Lynn Mather, and Craig A. McEwen. 1992. "Gender and Specialization in the Practice of Divorce Law." *Maine Law Review* 44:39–61.

Maine Bar Rules. 1994.

Maine Commission on Legal Needs. 1990. *Report of the Maine Commission on Legal Needs*. Augusta, Me.: Maine Bar Foundation.

Mather, Lynn. 1979. *Plea Bargaining or Trial? The Process of Criminal Case Disposition*. Lexington, Mass.: Lexington Books.

————. 1998. "Theorizing About Trial Courts: Lawyers, Policymaking and Tobacco Litigation." *Law and Social Inquiry* 23:897–940.

Mather, Lynn, Richard J. Maiman, and Craig A. McEwen. 1995. " 'The Passenger Decides on the Destination and I Decide on the Route': Are Divorce Lawyers 'Expensive Cab Drivers?' " *International Journal of Law and the Family* 9:286–310.

Mather, Lynn, and Barbara Yngvesson. 1980–1981. "Language, Audience, and the Transformation of Disputes." *Law and Society Review* 15:775–822.

McEwen, Craig A., Lynn Mather, and Richard J. Maiman. 1994. "Lawyers, Mediation, and the Management of Divorce Practice." *Law and Society Review* 28:149–86.

McEwen, Craig A., Nancy H. Rogers, and Richard J. Maiman. 1995. "Bring in the Lawyers: Challenging the Dominant Approaches to Ensuring Fairness in Divorce Mediation." *Minnesota Law Review* 79:1317–1411.

McIntyre, Holly Marie. 1996. "Fleming vs. Asbill: South Carolina Guardian Ad Litem Not Immune from Civil Liability." *Creighton Law Review* 29:1711–1759.

Melli, Marygold. 2000. "Guideline Review: The Search for an Equitable Child

Support Formula." Pp. 113–127 in *Child Support*, edited by J. Thomas Oldham and Marygold S. Melli. Ann Arbor: University of Michigan Press.

Menkel-Meadow, Carrie. 1984. "Toward Another View of Legal Negotiation: The Structure of Problem Solving." *UCLA Law Review* 31:754–842.

———. 1985. "Portia in a Different Voice: Speculations on a Women's Lawyering Process." *Berkeley Women's Law Journal* 1:39–63.

———. 1989. "Exploring a Research Agenda of the Feminization of the Legal Profession: Theories of Gender and Social Change." *Law and Social Inquiry* 14:289–319.

———. 1995. "Portia Redux: Another Look at Gender, Feminism, and Legal Ethics." Pp. 25–56 in *Legal Ethics and Legal Practice: Contemporary Issues*, edited by Stephen Parker and Charles Sampford. Oxford: Clarendon Press.

Merry, Sally. 1990. *Getting Justice and Getting Even: Legal Consciousness Among Working-Class Americans*. Chicago: University of Chicago Press.

Mnookin, Robert H., and Lewis Kornhauser. 1979. "Bargaining in the Shadow of the Law: The Case of Divorce." *Yale Law Journal* 88:950–997.

Mossman, Mary Jane. 1988. "Portia's Progress: Women as Lawyers—Reflections on Past and Future." *Windsor Yearbook of Access to Justice* 8:252–266.

Muhlhauser, Tara Lee. 1990. "From 'Best' to 'Better': The Interests of Children and a Guardian Ad Litem." *North Dakota Law Review* 66:633–647.

Nacht, Arthur, et al. 1990. *Improving Accounts Receivable Collection: A Practical System*. Chicago: American Bar Association.

Nelson, Robert L. 1985. "Ideology, Practice, and Professional Autonomy: Social Values and Client Relationships in the Large Law Firm." *Stanford Law Review* 37:503–551.

Nelson, Robert L., and David M. Trubek. 1992a. "Arenas of Professionalism: The Professional Ideologies of Lawyers in Context." Pp. 177–214 in *Lawyers' Ideals/Lawyers' Practices*, edited by Robert L. Nelson, David M. Trubek, and Rayman L. Solomon. Ithaca, N.Y.: Cornell University Press.

———. 1992b. "Introduction: New Problems and New Paradigms in Studies of the Legal Profession." Pp. 1–27 in *Lawyer's Ideals/Lawyers' Practices*, edited by Robert L. Nelson, David M. Trubek, and Rayman L. Solomon. Ithaca, NY: Cornell University Press.

New England School of Law. 1999. "Online Lawyer Income Statistical Report: Table 8—Incomes of Attorneys Engaged in the Private Practice of Law by Specialty." *http://www.nesl.edu/FACULTY/table8.htm#specialty*.

New Hampshire Bar Association. 1990. *The 1990 Desktop Reference on the Economics of Law Practice in New Hampshire*. Concord: New Hampshire Bar Association.

New Hampshire Rules of Professional Conduct. 1995.

Newberry, Jon. 1996. "Working the Percentages: By Learning How to Divide Time Between Practicing Law and Managing a Practice, Any Lawyer Can Improve the Chances for Becoming a Success." *ABA Journal* 82:62–65.

Olson, Susan M. 1984. *Clients and Lawyers: Securing the Rights of Disabled Persons*. Westport, Conn.: Greenwood Press.

O'Gorman, Hubert. 1963. *Lawyers and Matrimonial Cases: A Study of Informal Pressures in Private Professional Practice*. New York: Free Press.

Parsons, Talcott. 1939. "The Professions and Social Structure." *Social Forces* 17:457–467.

————. 1962. "The Law and Social Control." Pp. 56–72 in *Law and Sociology*, edited by William M. Evan. Glencoe, Ill.: The Free Press.

Paterson, Alan A. 1996. "Professionalism and the Legal Services Market." *International Journal of the Legal Profession* 3:137–68.

Pawluch, D. 1983. "Transitions in Pediatrics: A Segmental Analysis." *Social Problems* 30:449–465.

Pearson, Jessica. 1993. "Ten Myths About Family Law." *Family Law Quarterly* 27:279–299.

Postema, Gerald J. 1980. "Moral Responsibility and Professional Ethics." *New York University Law Review* 55:63–89.

Pue, W. Wesley. 1998. "Lawyering for a Fragmented World: Professionalism After God." *International Journal of the Legal Profession* 5:125–140.

Racusin, Robert, et al. 1989. "Factors Associated with Joint Custody Awards." *Journal of the American Academy of Child and Adolescent Psychiatry* 28:164–170.

Ramos, Manuel R. 1994. "Legal Malpractice: The Profession's Dirty Little Secret." *Vanderbilt Law Review* 47:1657–1750.

Rand Institute for Civil Justice. 1995. "California Lawyers View the Future: Special Issue." *Facts and Trends* 3(4).

Reed, Richard C. 1996. *Billing Innovations: New Win-Win Ways to End Hourly Billing*. Chicago: American Bar Association.

Rhode, Deborah. 1985. "Ethical Perspectives on Legal Practice." *Stanford Law Review* 37:589–652.

————. 1994. "Gender and Professional Roles." *Fordham Law Review* 63:39–72.

————. 1999. "Symposium Introduction: In Pursuit of Justice." *Stanford Law Review*, 51:867–873.

Ritzer, George. 1972. *Man and His Work: Conflict and Change*. New York: Appleton-Century-Crofts.

Rogers, Nancy H., and Craig A. McEwen. 1994. *Mediation: Law, Policy, Practice* 2nd ed. New York: Clark Boardman Callaghan.

Rosenthal, Douglas E. 1974. *Lawyer and Client: Who's In Charge?* New York: Russell Sage Foundation.

Rostain, Tanina. 1999. "Waking Up From Uneasy Dreams: Professional Context, Discretionary Judgment, and the Practice of Justice." *Stanford Law Review*, 51:955–973.

Rothman, Robert A. 1987. *Working: Sociological Perspectives*. Englewood Cliffs, N.J.: Prentice-Hall.

Rubin, Alvin B. 1975. "A Causerie on Lawyers' Ethics in Negotiation." *Louisiana Law Review* 35:577–593.

Sarat, Austin, and William L. F. Felstiner. 1995. *Divorce Lawyers and Their Clients: Power and Meaning in the Legal Process*. New York: Oxford University Press.

Sarat, Austin, and Stuart A. Scheingold (Eds.). 1998. *Cause Lawyering: Political Commitments and Professional Responsibilities*. New York: Oxford University Press.

Schon, Donald. 1983. *The Reflective Practitioner: How Professionals Think in Action*. New York: Basic Books.

Schwartz, Murray L. 1978. "The Professionalism and Accountability of Lawyers." *California Law Review* 66:669–697.

Seron, Carroll. 1996. *The Business of Practicing Law: The Work Lives of Solo and Small Firm Attorneys.* Philadelphia: Temple University Press.

Shaffer, Thomas L. 1999. "Should a Christian Lawyer Sign Up For Simon's Practice of Justice?" *Stanford Law Review,* 51:903–919.

Shamir, Ronen. 1995. *Managing Uncertainty: Elite Lawyers in the New Deal.* Durham: Duke University Press.

Shanelaris, Catherine E., and Henrietta Walsh Luneau. 1998. "Ten Year Gender Survey." *New Hampshire Bar Journal* 39:56–88.

Shapiro, Martin. 1990. "Book Review Essay: Lawyers, Corporations and Knowledge." *American Journal of Comparative Law* 38:683–716.

Silbey, Susan S. 1992. "Making a Place for Cultural Analyses of Law." *Law and Social Inquiry* 17:39–48.

Simon, William H. 1978. "The Ideology of Advocacy: Procedural Justice and Professional Ethics." *Wisconsin Law Review.* 1978:29–144.

———. 1984. "Visions of Practice in Legal Thought." *Stanford Law Review* 36:469–507.

———. 1998a. "The Kaye Scholer Affair: The Lawyer's Duty of Candor and the Bar's Temptations of Evasion and Apology." *Law and Social Inquiry* 23:243–295.

———. 1998b. *The Practice of Justice: A Theory of Lawyers' Ethics.* Cambridge: Harvard University Press.

Skolnick, Jerome. 1967. "Social Control in the Adversary System." *Journal of Conflict Resolution* 11:52–70.

———. 1994. *Justice Without Trial: Law Enforcement in Democratic Society.* 3d ed. New York: Macmillan.

Solomon, Rayman L. 1992. "Five Crises or One: The Concept of Legal Professionalism, 1925–1960." Pp. 144–174 in *Lawyers' Ideals/Lawyers' Practices,* edited by Robert L. Nelson, David M. Trubek, and Rayman L. Solomon. Ithaca, N.Y.: Cornell University Press.

Sommerlad, Hilary, and Peter Sanderson. 1998. *Gender, Choice and Commitment: Women Solicitors in England and Wales and the Struggle for Equal Status.* Hampshire, Eng.: Dartmouth Publishing Co.

Spangler, Eve. 1986. *Lawyers for Hire: Salaried Professionals at Work.* New Haven: Yale University Press.

Strauss, Marcy. 1987. "Essay: Toward a Revised Model of Attorney-Client Relationship: The Argument for Autonomy." *North Carolina Law Review* 65:315–349.

Suchman, Mark C., and Mia L. Cahill. 1996. "The Hired Gun as Facilitator: Lawyers and the Suppression of Business Disputes in Silicon Valley." *Law and Social Inquiry* 21:679–712.

Sullivan, Timothy J. 1987. "Lawyer Professionalism." *Virginia Bar Association Journal* 13:13–15.

Swent, Jeannette F. 1996. "Gender Bias at the Heart of Justice: An Empirical Study of State Task Forces." *Southern California Review of Law and Women's Studies* 6:1–87.

Taber, Janet, et al. 1988. "Gender, Legal Education, and the Legal Profession: An Empirical Study of Stanford Law Students and Graduates." *Stanford Law Review* 40:1209–1297.

Taylor, Michael. 1989. "Structure, Culture and Action in the Explanation of Social Change." *Politics and Society* 17:115–62.

Tobol, Amy Ruth. 1996. "Cause Lawyering Creating Community: The Role of Professional Organizations." Annual Meeting of the Law and Society Association. Glasgow, Scotland.

Trevethick, Thomas V. 1995. "Is There a Pattern in the Madness? A Statistical Survey of Conduct Complaints." *New Hampshire Bar Journal* 36:13–22.

Trotter, Michael H. 1997. *Profit and the Practice of Law: What's Happened to the Legal Profession*. Athens: University of Georgia Press.

Udry, Richard. 1967. "Research Notes: Marital Instability by Race and Income Based on 1960 Census Data." *American Journal of Sociology* 72:673–674.

U.S. Bureau of the Census. 1994. *Statistical Abstract of the United States*. 114th ed. Washington, D.C.: U.S. Government Printing Office.

Utz, Pamela J. 1978. *Settling the Facts: Discretion and Negotiation in Criminal Court*. Lexington, Mass.: Lexington Books.

Van Hoy, Jerry. 1993. "Intraprofessional Politics and Professional Regulation: A Case Study of the ABA Commission on Professionalism." *Work and Occupations* 20:90–109.

———. 1997. *Franchise Law Firms and the Rise of Personal Legal Services*. Westport, Conn.: Greenwood Press.

Wendt, Alexander. 1998. "On Constitution and Causation in International Relations." *Review of International Relations* 24:101–17.

Wenger, Etienne. 1998. *Communities of Practice*. Cambridge: Cambridge University Press.

West, Robin. 1988. "Jurisprudence and Gender." *University of Chicago Law Review* 55:1–72.

———. 1999. "The Zealous Advocacy of Justice in a Less Than Ideal World." *Stanford Law Review* 51:973–991.

White, James J. 1967. "Women in the Law." *Michigan Law Review* 65:1051–1122.

Wilkins, David B. 1990. "Legal Realism for Lawyers." *Harvard Law Review* 104:468–524.

———. 1994. "Book Review: Practical Wisdom for Practicing Lawyers: Separating Ideals from Ideology in Legal Ethics." *Harvard Law Review* 108:458–476.

———. 1998. "Fragmenting Professionalism: Racial Identity and the Ideology of Bleached-Out Lawyering." *International Journal of the Legal Profession* 5:141–73.

Winter, Greg. 2000. "Legal Firms Cutting Back on Free Services for Poor." *New York Times*, August 17, A1.

Zacharias, Fred C. 1995. "Reconciling Professionalism and Client Interests." *William and Mary Law Review* 36:1303–1378.

INDEX

Abbott, Andrew, 65–66, 68, 84–85, 209n.1
Abel, Richard L., 46, 90, 184, 203n.3, 204n.3. 209n.1, 224n.10
Adversariness in divorce
indicators of, 58, 209n.23
Advocacy in divorce, 110–132
and client resources, 122–125, 131
debate over rules governing, 111–113
influence of legal rules on, 118–121, 131–132
and lawyer's reputation, 127–131
lawyers' responses to questions about, 114–118
and negotiation, 116–117
"partisan," 110–111
and reasonable lawyer norm, 48–51, 113–115
and women divorce specialists, 125–127, 131–132

American Academy of Matrimonial Lawyers (AAML)
as community of practice, 189–190, 206n.1
mission of, 222n.20
Bounds of Advocacy, 113, 172, 217n.23
American Bar Association (ABA)
Commission on Professionalism, 7, 56–57, 133, 188–189
Family Law Section, 222n.19
and law practice management, 134, 154–155
Model Code of Professional Responsibility, 111–112, 134, 146, 224n.7
Model Rules of Professional Conduct, 88–89, 111–112, 118, 134, 144, 146, 204n.6, 207nn.7, 11, 212n.3, 224nn.7, 13

239

American Bar Association (ABA)
(*cont.*)
and pro bono service, 134
Young Lawyers Division, 220n.5
Arenas for judgment by lawyers in
divorce work, 37–40
Atkinson, Rob, 215n.1

Bogoch, Bryna, 83
Brockman, Joan, 83, 170

Cain, Maureen, 204n.7
Carlin, Jerome, 7, 9, 11, 12, 173,
223n.6
Chambers, David L., 17, 211n.23
Chambliss, Elizabeth, 96, 114
Child support guidelines, 118–119,
216n.9
Chodorow, Nancy, 222n.16
Client-adjustment orientation, 164–
171
characteristics of, 166–168
as community of practice, 172
and gender of lawyer, 168–171
and specialization, 169–171
See also Legal-craft orientation
Client control by lawyers, 14, 87–109
client resistance to, 107–108
and client screening, 92–96
tactics for, 96–104
Clients
counseling of, 165–167
education of, 96–98
emotions of, 68–69, 91–92, 165–
167
gender of, 91, 212–213n.8
lawyer's control of, 87–109
and negotiation, 69–71, 78
resistance to lawyer's control by,
107–108
resources of, 14, 77–78, 121–125,
139–142, 191
screening of difficult, 92–96
unreasonable demands by, 89–109
See also Sensitive listening to clients
Codes of professional conduct, 6, 7,
45–47, 88–89, 111–113, 134,
144, 146–147
Collegial control (and influence) over
work, 6, 177–181

and communities of practice, 10–
12, 108–109, 132, 175–181,
188–193
forces for change in, 181–188
and legal professionalism, 188–193
See also Community(ies) of practice
Community(ies) of practice, 6, 10–12,
14–15, 41–63, 180–181, 188–
193
bar as, 6, 42–47, 61
and collegial control of lawyer's
decisions, 6, 10–12, 61–63, 108–
109, 132, 171–73, 175–181,
188–193, 203n.1
divorce lawyers as, 47–56
and entry of women into legal
profession, 125–127, 183–184
geographic locales as, 6, 57–61
law firms as, 6, 56–57, 151–154,
180, 184–185, 191–192,
208n.18
and lawyers' standards for judging
success, 160–161
and reasonable lawyer norm, 48–
51, 62
and rise of divorce specialization,
182–183
Cunningham, Clark D., 89

Delaying cases, 101–102, 214n.21.
See also Client control by lawyers
Dingwall, Robert, 65, 177
Divorce law
and advocacy, 118–121
changes in, 185–186
importance of knowledge of, 71–72,
79–81
Divorce law nonspecialists
clients of, 54–55
competition with specialists, 85
contrasts with specialists, 52–56
and divorce law expertise, 79–81,
137–142
and reasonable lawyer norm, 52–
56
See also Divorce law specialists,
Women lawyers
Divorce law specialists
clients of, 54–55
competition with nonspecialists, 85

contrasts with nonspecialists, 52–
56
and divorce law expertise, 79–81,
137–142
and reasonable lawyer norm, 52–
56
women as, 52–56, 81–84
See also Divorce law nonspecialists,
Women lawyers
Dual representation, bar rule against,
46–47

Eisenstein, James, 180, 209n.25
Ellmann, Stephen, 68, 89, 91, 107
Epstein, Cynthia Fuchs, 125, 222n.17
Erlanger, Howard S., 96, 114
Expertise of lawyer in divorce work,
64–86
and communities of practice, 76–84
and gender of lawyers, 76, 81–84,
211n.27
and knowing divorce law, 67, 71–
72, 79–81
and knowing judges, 67, 73–74
and knowing other lawyers, 67, 74
and litigation skills, 67, 72–74,
211nn.22, 24
and market competition, 84–86
and negotiation skills, 67, 69–71,
74
ratings of importance of lawyer
skills, 67
and sensitive listening to clients, 67–
69, 74
and specialization, 78–81,
211nn.24, 25
and type of clientele, 77–78,
211nn.20, 22

Fairness in divorce settlements, 114–
116
Family law movement, 172
Family Support Act of 1988, 119. *See
also* Child support guidelines
Fees, 133–156
and advocacy in divorce, 122–125
and clients with limited means, 139–
142, 155
law firm policies for setting, 150–
154

reduction of, 137–138
and retainers, 148–149
role in client education, 102–103
role in client screening, 147–148
techniques for collecting from
clients, 142–147
See also Clients, resources of
Felstiner, William L. F., 17, 92, 99–
100, 107, 114, 121, 129, 162,
210n.11, 214n.17, 215n.4
Fineman, Martha A., 75, 224n.11
Flemming, Roy B., 180, 209n.25
Flood, John, 204n.7
Frankel, Marvin E., 112
Freedman, Monroe, 8, 89
Freidson, Eliot, 12, 37, 50, 65, 130,
133, 155, 162, 177, 218n.14,
220n.1
Fried, Charles, 212n.4

Galanter, Marc, 113, 158
Gender of lawyer
and definitions of professionalism,
55–56
and expertise in divorce work, 81–
84, 211n.27
and gender of clients, 212–213n.8
research on, 9–10, 82–84
and role orientation, 168–171
and specialization in divorce law,
125–127
See also Women lawyers
General practice lawyers. *See* Divorce
law nonspecialists
Genn, Hazel, 116
Gibeaut, John, 142
Gifford, Donald G., 215n.5
Gillers, Stephen, 224n.12
Gilligan, Carol, 9, 68, 81, 222n.16
Gilson, Ronald L., 11, 113–114, 123,
128, 129–130, 214nn.23, 26,
216n.15
Glendon, Mary Ann, 10, 90
Glick, Paul, 182
Goerdt, John, 206n.3
Goldschmidt, Jona, 206nn.3, 5
Goode, William J., 182, 205n.15
Gordon, Robert W., 89–90, 127, 189
Griffiths, John, 114
Guardians *ad litem*, 187

Halliday, Terence C., 86
Handler, Joel, 11–13, 205n.16
Harrington, Christine B., 90, 158, 192, 209n.4
Harter, A. A., 220n.5, 221nn.6, 10
Haskell, Paul G., 90, 112
Heinz, John P., 7, 90, 176, 209nn.2, 3, 220n.5, 221nn.6, 10
Hired gun role of lawyer. *See* Independent advisor role of lawyer
Hotel, Carla, 83, 170
Hughes, Everett C., 171
Hull, K. E., 220n.5, 221nn.6, 10

Independent advisor role of lawyer, 88–90
Ingleby, Richard, 114

Jack, Dana Crowley, 81
Jack, Rand, 81
Jacob, Herbert, 74, 185
Johnson, Terence C., 177, 203n.3, 223n.2

Kelly, Michael J., 8, 57, 153, 180, 185
Kornhauser, Lewis, 73, 118
Kressel, Kenneth, 18, 113, 210n.10
Kritzer, Herbert M., 8, 97, 116, 215nn.5, 29, 224n.7
Kronman, Anthony T., 90, 158, 163, 220n.1

Landon, Donald D., 12, 215n.2
Larson, Magali Sarfatti, 65, 203n.2
Laumann, Edward, 7, 90, 176, 209nn.2, 3
Law firms
    and collegial control of work, 7–8, 191–192, 224n.13
    as communities of practice, 56–57, 180, 184–185, 191–192, 208n.18
    and dissatisfaction among lawyers, 158
    growth of, 184–185, 224n.8
    and pressures for business-like practice, 14, 56–57, 151–154
Lee, Robert G., 57
Legal community
    as community of practice, 42–47

formal norms of, 45–47
informal norms of, 42–45
Legal-craft orientation, 164–171
    characteristics of, 165–166
    as community of practice, 171–172
    and gender of lawyer, 168–171
    and specialization, 169–171
    See also Client-adjustment orientation
Legal professionalism, 4, 6–10, 175–193
    and advocacy, 110–132
    and collegial control of work, 175–193
    and communities of practice, 10–12, 176
    different accounts of, 6–10
    and divorce law practice, 12–13
    and expertise, 64–86
    and lawyers' adversary roles, 88–90
    in practice, 6, 10–12, 18, 175–193
    and satisfaction of lawyers, 157–174
    and service to public, 133–156
Levinson, Sanford, 8
Lewis, Philip C. S., 204n.3
Linowitz, Sol M., 90
Llewellyn, Karl, 10
Local legal culture, 10–11. *See also* Community (ies) of practice
Luban, David, 9, 110–111

MacKinnon, Catherine A., 83, 222n.16
Maiman, Richard J., 58, 75, 85, 211n.19, 222n.14
Maine
    adversarial motions in, 58, 209n.23
    bar rules in, 112, 207nn.8, 9
    child support guidelines in, 119, 216n.10
    division of marital property in, 118, 216nn.10, 14
    divorce dockets in, 47–48
    mediation in, 74–76, 206–207n.6, 210–211n.16, 211n.19
    no-fault divorce in, 96, 118, 119–120

pro bono service in, 135, 218n.7
typical divorce in, 43, 206n.3
Mather, Lynn, 58, 75, 164, 222n.14
McEwen, Craig A., 58, 75, 85, 186,
    211n.19, 222n.14
Mediation
    and competition with divorce
        lawyers, 74–76
    as institutional change in divorce
        law, 186–187
    in Maine, 58, 74–76, 186, 187,
        206–207n.6, 210–211n.16
    in New Hampshire, 75–76,
        211n.17
Melli, Marygold S., 96, 114, 119
Menkel-Meadow, Carrie, 9, 81–82,
    118
Mnookin, Robert H., 11, 73, 113–
    114, 118, 123, 128–130,
    214nn.23, 26, 216n.15
Model Code. See American Bar
    Association
Model Rules. See American Bar
    Association

Nardulli, Peter F., 180, 209n.25
Negotiation
    between clients, 69–71, 141
    and child custody rules, 120–121
    and child support guidelines, 118–
        119
    and client resources, 77–78, 141
    and identity of opposing lawyer,
        128–129, 214n.21
    importance of skills in, 69–71, 77–
        78
    lawyer's goals in, 114–116
    and lawyer's reputation, 127–130
    lawyers' tactics in, 116–118
    and no-fault divorce, 119–120
    with pro se litigants, 44–45
Nelson, Robert L., 7–8, 11, 85, 111,
    157, 203n.1, 205n.14
New Hampshire
    adversarial motions in, 58,
        209n.23
    bar rules in, 112, 207n.7
    child support guidelines in, 119,
        216nn.9, 10
    division of marital property in, 118,
        216nn.8, 10, 14

divorce dockets in, 47–48, 207–
    208n.13
mediation in, 75–76, 211n.17
no-fault divorce in, 96, 118, 119–
    120
pro bono service in, 135, 218n.7
typical divorce in, 43, 206n.3
withdrawing from cases in, 146
No-fault divorce, 118, 119–120, 185
Nonspecialists. See Divorce law
    nonspecialists

O'Gorman, Hubert, 8, 12, 18,
    209n.5, 210n.10, 213n.9,
    221n.12, 223n.6

Palay, Thomas, 158
Paterson, Alan A., 88
Pawluch, D., 173
Pearson, Jessica, 77, 206n.3
Personal identities of lawyers, 8–10
Personal property, division of, 70–71
Postema, Gerald, 9
Pro bono service, 103, 134, 135–
    139, 147–155
Pro se (unrepresented) parties, 43–45,
    206n.4
Professionalism. See Legal
    Professionalism
Public service. See pro bono service

Reasonable lawyer norm, 48–51,
    111, 113–114,
    characteristics of, 48–51
    lawyers' different understandings of,
        52–56
    and lawyer's reputation, 127–130
"Reflective practitioner," 37, 65, 189.
    See also Schon, Donald.
Resources for Divorced Families (RDF),
    172–173
Retainers, 148–149, 219n.25. See
    also Fees
Rhode, Deborah, 125
Rogers, Nancy H., 85, 186, 211n.19
Rosenthal, Douglas E., 8, 89, 204n.7
Rubin, Alvin B., 116
Rules of professional conduct. See
    Codes of professional conduct

Sarat, Austin, 17, 92, 99–100, 107, 114, 129, 162, 210n.11, 214n.17, 215n.4
Satisfaction of lawyers, 157–174
  and collegial norms, 160–161
  and communities of practice, 171–173
  and opinions of clients, 161–162
  and own assessments of work, 159–160
  and professional autonomy, 162–164
  and role orientations, 164–171
Schon, Donald, 10, 37, 65, 189
Schwartz, Murray L., 43, 112
Screening of clients, 92–96
Sensitive listening to clients, 67–69, 82–84, 165–167
  gender differences in rating importance of, 82–84
  lawyers' different versions of, 67–69, 117–120
Seron, Carroll, 7, 12, 66, 84, 163
Shamir, Ronen, 85–86, 209n.4
Simon, William H., 110–112, 189, 204n.6, 212n.4, 215n.1
Small-firm practice (and practitioners), 7, 12–13, 37, 56–57, 184
Sole practice (and practitioners), 7, 12–13, 37, 56–57
  characteristics of, 30
  long-term decline in, 184, 224n.8
Spangler, Eve, 8
Specialists. *See* Divorce law specialists
Specialization
  and collegial control of work, 189–191
  contrasts with general practice lawyers, 52–56
  and legal expertise, 79–81
  and market competition for clients, 85–86
  and professional rules, 224n.7

rise of divorce, 182–183
and women lawyers, 55–56, 86, 125–127

Trotter, Michael H., 205n.8
Trubek, David M., 7–8, 11, 111, 157, 203n.1, 205n.14

Udry, Richard, 180
Unreasonable lawyer, 51–56, 227–235. *See also* Reasonable lawyer norm

Van Hoy, Jerry, 12
Visitation schedules, negotiating terms of, 70

White, James J., 183
Wilkins, David B., 9, 11, 83, 158, 190, 205n.14
Women lawyers
  and advocacy, 125–127
  and divorce law specialization, 55–56, 125–127, 183–184
  and divorce law expertise, 81–84
  gender bias against, 217nn.19, 20
  increase in numbers of, 183–184
  and listening to clients, 82–84
  organizations of, 223n.3
  and professional identity, 179
  representation of female clients by, 56, 208n.16
  and role orientations, 168–171
  See also Divorce law specialists, Gender of lawyer
Workplace influence on lawyer behavior, 7–8, 11–12, 41, 189–193

Yngvesson, Barbara, 164

Zacharias, Fred C., 88, 203n.2, 204n.5